AF271758

DON BACHARDY
A LIFE IN PORTRAITS

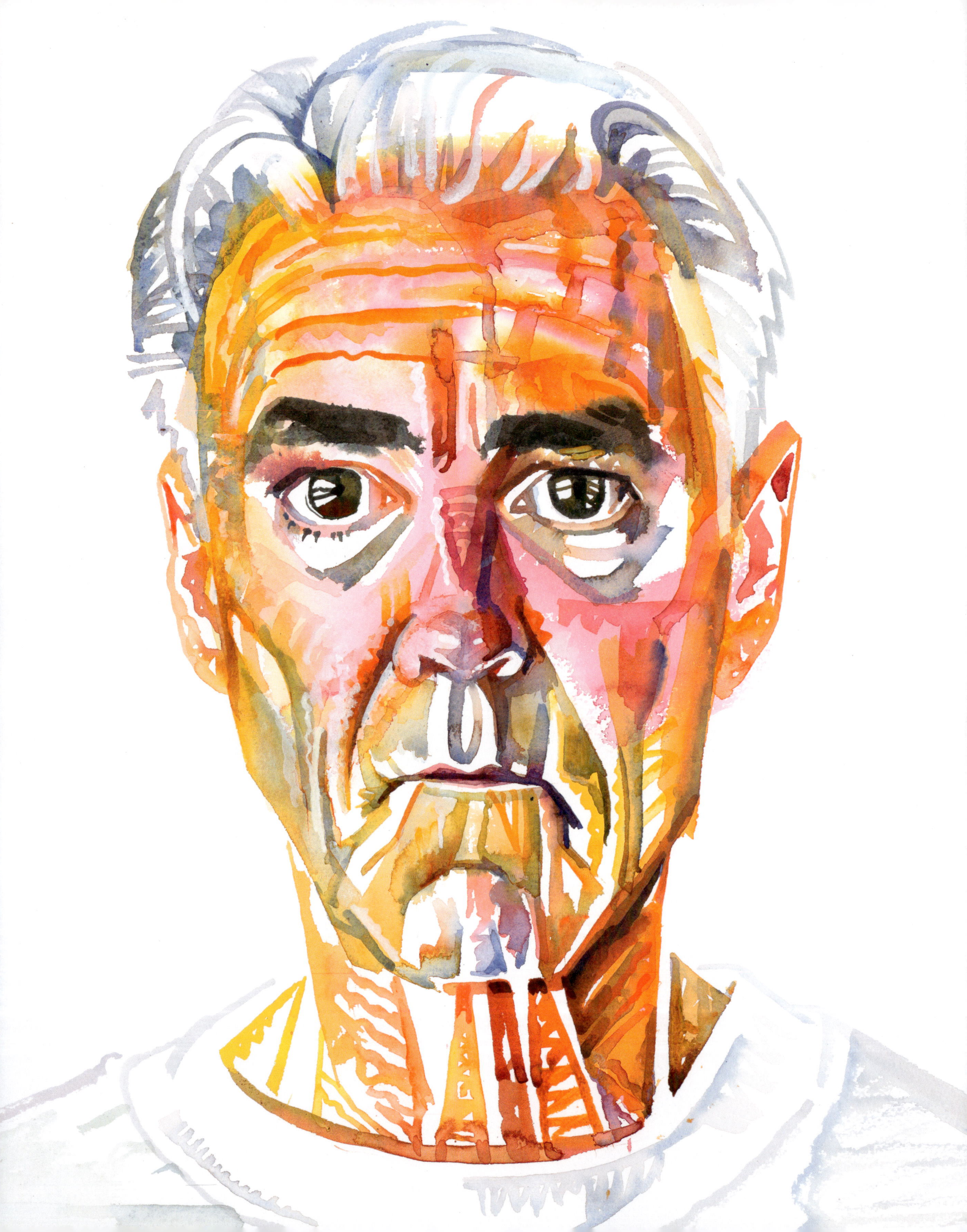

DON BACHARDY
A LIFE IN PORTRAITS

EDITED BY

Dennis Carr

Karla Nielsen

WITH CONTRIBUTIONS BY

Katherine Bucknell

James Cahill

Simon Callow

Mary Agnes Donoghue

Gregory Evans

Tina Mascara

THE HUNTINGTON
SAN MARINO, CALIFORNIA

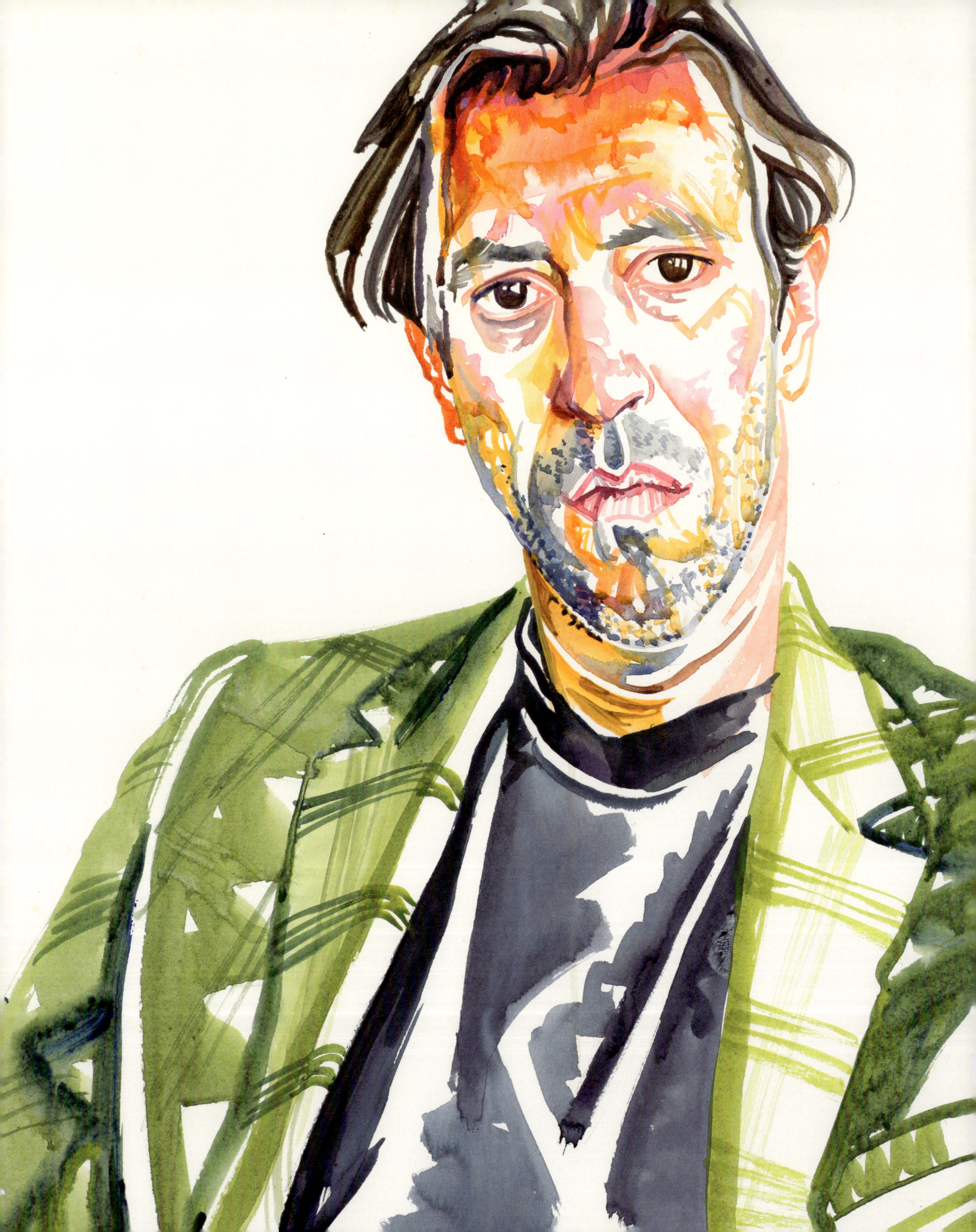

CONTENTS

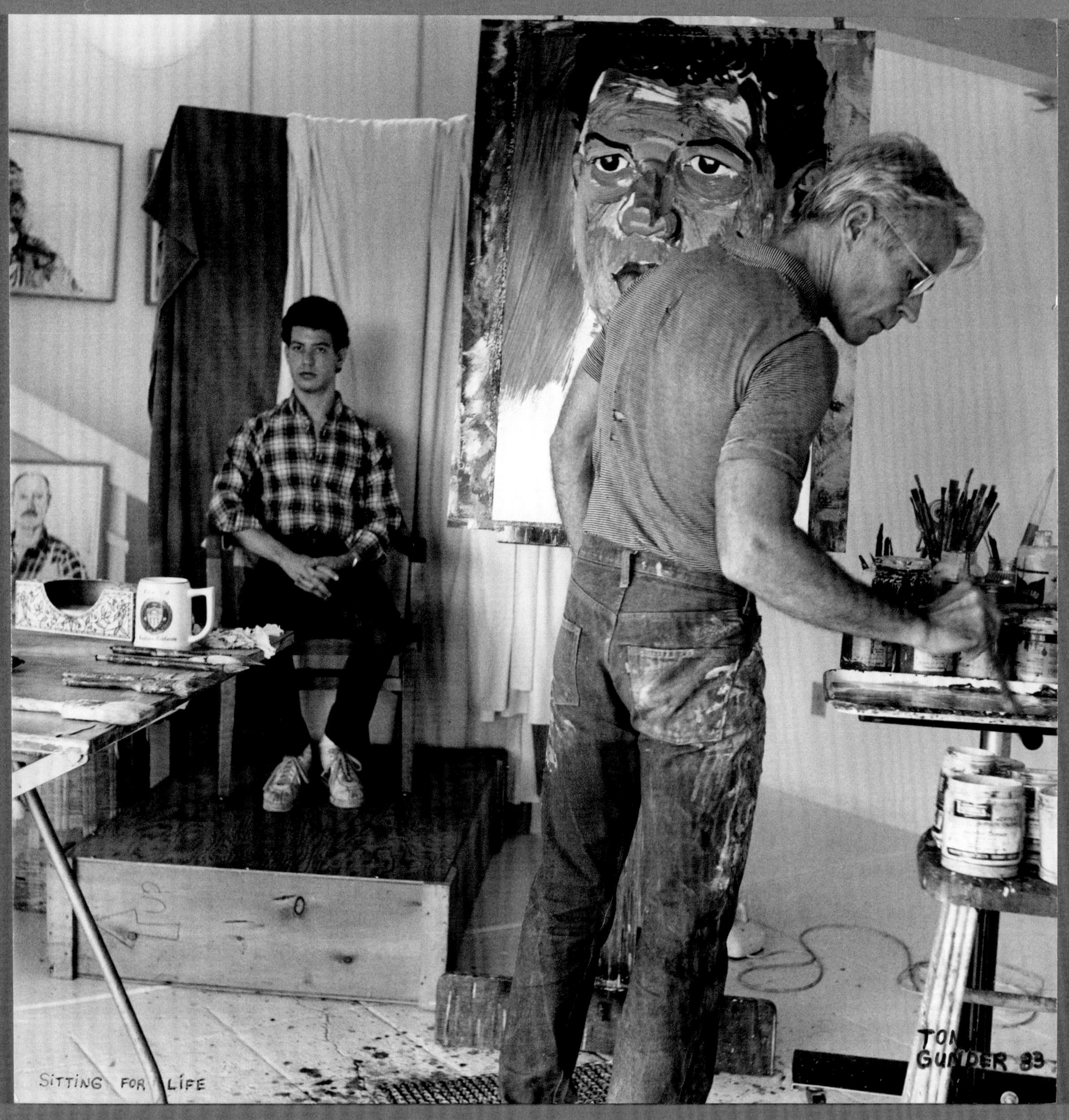

SITTING FOR LIFE
TOM GUNDER 83

This retrospective exhibition of the work of Don Bachardy marks a very special milestone in a long association between the artist and The Huntington. This warm and fruitful relationship began over two decades ago when, in 1999, Bachardy honored The Huntington by choosing it as the home for the papers of Christopher Isherwood, his companion of more than thirty years, who had died in 1986. Bachardy's own life and creativity are deeply woven throughout the Isherwood Papers, and conversations began early on about The Huntington's hope of ultimately acquiring the artist's own personal papers to sit alongside those of Isherwood. Thanks to Don Bachardy's generosity, we are thrilled to see that hope now becoming a reality.

A brilliant practitioner of the art of portraiture, Bachardy has devoted himself to a lifetime of capturing individuals through focused and meditative in-person sittings. Bachardy's artistic practice is deeply traditional and, paradoxically, ever more radical in an age of ubiquitous instant photography. Life sittings require a rapprochement: a coalescence of perspicacity and vulnerability. Sitting for a portrait makes for a unique mode of human interconnection. It is a process that has the power to reveal much more than mere likeness and one that sitters can't seem to forget. Bachardy is a master, and the results can be seen throughout the galleries and the book in your hands.

Beginning in 1999 with a cache of drawings selected by Bachardy to accompany the Isherwood accession—portraits of W. H. Auden, Stephen Spender, Aldous Huxley, and many others—the Library has gradually grown its Bachardy holdings for the past twenty-six years, including a stellar group of more than five hundred nudes donated by Don Howarth and Suzelle Smith in 2023. *Don Bachardy: A Life in Portraits*, however, showcases a large group of works given by Bachardy himself to The Huntington in 2024. These works, selected by guest curator Gregory Evans, are the first tranche in what will ultimately be an astounding Don Bachardy archive at

DIRECTORS' FOREWORD

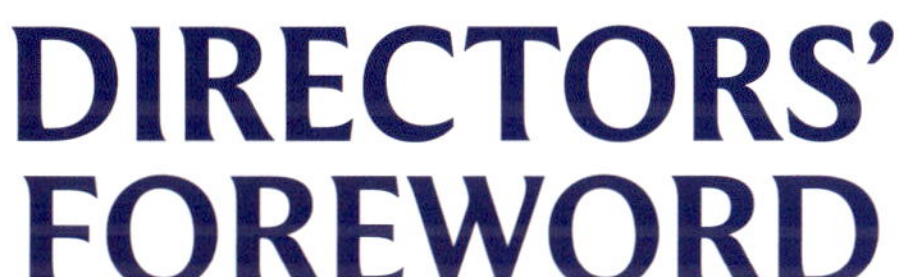

Fig. 1 Mark Sufrin and Don Bachardy in studio, photograph by Tony Gunder, November 28, 1982. Christopher Isherwood Papers

The Huntington, containing upwards of fifteen thousand works documenting a lifetime of human connection and artistic practice.

This exhibition would never have been possible without the vision and beneficence of Don Bachardy, for which we are deeply grateful. We are also indebted to guest curator Gregory Evans for the tremendous effort of surveying thousands of Bachardy's drawings and making this insightful selection. Evans's aesthetic eye, knowledge of the people, places, and times depicted, and dedication to this project were invaluable. The exhibition also could not have happened without Katherine Bucknell, director of the Christopher Isherwood Foundation, which preserves the creative legacies of both Isherwood and Bachardy. Ever gracious and perceptive, Bucknell was an indispensable collaborator and authoritative resource for both the exhibition and the catalogue. Tina Mascara, documentary filmmaker and longtime associate of the artist, was an amiable and knowledgeable partner. She provided expert facilitation for our work with Bachardy, aided by his studio assistant, Meredith Freeman. It has been a pleasure to work with critic, art historian, and novelist James Cahill, who brings to his study of Bachardy an expansive engagement with art from classical antiquity to the present. And an especially warm thank-you is due to actor Simon Callow and filmmaker and playwright Mary Agnes Donoghue for providing their lively reflections on Bachardy as an artist and friend.

Huntington curators Dennis Carr, Virginia Steele Scott Chief Curator of American Art, and Karla Nielsen, Senior Curator of Literary Collections, worked closely with Evans as co-curators, helping to shape the vision for the show and working to make that vision come to life. In this they were aided by assistant library curators Kristen Anthony and Sarah Francis. Lana Johnson, head of Exhibition Management, Anna Rose Canzano, senior exhibition coordinator, and Cynthia Tovar, head of Registration and Collections Management, handled a complex exhibition process with aplomb. Many other Library and Art Museum staff helped bring in Bachardy's archive on a quick timeline—processing, treating, imaging, and preparing items for the show. These include Kelly Kress, Jenny Werner, Jessamy Gloor, Jacob Yanes, Kristi Westberg, Jacklyn Chi, Mario Einaudi, Holly Mendenhall, and Sean Kennedy and the art preparators. Exhibition designer Stephen Saitas created a beautiful setting for Bachardy's work in the Boone Gallery, and Jean Patterson, manager of book publishing, has done the same with this publication. A special debt is owed to David Zeidberg, retired Avery Director of the Library, who was instrumental in bringing Isherwood's and Bachardy's archives to The Huntington and who, with Don, first envisioned mounting a retrospective exhibition of Don's work here.

Generous support for this exhibition and catalogue has been provided by the Douglas and Eunice Erb Goodan Endowment and the Robert F. Erburu Exhibition Endowment. Additional funding has been provided by The Ahmanson Foundation Exhibition and Education Endowment, The Melvin R. Seiden–Janine Luke Exhibition Fund in memory of Robert F. Erburu, and the Boone Foundation.

We are excited to share this retrospective tribute to California artist Don Bachardy with thousands of Huntington visitors and the reading public. Many will know him already. Those who are just getting acquainted have a marvelous treat in store.

Sandra Brooke Gordon
AVERY DIRECTOR OF THE LIBRARY

Christina Nielsen
HANNAH AND RUSSEL KULLY DIRECTOR OF THE ART MUSEUM

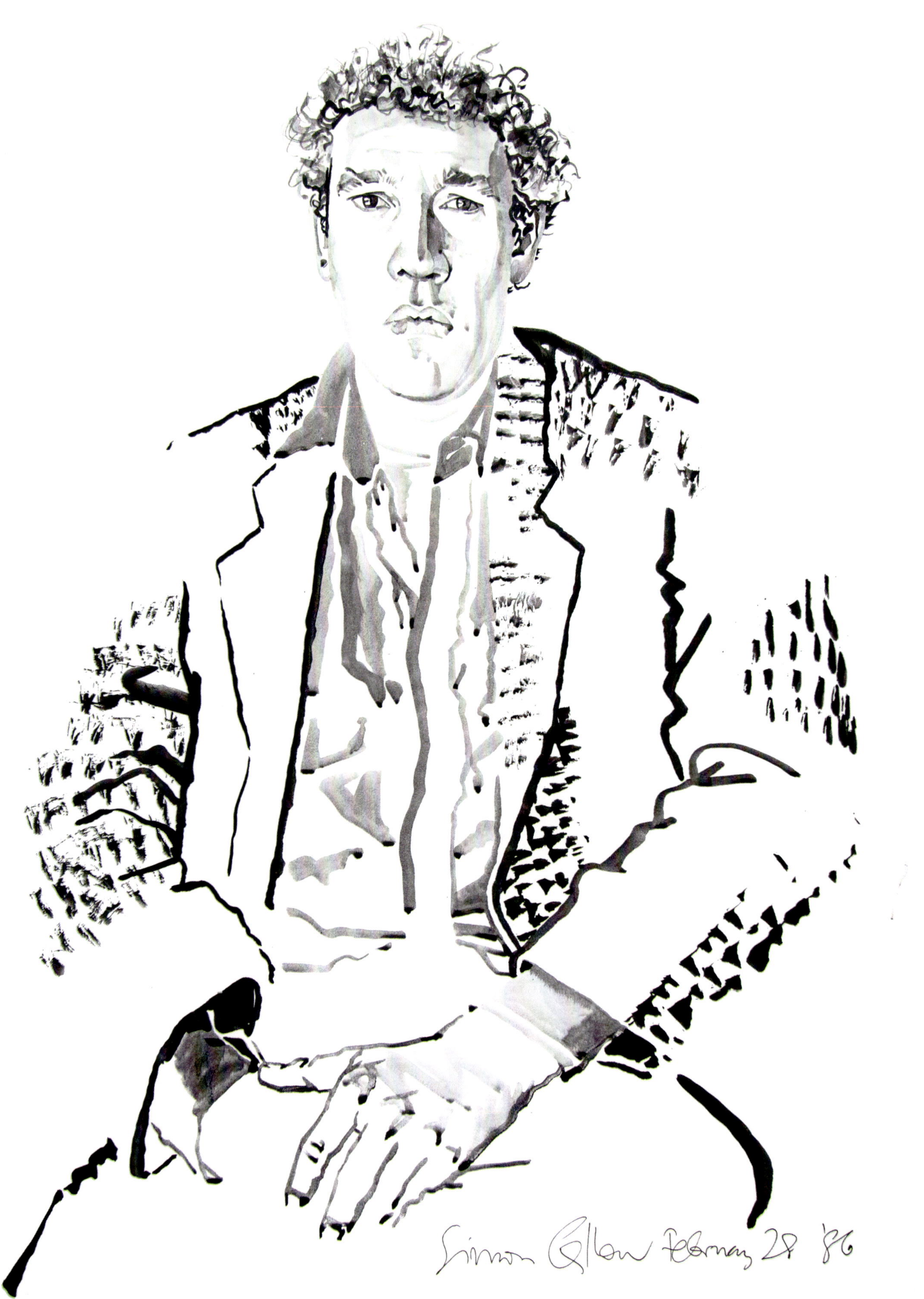

Simon Callow February 28 '86

SITTING FOR DON

Simon Callow

When I started writing about Charles Laughton (see p. 86), in 1985, I knew that I needed to talk to Christopher Isherwood. At the time of Laughton's death, the great actor had been working with Isherwood on an adaptation of three of Plato's *Dialogues*, a project very dear to Laughton's heart. This, I thought, was a unique opportunity to discover something both about Laughton's attitude toward his sexuality, a subject on which he was—publicly, at any rate—in complete denial, and also about the cast of his mind; Isherwood, master observer of gay lives within straight society, would surely have much to tell me on the subject of his old friend. He also happened to be my favorite English writer of the twentieth century: a bit of an idol, in fact.

By happy chance, just before I planned to go to Los Angeles, where he lived, I was working with Isherwood's friend Claire Bloom. She gave me his phone number but said, very firmly, "Speak to Don first. He'll smooth the way." I knew of course who Don Bachardy was, knew, indeed, all about him—his romance with Isherwood, the extraordinary age gap between them, their writing collaboration on the dramatization of *A Meeting by the River*. He and Isherwood were an exceptionally rare example of an openly gay couple; his elegant, exquisitely refined drawings adorned the covers of most editions of Isherwood's novels, and his drawings of the stars of John Osborne's eagerly awaited brace of plays at the Royal Court Theatre, *A Hotel in Amsterdam* and *Time Present*, had advertised them on programs and posters all over London. He was a star in his own right.

The day I arrived in Los Angeles, I called the number Claire had given me. "Hello," said a crisp English voice. "Oh, hello," I said. "Could I speak to Don Bachardy?" "Don's not here at the moment. This is Christopher Isherwood. Can I help?" "Well," I stumbled, "my name is Simon Callow. Claire Bloom gave me your number." "Oh, how is Claire?" "Well, very well. The truth is, Mr. Isherwood, it's you I want to talk to. I'm writing a book about Charles Laughton and—" "I don't want to talk about Charles," he said, briskly. "I assure you," I burbled, "I'm not interested in anything prurient." "I don't want to talk

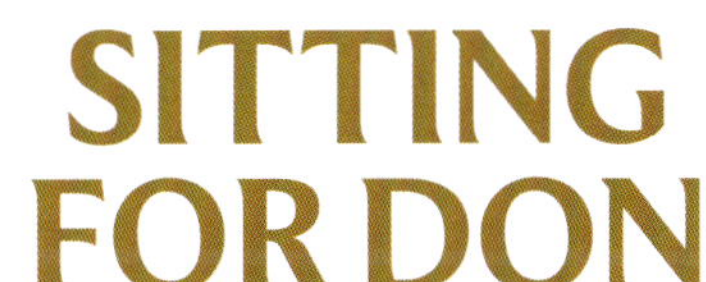

see p. 86

Fig. 1 *Simon Callow*, February 28, 1986. Acrylic on paper, 30⅛ × 22¼ in. (76.5 × 56.5 cm). Courtesy of Don Bachardy

about Charles," he said again, more firmly. "I can give you Mrs. Laughton's number." I knew, as he must have done, that Elsa Lanchester was long gone in Alzheimer's, and accepted defeat as graciously as I knew how. "Thank you," I said, pretending to note down the number. "You've been very helpful." I had taken care not to mention my Isherwoodolatry; I sensed it would only make things worse. I did the only thing I could do: Claire had given me Isherwood's address, and I took a cab to Adelaide Drive in Santa Monica, where he lived, just across the road from the Laughtons' house, and pushed a copy of my first book, *Being an Actor* (1984), through the letter box. I inscribed it "To Christopher Isherwood from Simon Callow. In no sense an inducement to talk about Laughton, simply a very small token of profound admiration and gratitude."

I never spoke to him again. Some months later his death was reported, and I realized why he hadn't wanted to talk: he died of cancer, also what Laughton had died of. Time passed; nearly a year. I was asked, before the book came out, to make a television documentary about the great actor. This involved going to New York to interview people who had worked with him—Rex Harrison, Peter Ustinov; wonderful. But I still regretted the absence of an interview with Isherwood. Then it suddenly occurred to me that Don Bachardy must have known Laughton almost as well as Isherwood did, so I called the number I had called before. "Hello," said a crisp English voice—Isherwood's voice. Bewildered, I stuttered, "Could I speak to Don Bachardy?" "This is Don. Who am I speaking to?" "My name is Simon Callow. I'm a British actor and—" "I know exactly who you are. Christopher was, uh, uh, reading your book for the second time when he died." "Goodness." "He found it, uh, fascinating." He laughed. "How can I help you?" I told him about the documentary. Would he talk? "Uh, uh, I don't know what I'd say." I suggested that we could discuss it when I came to Los Angeles the following week. When I called him, he said, quite abruptly, "I don't want to talk about Charles. He was, uh, uh, an enthusiasm of Christopher's I didn't share." "Oh," I said. "I'm very sorry," he replied. "But may I ask you an odd thing; would you, uh, uh, allow me to paint your portrait?" "Gosh. Of course."

As soon as I got to Los Angeles, I found my way to Santa Monica. Don was smaller than I had imagined, but compact and powerful in his white singlet and gray jeans. There was a fierce gravity about him, disrupted by sudden gurgles and gasps of laughter. And he spoke with the unmistakable accent of the upper middle-class Englishman with whom he had lived for over thirty years. "I know I talk like Christopher," he said. "I don't care." The house was hung like a laundry with large sheets of paper, filled with images in rough strokes, gray and black, a mixture of Japanese brush and black acrylic paint. The images were unmistakably of Isherwood: in pajamas, mostly, sometimes naked. I had seen innumerable images of the writer, many—perhaps most—by Don, but this was something altogether different: the writer's habitual spryness and quizzicality, sexy and elfin, replaced by something almost monumental, the face contorted with pain, but occasionally almost blank, the body sometimes clothed, often not, his *membrum virile* dangling in the foreground, slack, majestic, redundant. Here was Isherwood awake, Isherwood slumbering, Isherwood locked in pain, Isherwood dying, Isherwood dead. "I embarked on this, uh, uh, sequence during Christopher's last illness. It was something I knew had to be done. He was in great pain, but I insisted. It was very difficult for us both." Seeing the drawings at such close quarters, in the house in which Isherwood had lived and died, was overwhelming, the experience both intimate and impersonal, being suddenly taken to the heart of this exceptional relationship, admitted into his confidence by a man I had only just met, describing, in his searching way, some pretty deep truths not only about Chris but also about what it is to be so viscerally connected to another person.

It was all the more extraordinary that these profound truths were coming from the mouth of someone who, though his hair was becoming silvery, was still slim-hipped and bright-eyed, almost boyish. He expressed his hard truths with something like joy, the joy of having precisely nailed experience. Silence fell. He laughed, a sort of private laugh, reflecting on what he had lived through. "Shall we do the drawing?" he said, brightly. He put me next to a window that looked out over the Santa Monica Valley. I quickly sensed that he preferred not to talk, so we sat together for nearly two hours in that strange intimacy that exists between subject and artist: who else apart from a mother or a lover—or perhaps a doctor—looks at one with such penetrating scrutiny? "It's done," he suddenly announced. "You're a very good sitter." "The silence was wonderful," I said. "Yes!" he cried. "I only recently realized that the reason I paint portraits is because it's the only way I can get that silence." After finishing a portrait, Don famously asks his sitter to sign it, as if he or she were somehow its co-creator. When I went to put my name to the one he had made of me, I was taken aback: he had drawn a sort of double portrait of me and Charles Laughton—as if Laughton and I had had a child together. I pointed this out. He said, "Oh, really? I never know what I've done. I rely on people to tell me."

As if all that were not enough, as we were making our farewells he suddenly, unprompted, started talking about Laughton, how pompous he was, and how he failed to relate to Don at all. And then, with wonderful precision, he talked about the relationship between Charles and Elsa. "They tormented each other, that was their whole life's work, and they were, uh, uh, perfectly innocent that this was what they were doing." In ten minutes of sustained and brilliantly observed analysis, he told me everything I needed to know about them in these later years of their life. I understood then that Don's portraitist's eye went far beyond the surface.

I left him having been brought abruptly closer to my literary hero, Christopher Isherwood, and my biographical subject, Charles Laughton. Not bad for three hours, which also produced an extraordinarily striking image of me as I had certainly never seen myself. I wasn't sure where our acquaintance would go after that. As it happens, I was summoned a day or two later to the Hollywood mansion of Tony Richardson, the cavalier English film director, whom I had never met but who had, he said, a wonderful new play in which he wanted to direct me. When I arrived, he told me he had found out that Don and I knew each other and that he would be arriving at any moment, which was delightful to me. Then Richardson, with what I knew from other people was entirely characteristic behavior, told me that he wanted me to read the play there and then. I was reluctant to do so at pistol point, so to speak, and told him that I'd read it overnight and call him first thing in the morning. This did not please him. At this point Don arrived, and Tony left the house huffily, urging us to avail ourselves of the contents of his drinks cabinet and instructing me to call him the following morning *without fail*.

So here Don and I were, in someone else's house, sitting on the floor, there being, for unfathomable reasons, no chairs to sit on. We got drinks and started to talk. Don was somewhat subdued; inevitably, the conversation turned to Christopher. I ventured that of all his books, the one I was least able to connect to was *My Guru and His Disciple* (1980)—a highly enjoyable study of his discipleship with Swami Prabhavananda. As an account of pupil and guru, it was entirely compelling. The difficulty was trying to connect that aspect of Isherwood's life with all the rest of it. "It was, uh, uh," said Don, "the only area of him of which I couldn't be part." I said that I could see how that might be so. There was, however, I said, one exchange in the book that I found infinitely touching. At one of their first meetings, Isherwood had asked Prabhavananda whether his being involved in a sexual relationship with a young man was an obstacle to his spiritual development. After briefly sighing, Prabhavananda had replied, "You must try to think of him as the Lord Krishna."

When I said this, Don's face broke up and he wept. "I'm sorry," he said. "It's still so fresh." I hugged him—we were still sitting on the floor—and I said, "What you're feeling is unimaginable. So many years of being intertwined." He said, "I think we'd better go to supper." I was meeting friends; he joined us. Over the meal, we talked about everything but Christopher; Don drank a great deal and laughed a great deal, as did we all.

Since then, I have seen him pretty well whenever I've been in Los Angeles. I've seen him in London, and in Berlin, where I read from the collection of his and Christopher's letters, *The Animals* (2014); oddly, at his behest, I read his letters and he Christopher's. Later, at The Metropolitan Museum of Art in New York, Alan Cumming read Don and I Christopher, which seemed a better fit.

I have rarely traveled so fast and so deep into friendship as I did with Don. The odd circumstances—the last drawings of Christopher in the house, the intense portrait session, our abandonment by our host in Hollywood, his sudden access of grief—seemed to take us very rapidly to a position of great frankness and emotional freedom. I have since discovered that all his friendships are of this order. He is an uncommonly present individual. It is impossible to imagine him having a casual friendship, or indeed a casual conversation. He brings the entirety of his being to whatever he's doing—painting, talking, writing. There is always about him that sense of discovery, of nailing, or doing his utmost to nail, a particular truth. To be with him is to join him on that exhilarating and unending voyage.

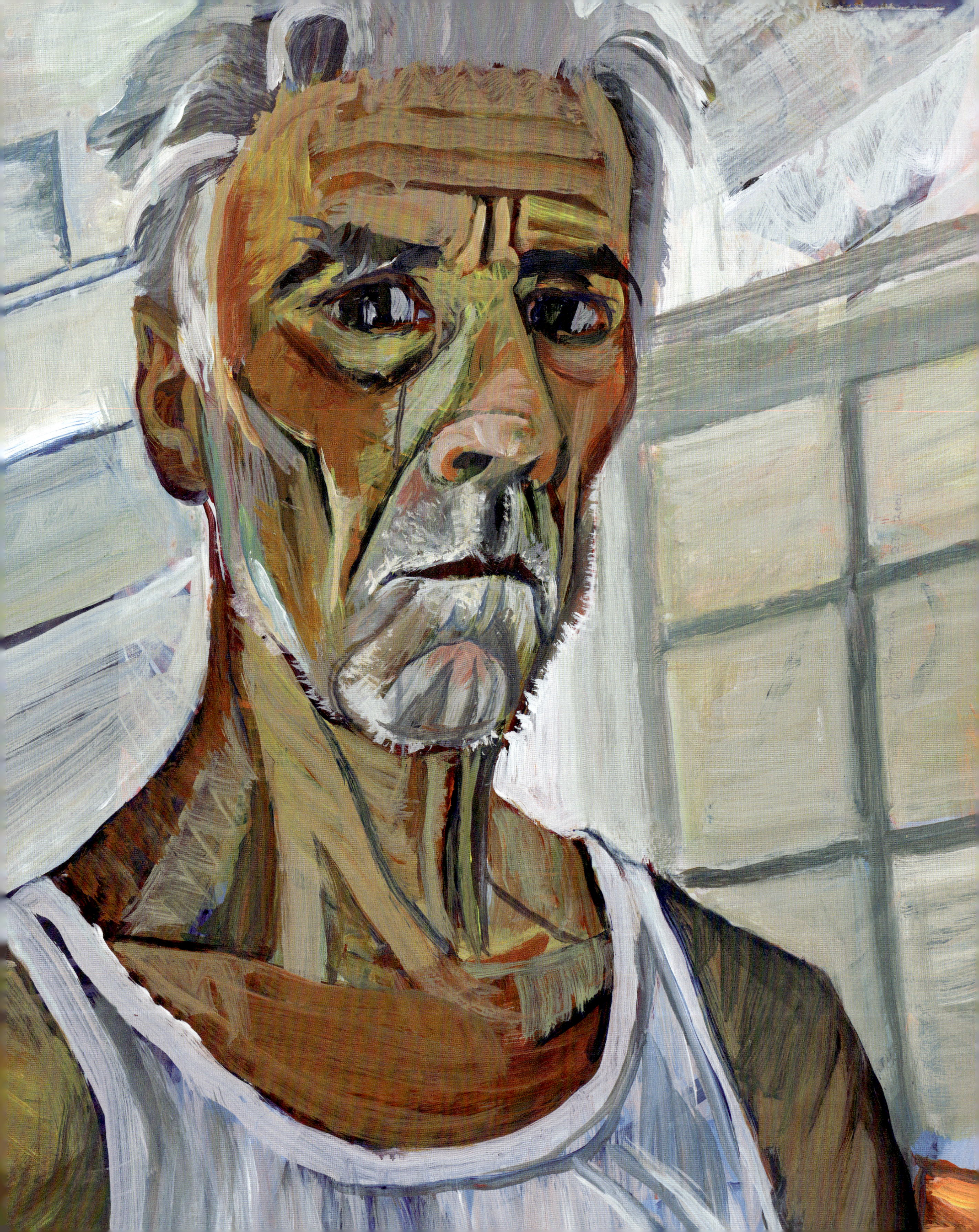

GREGORY EVANS TALKS WITH DON BACHARDY AT NINETY

Excerpts from
three conversations about
Bachardy's work, edited by
Tina Mascara and
Katherine Bucknell

Gregory Evans Two years ago, Katherine Bucknell asked me if I would help update your website by selecting a group of newer images. I was delivered an external hard drive that contained a copy of your personal archive database. It was approximately seventeen thousand images. YIKES!! What had I gotten myself into?!

After recovering from the shock, I realized the rare opportunity that was at my fingertips—the opportunity to discover the life's work of artist Don Bachardy. Eighty-two years of work (1940–2022)! I went through the entire database several times, moving from 1940 to 2022, then from 2022 back to 1940, and then again from 1940 to 2022. I started making my selection of works that I liked. My choices were not based on any criteria other than what captivated me. Which works reached out to me. Which works I felt a strong connection to. I became so engrossed in what I was seeing that ideas started swirling in my head. It seemed as if there were endless themes for publications.

The deeper I delved into your database, the more exciting it became. From 1970 until this time, I had always known you as my friend Don, who happened to be an artist. I was familiar only with what I had seen in your exhibitions and publications. But now, I was looking at the work of artist Don Bachardy—works that were mostly unfamiliar to me. I was now looking at and experiencing thousands of faces, bodies, eyes, lips, noses, hands, feet…one after another after another. Thousands of days of private moments spent between the artist and the model. It hit me that most of these works had never been seen by anyone other than you, the sitter, and perhaps by Christopher [Isherwood]. Thousands of works neatly filed away for years, decades, waiting to be uncovered and exposed to life once again.

I [knew I] would love to make an exhibition. I was and remain deeply moved by this rare experience. We found that most of the works I selected are works that you still own. There's no record of how many works you've made in total, because I don't think you've kept records of what you sold, gifted, or traded over the years. It occurred

Self-Portrait (detail), July 4, 2004
Acrylic on paper, 28⅞ × 23 in. (73.3 × 58.4 cm)
Don Bachardy Papers

to me that just because I found images in the database that I personally liked, there was no way to confirm their location. This forced us to do a physical inventory. My first edit of the 17,000 resulted in a selection of 2,850. But, of these, about 250 could not be located.

Don Bachardy I think I've been very irresponsible in not keeping proper lists of works that I let go.

GE Because there is no record of these missing works in your archive, I'm going to make a guesstimate that you've probably produced well over twenty thousand works since the age of four.

DB Twenty?! My brain can't even handle it [*laughter*].

GE Maybe that is a good segue into this creative drive that you've always had. Once you said that the first time you can remember being inspired was when you were four years old. It was the movie *Jezebel* [1938]. What inspired you?

DB Yes. My brother, Ted, and I were taken to the movies very early by our mother, and for years we were a threesome. And secretly my mother was taking me and Ted downtown to first-run movies, which would have horrified my father—paying general admission at first-run! We were down there for the early-morning show; they weren't nearly as expensive in the morning as they were at night, so she could hide the money she was spending on our movies—because my father required her to make lists of everything she spent in a week, and Friday night was the showdown each week. And sometimes it was a real showdown because my mother was hiding things—hiding money she was spending.

GE So there was no budget for movies?

DB No budget whatsoever, so everything had to be padded. All the other expenses.

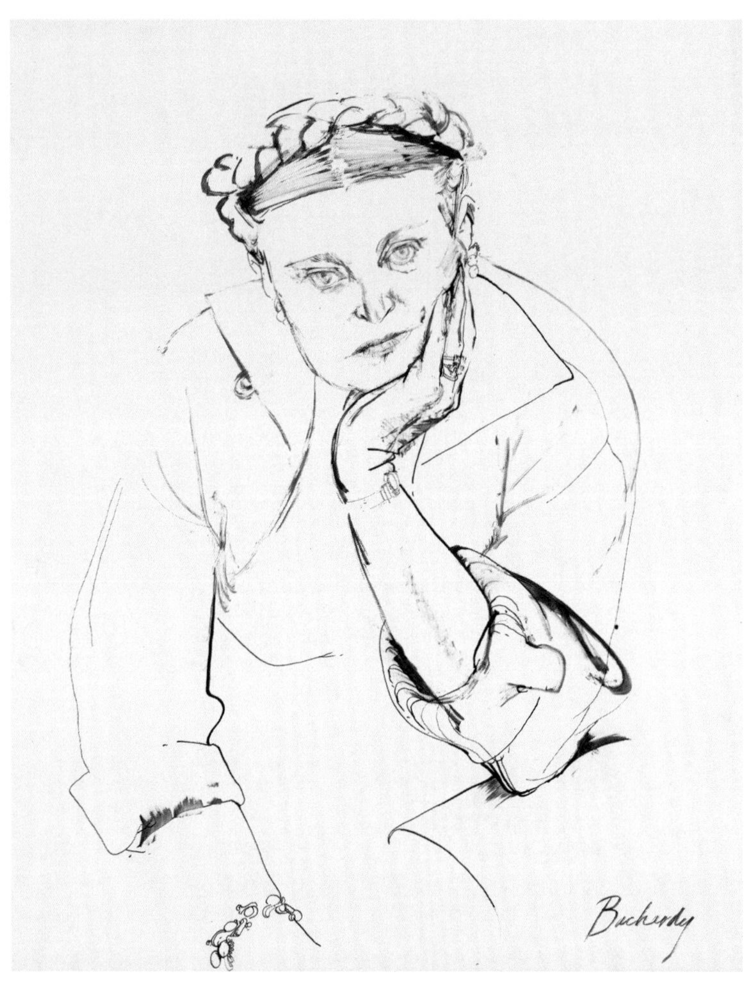

Glade Bachardy (Don's mother), 1960
Graphite on paper, 28 × 22 in. (71.1 × 55.9 cm)
Courtesy of the Christopher Isherwood Foundation

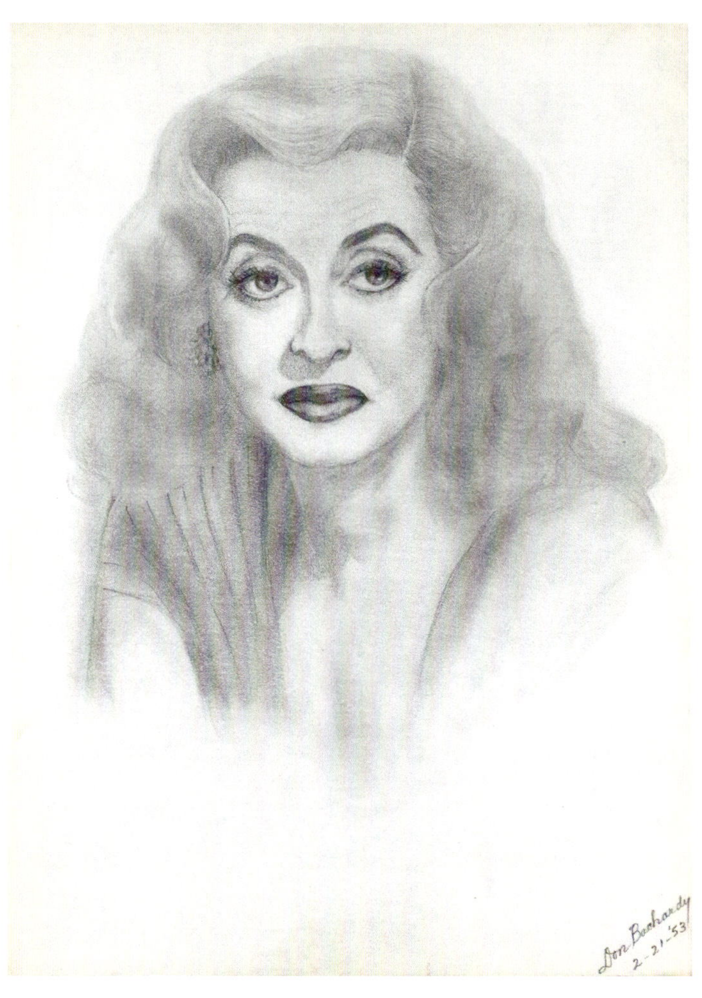

GE Our age gap is nineteen years. People in my generation would say the first movie they were inspired by or could remember was Disney. "Oh, I saw *Bambi*." But for you, at the age of four, it was *Jezebel*! What was it that impacted you?

DB It was the "sausage curls" on Bette Davis. And the gown she wore to the ball that shocked everybody, because it was red. And in a black-and-white film, it was black, but it still looked pretty impressive. And that was a very early but indelible impression for Ted and me.

GE Were you able to distinguish color in black-and-white films?

DB No, but I could imagine. I was a very visual person at a very early age. Probably because I was taken to the movies all the time and loved it. And because it was secret from my father. Both Ted and I—the three of us—almost criminals.

GE We found these early works starting in 1940. You may have started painting and drawing before that, but this is the earliest we have been able to locate. You were probably six years old at that time. It is not unusual that five- and six-year-olds would do these tempera paintings in kindergarten on construction paper.

DB I was always working, drawing.

GE It's not unusual that you would have made these. But what struck me about them is that at the age of six, you already had an eye. A sense of balance and proportion. In these flower paintings, you are totally aware of the edges of the paper. You were daring to take things right up to the edge, as though you had already seen the work completed before you had even started. This is quite sophisticated for a six-year-old.

DB I was so lucky to not only have a brother who could draw but who drew all the time and didn't pull me down. He encouraged me to join him. I was trying to keep up with him. He was so much better in the

Bette Davis, February 21, 1953
Graphite on paper, 14 × 10 in. (35.6 × 25.4 cm)
Don Bachardy Papers

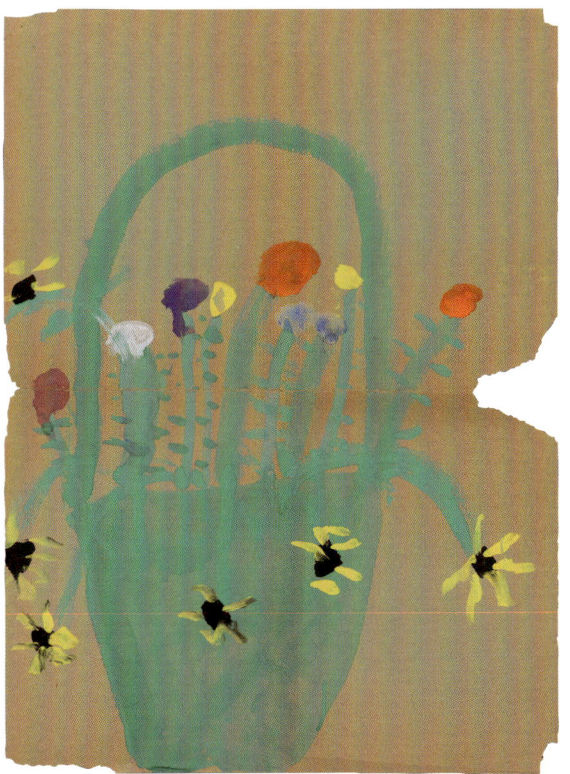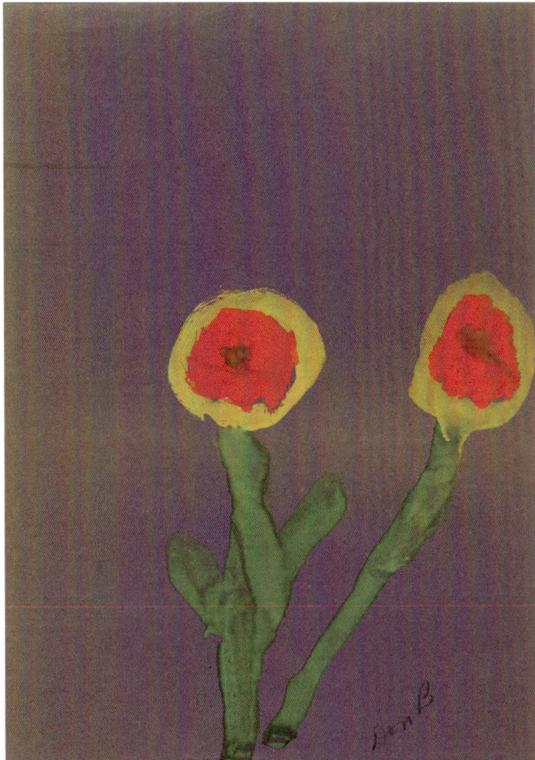

beginning, and eventually, I was as good as he was. And that was fun for both of us.

GE Your school works seem much more accomplished than those of other students your age.

DB It was fortunate for me to have a brother I wanted to imitate and who challenged me. And I carried what I learned from Ted into kindergarten, then first and second grade. Nobody in my classes could draw like I could. Especially the girls. And the girls were always my friends. And they encouraged me. They asked me to do drawings for them, and I was so pleased to do it. It took me a long time before I could get a likeness, but I was right in there, working.

GE I see in your drawing a big jump from the '40s. The year 1953 was a watershed for you because that is the year you met Chris. Chris's entry into your life made an enormous impact on your work.

Fig. 1   Childhood drawing, 1940. Gouache on paper, 23 × 18 in. (58.4 × 45.7 cm). Don Bachardy Papers

Fig. 2   Childhood drawing, 1940. Gouache and graphite on paper, 15½ × 11 in. (39.4 × 27.9 cm). Don Bachardy Papers

DB He encouraged me immediately. When he found out that I could draw, he made up his mind that I was going to be an artist.

———————

DB He was my first live sitter. I'd been copying photos of movie actors for many years before I met him (see pp. 19, 32). And he made me realize that there was nothing equivalent to working from life. A photograph of somebody is somebody else's idea of what the subject looks like, so I had to work from life in order to prove myself a portraitist. And Chris was my very first sitter from life. And I did a hair-raising drawing that even staggered him. What could I say? I knew that he was really taken aback, but to me, I was not trying to please him. I was trying to do what he told me he believed portraiture was. It was a naked revelation of how I saw him. And even though it was very unattractive to me, it was still very accurate—or as accurate a likeness of him that I could do. So he became his own victim. And I knew it set him back. I knew him well enough to know that that first look at that picture really shocked him.

    You see, after all those years of drawing mostly from movie actors, this was the first time I had a real, steady subject who was willing to sit for me every day if I asked him to. And that's what got me going. And people I met with him, I could ask them to sit for me.

    He was telling me, "You can do it. Don't hesitate." And then when I came home, "Show me what you did." He cared and he praised.

———————

DB By the time I was working from life, I had a very strong sense of what a likeness was, and other people might not see a likeness in my work, but I always knew whether or not my own work was a defensible likeness.

GE You've always been very disciplined. Sometimes the hardest part is getting from your bed to the studio to work but once you get to that sheet of paper and the sitter, you are off. Did you have sittings where you thought, "I wish I'd never arranged a sitting with this person"?

DB Continually.

GE Where you were totally turned off by the sitter?

DB That is something that never ended. There was no way of lying to myself, because I had to believe in my own sense of what a likeness is, and, of course, people who looked at my portraits of people they knew—they couldn't see any likeness at all, or there was something wrong…

GE Representation.

DB Yes.

GE That you became bored with the sitter?

DB I couldn't afford to be bored with the sitter. Because as soon as I started working from life, some of my most challenging sitters were people I exposed myself to. I always did. I never shirked from anybody who was willing to sit for me.

   I will tell you a good test of that. I did several sittings with [Swami] Prabhavananda (see p. 102), and Chris had to admit that at least the first three or four results had not pleased him. I knew he felt that I missed something essential in Prabhavananda. And it took me many efforts. And it was terribly tough to ask him to sit, and then to go up there and do a sitting with him, all by myself. That was an absolutely agonizing test to me.

GE What did he feel that you had gotten…?

DB Well, how could he express it? Except by saying, it wasn't his way of seeing Prabhavananda. And it took me at least three or four sittings before I did one that Chris could sincerely praise.

GE That is why I was asking you earlier if you were involved with the Vedanta Society and if you learned [about] nondualism, which is a central teaching of Vedanta.…And I don't know what year that happened, but maybe what you were referring to is what Chris was frustrated with in the portraits. If I get this correctly, nondualism is really seeing beyond the body and seeing the true innermost self. And I do see that occurring in your work, because in your earlier works, you really mastered the traditional, the literal representations of your sitter; then there is a transition where you start to move below the physicality.

DB Even when I achieved that, I could never be certain that I could hang onto it and repeat it each time I did another drawing of anybody; it was elusive. I could do it sometimes, well enough to please myself, and other times I couldn't. And even Chris had to tell me that those early attempts at Prabhavananda had failed. And it was painful for him to be truthful with me.

GE Tough critic.

DB Well, I insisted on it, and he knew he couldn't lie to me. And I already knew him too well to know that even if he praised something that wasn't really right, I would guess. And I could; I knew if he was making it easy on me.

GE There are many people who will say that all portraits are really self-portraits. What do you think?

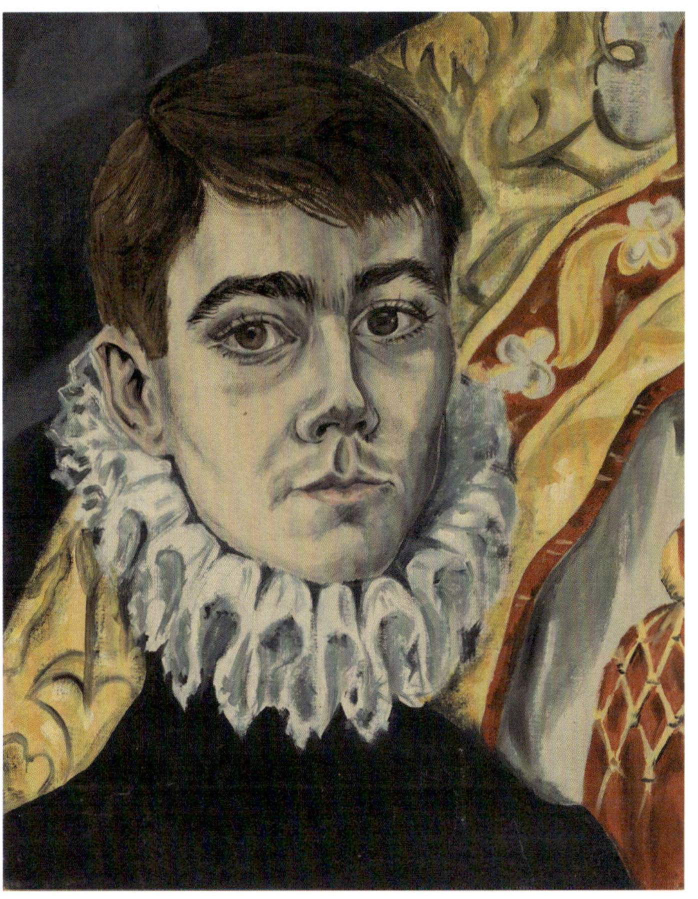

DB That doesn't mean anything, because it doesn't take into consideration the ability to be objective about a sitter. And there is no such thing as a perfect portrait of somebody that everybody agrees is a likeness. You might get a huge majority of people to say, "Yes." But there are still those who look at it and say, "I can't see who it is."

GE Going back to this idea of nondualism: In many of the drawings I was attracted to in my selections, it is this merging of the artist—you—and the sitter, where you become one. The merging of the sitter and the painter. And as a viewer, an observer of the piece, I feel it adds another dynamic to that work.

DB There is no way of becoming absolute because there is always an area for disagreement. There is no absolute where I can, say, look at that [John Singer] Sargent portrait and know it is a perfect likeness of her, but that doesn't mean it proves it for anybody else. That is still my opinion.

GE In many cases, I would rather walk into a room of art and not know who the art is by, who the sitter is, what the subject is. It is only after I've seen it that if there was something that I was really taken by, then I might want to know more about it. But I would rather not have information up front.

DB The information is irrelevant.

GE Who it is supposed to be or what year it was. Any of the backstory. But that is me. I know there are a lot of people who want to know that up front. They want to know what they will be looking at before they look at it.

DB If they think they know everything, they are wrong. There is no way a portrait likeness is absolute.

GE That is where the words "wrong" and "right," "good" and "bad" come into play. Good restaurant, bad restaurant. No, I like that restaurant. Or, that's one of my favorite works of art. It isn't good, bad, right, wrong. It doesn't mean anything. It is my opinion.

Fig. 3 *Untitled*, 1956. Paint on board, 19 × 16 in. (48.3 × 40.6 cm). Don Bachardy Papers

DB I learned that the hard way, by becoming a portrait artist. And the only way to become a portrait artist is to realize the absolute is impossible to achieve.

GE The first painter whose work you loved was Francis Bacon. Can you speak to what in his work had an impact on you?

DB It just wasn't like that of anybody else. Imagine the courage it demanded of me to do a sitting of him (see p. 88). I've really been through a lot. I really have exposed myself to hideous situations. "Can I do this or not?" And it scared the hell out of me.

GE Did you meet him when you were at the Slade [School of Fine Art]?

DB I had already met him, and I knew he would never have sat for me. But I knew he couldn't get out of it because he loved Chris, and I knew that Chris loved him, so I was taking advantage of him. And there was no way he would ever have done it without Chris. And that is an awful, heavy piece of knowledge to take with me into a sitting. And if any-thing, it made a man of me. To dare to do a sitting with him, Francis Bacon, even though I knew his fondness for Chris would protect me, and he would not be able to wriggle out of it. That only made it all the more challenging.

GE Did he comment on the portraits?

DB I can't remember. He signed it because I asked him to, just to prove that he had participated in it. That's always been my reason for having my sitters sign my pictures, because if they are genuinely good likenesses, that is the only way to authenticate it. I wasn't working from a photograph.

GE Did Lucian [Freud]'s sitting come after Bacon's?

DB Yes, it did. And surviving that sitting with Bacon—that was an event for me. If I had done a sitting with Francis Bacon, I could face anything as an artist. I had the required guts to do it. And if I do say so myself, I did at least a passably good likeness of him.

GE You did two, if not three.

DB They may not be my best work but they are undeniably portraits of him, and they have his signature and date on it. So in court, I could win.

GE So there! Not done from a photograph.

DB Not done from a photograph!

GE You had your first gallery exhibition in London [in 1961].

DB Yes.

GE At the Redfern [Gallery].

DB I must have had a show here, and I might have had a show in New York. But that London show was the real test.

GE Were you nervous about that?

DB Yes.

GE But it was quite successful?

DB Yes, it was. And because of Chris, so many people showed up. The gallery was dazzling. I was stunned.

GE How old were you when you gave up the belief that people were showing up for Chris and not your art?

DB I don't think I know it even now. No, he is part of my history. How could I remove him from my biography?

GE I've written my own narrative by looking at thousands of your works. I created my own narrative and I do come across periods where I can see you going in a new direction. And I can almost feel you becoming insecure and reverting to a previous, more comfortable area. I see advancements and then retreats.

DB Isn't that life? Every one of us has that experience in living our own life.

GE I notice in '85 that you are working mostly in black and white, with a few watercolor and color drawings, but mostly black and white. But '85 is a significant year because Christopher is ill, and you are both aware that his time is limited. You devote quite a few months exclusively to Christopher dying (see pp. 122–24).

DB Well, I was working with him every day. Often doing several drawings. And it didn't stop once he was dead. I went on working, so there was no escaping.

GE I think the point is, in '85, there is very little color in your work. All those works you did of Chris were black and white.

DB They had to be.

GE The color was disappearing from your work. And even going in after—I think it was one full month, almost to the day, of Christopher's death—there were no works. And the first work that appears—I have the name here, we can reference it later—it was a gentleman

[Rogers Albritton]. It was February the 7th, the first one I could find. But for that entire year, almost all the works you did, you continued on in black and white, with very few in color.

DB I was working under such pressure, such an uncomfortable setup, and worrying about him—that I was making it hard on him as well as myself. But just to keep going was hard work. But can you imagine the working conditions while he was dying? And trying to even justify myself for doing what I was doing.

GE Why do you say justifying?

DB I realized by drawing him, I couldn't get closer than that doing anything else. And that is why I quit working in color. I didn't want to wonder, "Which color now?" If I was doing it just in black and white, I could concentrate on him, and not have to wonder, "Blue or purple"?

GE I understand that with him, but what I am referring to is after his death, you continued on in black and white. And the drawings and the paintings seemed—pretty much consistently—the sitters seemed somber.
　　　　Then in '87, I see that you are trying to break into a new style, and you are using color, and it is very different. And it is heavier color. It is almost like the connection to the sitter is secondary. It seems like you are using more of their faces as a palette for this new style that you are trying to find; you are making color marks. It goes on for a couple of years but I can feel you never gave up. You felt determined. You didn't abandon it. Then by the late '80s, you hit it. It is like you catch your stride again. It must have been a very difficult time for you, because you had always had Christopher to critique, to encourage, and to talk about your work. And so here you are now on your own. You lost your major support and you are left with your own decisions, but you also find your own inner strength and your determination and your discipline. You didn't give up. I suppose like with many artists, something happens like that with the life of a partner, maybe a loss of inspiration; there may be a big void in their work. Like they didn't work for two years, and there were only a couple of works. But you didn't. You produced as much work as you always had.

————

DB Seeing the images here with you is startling to me. I don't know what to say about my work, and it seems to me, if it has to be explained…I really don't want to even—

GE Well, you've already explained yourself by making the work.

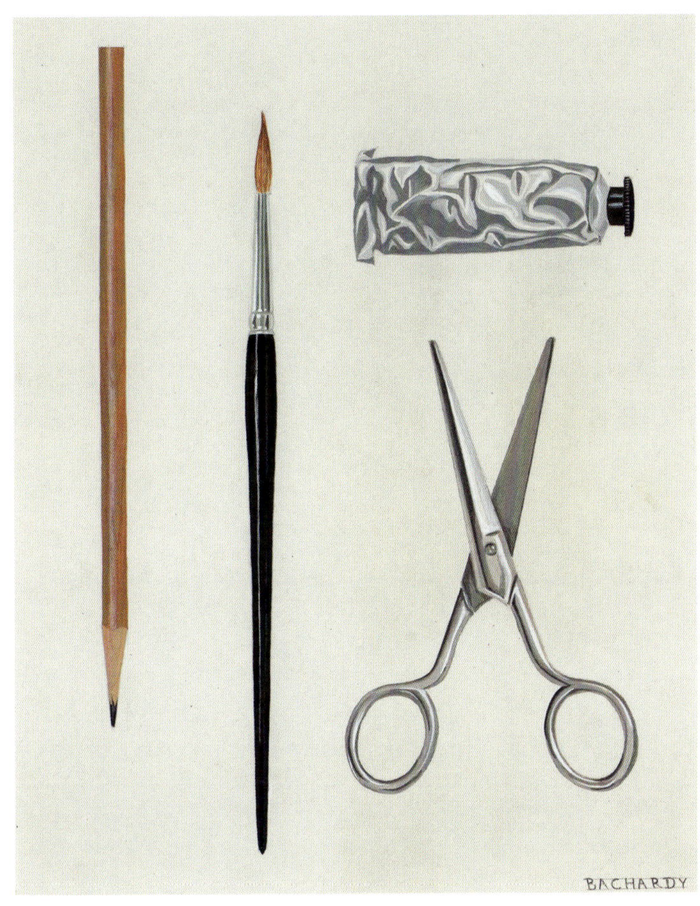

DB Yes. The work is the work, and I'm interested to hear what anybody else has to say about it, but not in what I say. I kind of go mum when I look at my work. If the work doesn't tell the story, there is no story to tell.

GE Yes, I agree with you on that. I almost loathe to even put labels or introductions to exhibitions to tell people what it is they are looking at. Because I think, Shouldn't the work just speak for itself? A picture is worth a thousand words.

DB I never have any intention when I start working until I'm looking at my sitter, and then I know what to do.

GE Nothing is premeditated.

DB I'm not saying, "Oh, it feels like a green day." I'm speechless and thoughtless when I pick up the brush, and I find out what I want to do by using the brush. I'm not the least bit equipped to talk about my work, I guess, except I can talk about the subject and what I convey of the subject once I see it, but when I start out, I have no intention at all until I find something to concentrate on in my sitter.

It's almost all on paper, and it's the size of the paper that tells me how much I can do or how to…considering all the work I've done, there is very little variation in the scale, because it is all dictated to me by the paper itself. I almost never painted on canvas. I've just had enough experience working on it to know that I don't like working on any kind of surface but smooth. I don't want a surface to—it has to demand something from me.

GE The moment determines the medium and the palette. So you did the series of eight hundred nudes back in the early 2000s (see pp. 141, 145, 148), and most of them are of the same palette. There is a lot of white, but every once in a while, there appear more dense, opaque nudes. Do you recall what caused the break from that?

DB It is the demand of the moment. Yes. I don't think about it; I think about it after I've done it. I say to myself, "Yes or no, or take it away or destroy it?"

Fig. 4 *Untitled*, 1957. Gouache on paper, 9¼ × 7⅜ in. (23.5 × 18.6 cm). Don Bachardy Papers

27

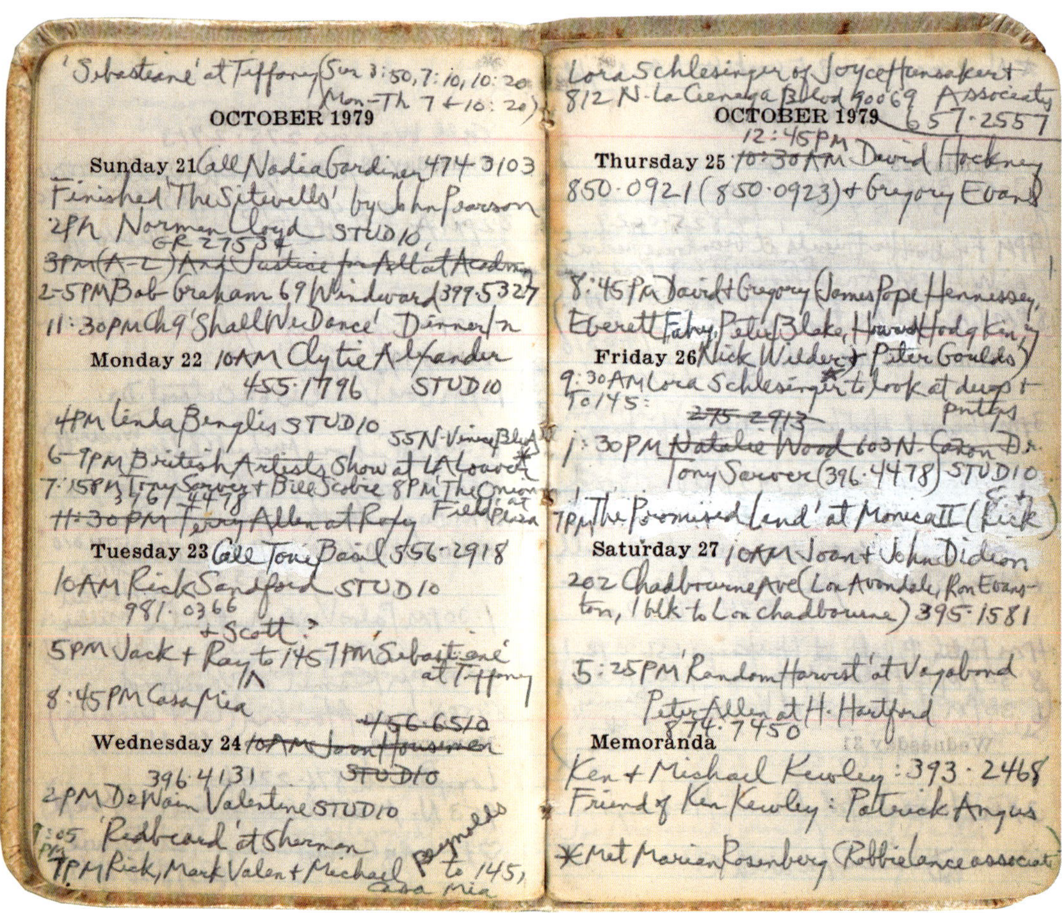

GE These are all part of the upcoming Don Bachardy exhibition, which is both exciting and painful for me, because it is such a limited number of works out of such a huge body of work. One last question: What was it like for you to paint yourself?

DB Only when I am desperate. When I feel I have a fierce need to work, and it is so fierce I can even get myself to do another self-portrait. The subject just couldn't interest me less. But if I have to work, I have to find something there to work with.

GE So you are an unwilling sitter?

DB Yes. If I think too much about the way I want to do a picture, I get lost. But if I have somebody to look at for that length of time, I always know what to do. And I guess I'm also trying to amuse myself by maybe taking some kind of different approach, but it is only when the sitting begins that I can think in those terms. Before I start a sitting,

Fig. 5   Don Bachardy datebook, October 1979.
Courtesy of Don Bachardy

I can't say to myself the kind of picture I want to do. It's all dictated by the experience. I have no intention except to release in myself the energy to go at it.

GE Perfect.

DB And now I'm thinking of a cabinet of drawers of abstract work. Now, what does that have to do with my portrait work? I started doing it out of desperation. I didn't have a sitter, and I was sick to death of starting another portrait of myself. I did many drawers of abstract work, just color, and very little difference in size. It's tough for me to talk about it.

GE I'm not going to show you works, but I'm going to point something out. I think you were doing abstracts long before you were aware you were doing abstracts. I find abstraction appearing in some of your portraits. I see this playfulness and looseness and freedom, mark making; you are using the sitter, but at the same time you are using your surroundings and becoming more playful. So maybe unknowingly, you are incorporating—at least in my eyes, I see abstraction in there. I see Abstract Expressionism. As you say, your brush does the talking.

DB I can't even talk about my work unless I'm looking at a particular picture. And it is still essentially for me about the experience I am having, looking at a particular person and often being astonished even with somebody that I've known for years, really what they look like to me. And even somebody—a friend I've known for years, who has sat for me many times—each new sitting is a totally new experience.

GE Do you feel satisfied?

DB By what?

GE Your last eighty-seven years of work?

DB Oh, no. No. There are individual pictures. I say to myself, "Yes, that has got something."

The interviews were conducted in Santa Monica in May 2024.

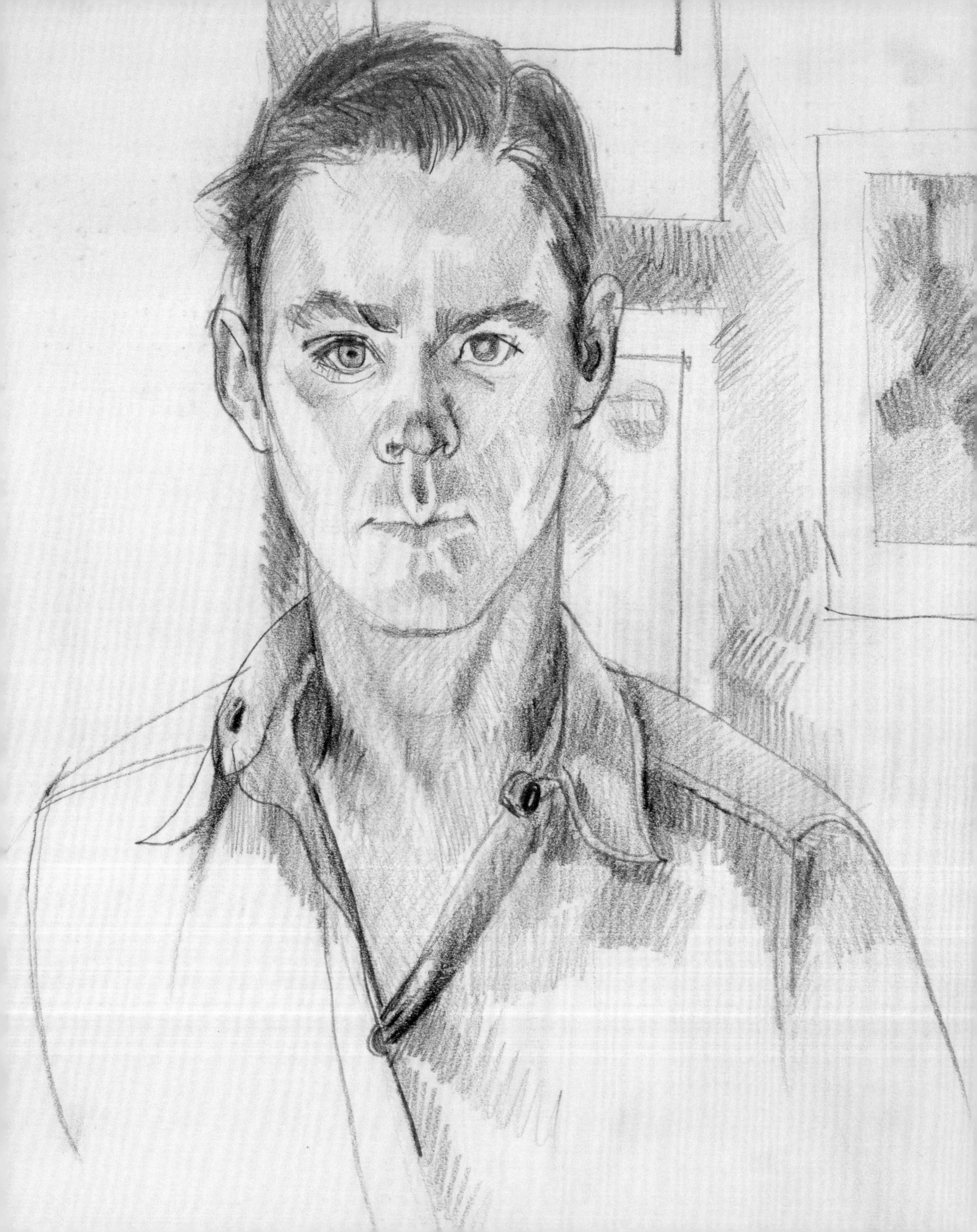

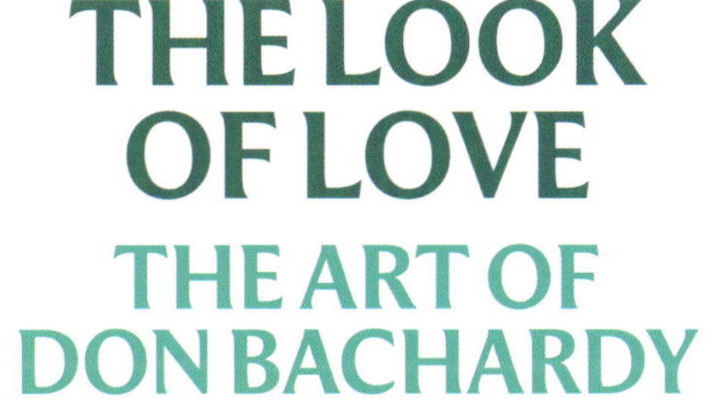

THE LOOK OF LOVE
THE ART OF DON BACHARDY

James Cahill

For Don Bachardy, Hollywood stars always seemed close enough to touch. As a boy, going to the movies with his mother and older brother, Ted, he saw their faces as larger-than-life projections. His earliest drawings were of actors in magazines. Throughout his teenage years, he and Ted went to premieres in the hope of obtaining photographs and autographs. A snapshot from March 1951 shows Bachardy at the age of sixteen—dressed in a double-breasted suit—grinning beside Marilyn Monroe, her own smile a little less assured than in later official shots, the tulle plumage of her black gown half obscured by a white fur (fig. 1).[1] The adolescent Bachardy has met—momentarily caught—Monroe in her own moment of becoming, as she hovers on the brink of superstardom.

Two years later, as he sat in a restaurant in Hollywood with Christopher Isherwood, Bachardy was awestruck to see Montgomery Clift walk through the door. He would recall, some fifty years after the event: "I was watching him as he came closer, until finally he was right at our table and he said: '*Hello, Chris!*' Well, I nearly fainted!"[2] Clift was one of the film stars who had haunted the young Bachardy's imagination, and Bachardy would go on to emulate the look of a 1950s leading man—suited, debonair—in a group of pictures taken by society photographer Carl Van Vechten in 1953–54 (figs. 2, 3). But in those few steps across the restaurant, Clift became something else—a knowable quantity, a real person.

The event might be regarded as symbolic of Bachardy's working method over the seven decades of his career—his practice of getting as close as possible to a sitter, sometimes positioning himself mere inches away, in order to transform the sitter from a "face" into a subject. Notoriously, Clift's on-screen personae belied—or only hinted at—the turmoil of his real life as a gay man seeking to pass as straight. By the time he sat for Bachardy in the mid-1960s, he had been permanently scarred by a car accident. Bachardy sensed that Clift wanted him to restore his beauty, but was able to record only what he saw. As he would later remark in relation to his final portraits

Self-Portrait (detail), 1959
Graphite on paper, 22 × 14 in. (55.9 × 35.6 cm)
Don Bachardy Papers

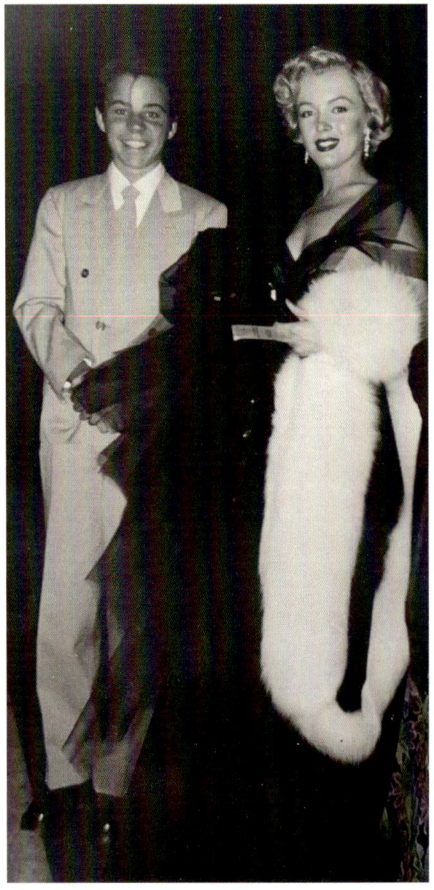

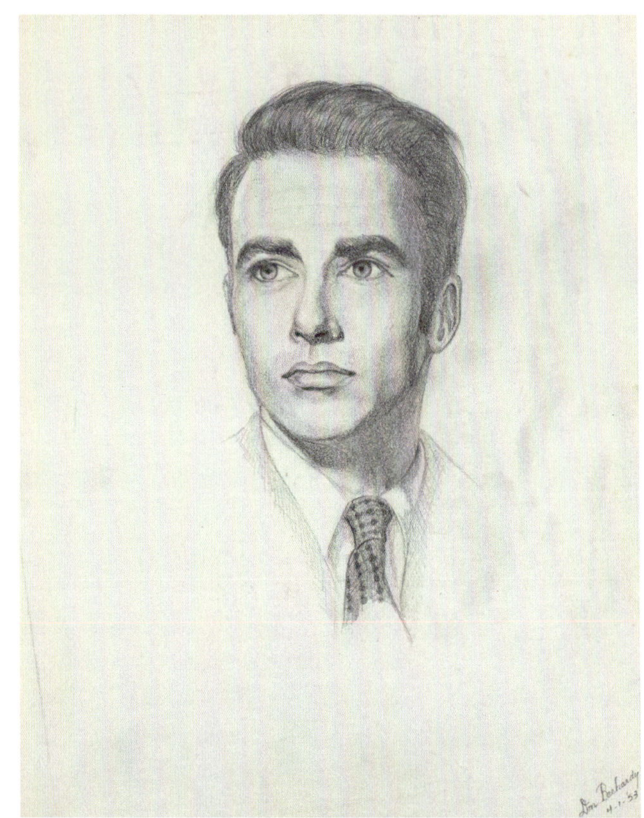

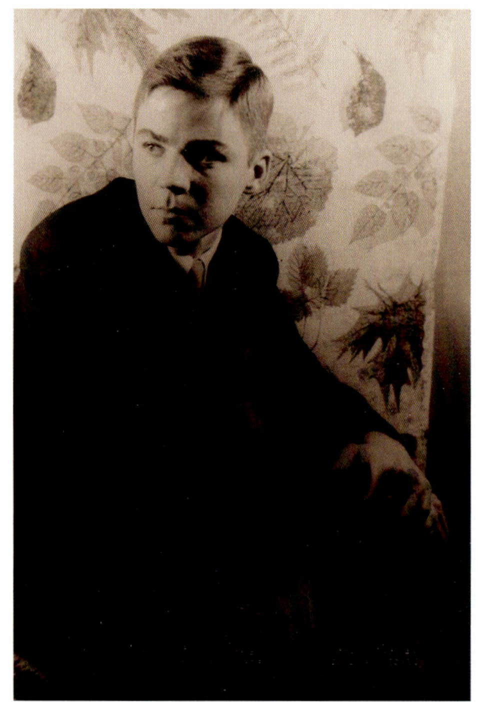

Fig. 1 Don Bachardy with Marilyn Monroe in the parking lot of the Pantages Theater, Hollywood, following the Academy Awards ceremony, photograph by Ted Bachardy, March 1951. Courtesy of Don Bachardy

Fig. 2 Sketch of Montgomery Clift, 1953. Graphite on paper, 12½ × 10 in. (31.8 × 25.4 cm). Don Bachardy Papers

Fig. 3 Carl Van Vechten (American, 1880–1964), *Donald Bachardy*, 1954. Photographic print, 12⅝ × 8½ in. (32.1 × 21.7 cm). Don Bachardy Papers

of Isherwood (see pp. 122–24): "all of my work is merciless and loving. And, since real love is merciless, one might just say my work is
loving—merciless is redundant."[3]

ART AND LIFE

At Isherwood's suggestion, Bachardy began to draw from life in
the early to mid-1950s, never again relying on photography: "Once
I started working from life, I couldn't bear to work from photographs any more. It was so thankless and uninspiring—totally dead
by comparison."[4] In a self-portrait in graphite from 1959, the young
artist confronts his image in the mirror, the casualness of his open-
necked shirt at odds with the coiled energy in his eyes and lips (see
p. 30). As a picture of a young man facing up to himself—wondering,
perhaps, who he intends to be—the drawing carries an echo of
Jean-Auguste-Dominique Ingres's *Self-Portrait Aged Twenty-Four*
(1804).[5] In this painting, Ingres fashions an image of himself as an
artist, standing back from an unfinished painting to regard himself—
and the world—with the same shining eyes that Bachardy would
display 150 years later.

Whether or not Bachardy was consciously placing himself in
such a lineage, he had developed a new cultural awareness on the
trip he and Isherwood took to Europe in 1955–56. This was a kind of
Grand Tour, encompassing Tangier, Italy, the south of France, and
England.[6] Traveling through Italy, they saw pornographic frescoes in
Pompeii, the Vatican Museums in Rome, Hadrian's Villa near Tivoli,
the Uffizi Gallery in Florence, and Tintoretto's *Crucifixion* (1565)—
along with Peggy Guggenheim—in Venice. In February 1956, on the
same day Isherwood experimented with mescaline for the first time,
they went to Westminster Abbey and later looked at reproductions
of Ingres's pictures. In his diary entry for the day, Isherwood gives
an account of studying Bachardy's face under the influence of the
drug that seems peculiarly prescient of the experience of viewing
the artist's portraits: "I spent some time studying Don's face. Amazing, how it changed from minute to minute! There was the bright-
eyed, sharp-nosed bobcat or fox at one end of the scale, and at the
other a hollow-cheeked, wearily composed mask that might have
been taken after death.…And yet—it was always a mask. I couldn't
penetrate it. I felt that the person inside was playing a game with
me, mockingly smiling."[7]

In Bachardy's self-portrait of 1959, the artist's older selves seem
to flicker inside his youthful face. At the same time, in the act of con-
fronting himself, he seems to be assuming a mask of maturity—

stepping into a role. Over the ensuing decades, he would seek to penetrate the masks he perceived in his sitters, hinting at the psychological layers beneath; and yet his images also remind us of the inescapability of such masks—of the capacity for a façade to seal a personality. After visiting Somerset Maugham's Villa Mauresque in December 1955, Bachardy recorded: "He was so unmistakably Maugham that I felt it was more a picture of him than the real thing and was surprised by how relaxed I felt."[8] The picture and the man had become mutually reinforcing. To draw from life, in Bachardy's case, has always been to observe life's theatricality, its absorption of art.[9]

The trip to Europe might be regarded as a formative moment in Bachardy's becoming an artist, awakening his consciousness to the Western canon. In the summer of 1956, he enrolled at the Chouinard Art Institute (later, California Institute of the Arts), where he studied for the next four years. Chouinard instilled in him the daily practice of drawing from life, usually from a female model.[10] He also began to make regular portraits of his and Isherwood's circle of friends, among them the writers Truman Capote (see p. 91) and Aldous Huxley (see p. 93), the actor Charles Laughton (see p. 86), and the historian, philosopher, and ascetic Gerald Heard (see p. 87).[11] At once graphically linear and alive to small incidents of physiognomy and gesture, these works strike a taut balance between stylization and naturalism. Far from being a mere training exercise, drawing from life was the means by which Bachardy began to assert a distinctive style.

A 1961 portrait of the Austrian actress and singer Lotte Lenya (facing page) depicts her squinting into the middle distance, her dark eyes mirrored (apparently multiplied) by the black glints of her fingernails. She raises one hand as if to hold a thought, while pressing the other against her knee. Bachardy's alternation between hard line and hazy tone finds a counterpart both in Lenya's pose (the stasis of her head offsetting the fluid torsion of her body) and in her facial expression, where alertness and dreamy insouciance seem to coexist. Lenya, who had been married twice to the composer Kurt Weill, had won a Tony Award in 1956 for her performance as Jenny in the Broadway production of Weill and Bertolt Brecht's *Threepenny Opera*.[12] In Bachardy's portrait, she continues to perform a practiced version of herself. Indeed, the drawing subtly evokes a photograph of Lenya by George Hoyningen-Huene from 1933, in which she adopts a stagier attitude—raising one hand on a ladder and staring raptly into space. In both the photograph and the drawing there is a note of

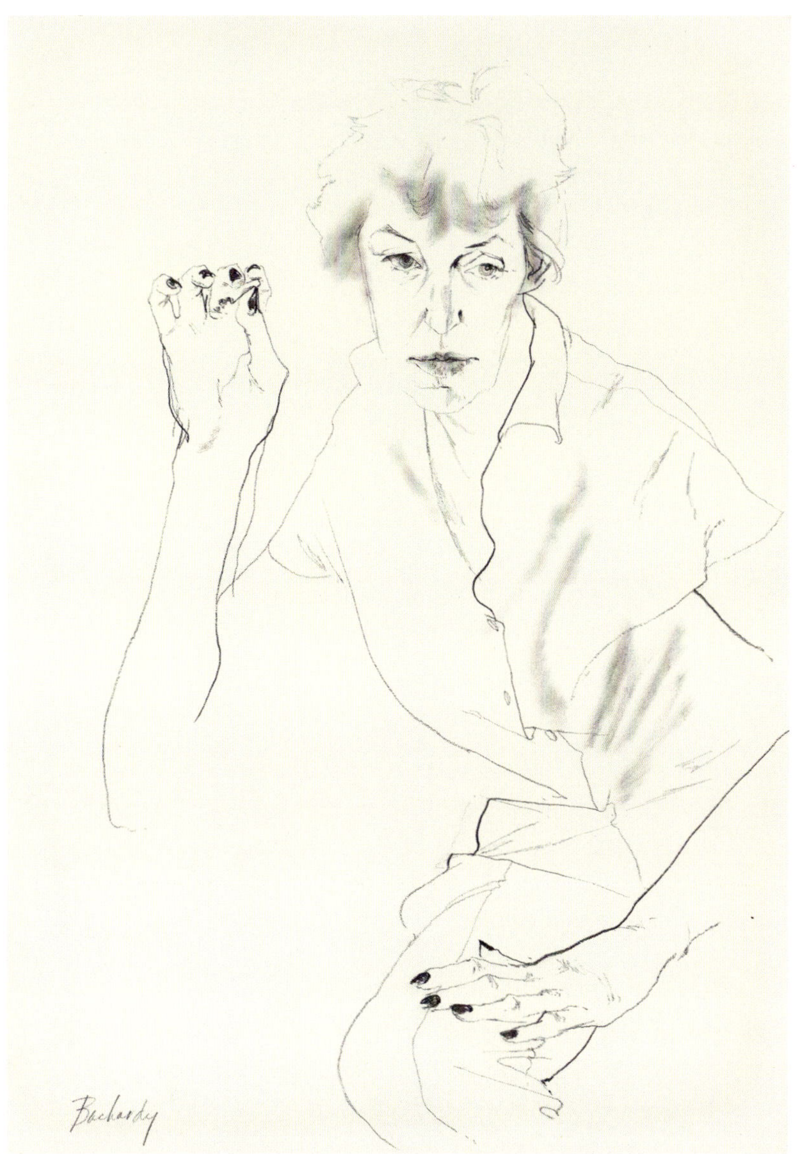

theatricality—alternately explicit and subliminal—to Lenya's pose, a "look" that betokens her bohemian world.

In their very lucidity of execution, Bachardy's drawings of this period achieve a sense of the preternatural that evokes the Neue Sachlichkeit (New Objectivity) art of Weimar Germany—and behind it, a longer tradition of Northern European realism stretching back to Hans Holbein. The portrayal of Lenya shares with Otto Dix's *Portrait of the Journalist Sylvia von Harden* (1926) a quality of ennui crossed with steely self-command, while Von Harden's spreading hands find a double in those of Igor Stravinsky in a pencil portrait by Bachardy of

Lotte Lenya, 1961 (no. 1)
Graphite on paper, 30½ × 22 in. (77.5 × 55.9 cm)
Don Bachardy Papers

1960 (see p. 89).[13] In each case, realism—a sense of the body closely observed—arises out of an absence of anatomical correctness. Bachardy's style is close, too, to that of Christian Schad in his drawing *Boys in Love* (1929), an image of two naked young men—portrayed from the waists up—embracing and kissing. There is a hyperreal air to the smooth shading and acute accuracy of Schad's silverpoint. The transgressive subject acquires, in his exacting depiction, a paradoxical otherworldliness.

Bachardy's first significant professional assignment came in September 1960, when the British director Tony Richardson commissioned him to make "bad" portraits of Angela Lansbury and Joan Plowright as props for a production of the play *A Taste of Honey* at the Biltmore Theater, Los Angeles. Richardson was so pleased with the results that he asked Bachardy to draw portraits of the remaining cast when the production moved to Broadway the following month.[14] In New York, the works were displayed in the theater lobby and attracted the praise of two of Bachardy's foundational influences— British photographer Cecil Beaton and Czech-born fashion illustrator René Robert Bouché, whose work had appeared in *Vogue* throughout the 1950s. "I thought Bouché was terrific," Bachardy recalls, "and not just the fashion drawings but the portraits he did, which were really first-class—really honest pictures. I had a whole collection of his drawings in fashion magazines before I ever met him."[15]

ANGLO-AMERICAN

In early 1961, Bachardy left Los Angeles for London and enrolled at the Slade School of Art, where he studied for six months.[16] His first impressions of the school were unflattering: "The Slade is really no different from any other school I've been to, sloppy, dirty, disorganized—bored teachers and bored students and bored models." But by March, he would admit: "I like working at the Slade now and feel quite relaxed there."[17] He was a "special student," as Beaton had been a few years earlier, not working toward a diploma but with use of the school's facilities. "It is assumed that I know what I'm about and don't need or want instruction—which was probably Cecil's set up," he wrote. "But one thing I have learned from being here—I must do it myself."[18]

Even at this early date, Bachardy was self-consciously an outsider, expressing a sense of self that would endure over the following decades as he pursued figuration against the prevailing tides of Abstract Expressionism, Minimalism, and Conceptualism. The move to London was an act of personal and artistic self-realization,

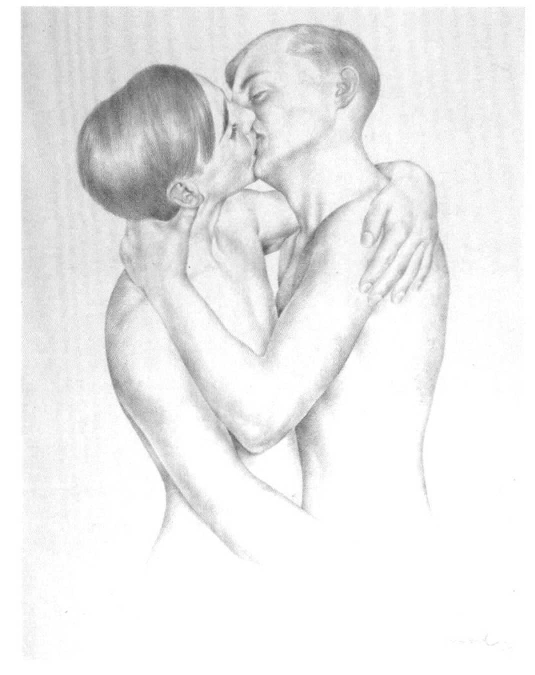

Fig. 4 Christian Schad (German, 1894–1982), *Liebende Knaben (Boys in Love)*, 1929. Silverpoint on paper, 11³⁄₄ × 9¹⁄₄ in. (30 × 23.5 cm). Museen der Stadt Aschaffenburg, Leihgabe Kurt-Gerd-Kunkel-Stiftung Aschaffenburg. © Christian-Schad-Stiftung Aschaffenburg (CSSA) / VG Bild-Kunst, Bonn. Photo: Ines Otschik (Museen der Stadt Aschaffenburg)

and a test of his relationship with Isherwood (then beginning its ninth year), who remained in Los Angeles. Isherwood's diaries make clear that Bachardy had long felt himself to be at the margins of their social milieu, although in time Bachardy's capacity to observe from a position of detachment would prove a defining attribute. The young artist's passage from Los Angeles to London was an attempt to emerge from his partner's shadow, as well as a reversal of Isherwood's own relocation from Europe to the United States with W. H. Auden in 1939.[19]

Classes at the Slade offered further opportunities for life drawing, but just as significant were Bachardy's inroads as a professional artist. "It was very exciting for me to go to London, and in that first year, I used to do two or three sittings a day, taking cabs and streetcars and buses all over," he recounts. "It's how I learned the geography of London."[20] In the process, he cultivated a new social circle, acquainting himself with many of Isherwood's old London contacts. His tutor at this time was the painter Keith Vaughan, who taught part-time at the Slade and whose own drawings and paintings—many of them of male nudes—were gravitating away from their Neo-Romantic origins toward a mode of semi-abstraction composed of blockish planes. Stylistically, Bachardy's work remained apart from that of Vaughan, and yet the boldness of Vaughan's nudes—their almost lackadaisical evocation of men's bodies in landscapes (and of the body itself as a kind of landscape, all firm masses and light-reflecting facets)—presages the uninhibited quality of Bachardy's own nudes of the 1960s. It was to Vaughan whom Bachardy confided his difficulties with oil painting, a medium he had struggled with since Chouinard.[21]

This first extended stay (the first of many throughout the 1960s) established him as a young American artist in the British capital. In March 1961, he was introduced to Harold Tatlock Miller, a director at the Redfern Gallery on Cork Street, and by June he had been offered an exhibition.[22] Opening on October 2nd, the show comprised fifty drawings of European and American literati and actors—from Angela Lansbury to John Gielgud to Truman Capote (see p. 91)—with a catalogue featuring a pen-and-ink study of Auden on the cover. The opening night was a society event, populated by celebrities and the press. "Willie Maugham created a major sensation by appearing for a short while with Alan Searle," Isherwood wrote. "[E. M.] Forster and Joe Ackerley stayed quite a long time.…After it was all over, we took Francis Bacon [see p. 88] out to supper at Gale's. He had stayed all through the show and somehow given it his blessing."[23]

Immersing himself in the society that Isherwood had left behind, Bachardy was redefining himself as an Anglo-American—the inverse of Isherwood. In this and other respects, the pair were mirror images of one another. It has often been observed that Bachardy unwittingly began to impersonate Isherwood in the early years of their relationship —a prelude to his ventriloquial approach as an artist, whereby he strives to impersonate his sitter. "I couldn't stop sounding like somebody who was putting on a British accent," he explains. "I'm a mimic. There's an unconscious sense of identification with whoever I'm looking at."[24]

THE UNCONSCIOUS IMPERSONATOR

Already in his 1959 self-portrait, Bachardy looks back at himself with the kind of absorption and intensity that would come to define his approach. The artist's gaze brings with it a depth of subjectivity—a capacity to be moved or even amazed. And amazement, in Bachardy's case, entails a *seeing through* to the reality of things rather than a dazzling or distortion of the senses: it constitutes a camera's-eye perspective akin to that described in the opening statement of Isherwood's novel *Goodbye to Berlin* (1939): "I am a camera with its shutter open, quite passive, recording, not thinking."[25] Years later, Isherwood would make the qualification that "what I was in fact describing was not my general attitude as a writer at all. It was my mood at that particular moment.…And indeed, [I] would never have written about people at all if I hadn't been fascinated by them and therefore, of course, to a degree, emotionally involved."[26]

In the same way, Bachardy's lucidity of vision—his propensity to record—operates in tandem with (or even through) close emotional involvement. His looking is not a matter of automatic capture, but a continuous succession of gazes and responses sustained over the two or more hours that a sitting lasts. By the same token, his works are never photographic, even at their most "photorealist": they attest, rather, to the look of a person through a sequence of infinitesimal moments, as attention gives way to inattention or as self-awareness subsides into obliviousness. The dynamic between artist and sitter, and its capacity to swing between empathy and subtle antagonism, forms a vital current throughout his art. He regards his sittings both as collaborations—asking each sitter to sign their own portrait—and confrontations.[27]

In Bachardy's pictures the sitter stands in for the artist, while the artist usurps (even *becomes*) the sitter: "I am impersonating the sitter, assuming that personality, as though I were making a portrait

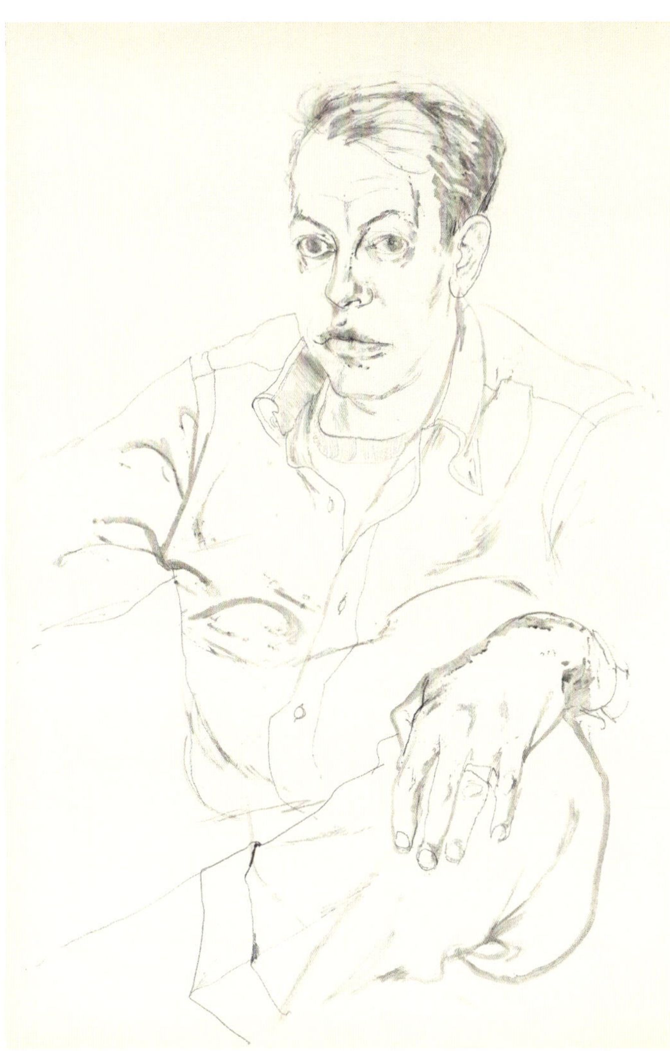

of myself in costume as my sitter."[28] The conflict inherent in the act of sitting is clear from a 1961 portrait of Chester Kallman, the American poet and (from 1939) partner of W. H. Auden. Evoked through sparing graphite lines and ink shading, Kallman stares back at the artist with an expression that seems morose, weary, disillusioned, perhaps pugnacious. The hardness of Kallman's gaze— its effrontery—comes to appear like a mirror, conveying a sense of the artist's own relentless looking. "Chester was much tougher than Wystan," Bachardy recalls. "It was harder to get him to sit still."[29] Kallman's eyes appear misaligned, as if caught between looking at Bachardy and looking away. A similar restlessness resides in the bagged, sagging contours of his shirt and the hand that he places on one knee.

The suggestion of a face-off is less explicit in Bachardy's portrait of Auden from the same year (see p. 91). By contrast with Kallman, Auden looks away, his tentatively outlined face suggesting a kind of abstracted concentration. And yet the avoidance of the artist's eye constitutes its own passive affront, with Auden retreating into himself just as Bachardy scrutinizes and seeks to capture him. The subliminal sense of a cat-and-mouse duel is characteristic. Bachardy has described his mode of working in terms of an "unedited dance number from a Fred Astaire and Ginger Rogers movie....I lead my partner into the spotlight to become the focal point of my inspection."[30] Auden's expression in the drawing (one of numerous depictions Bachardy made of the poet) is more placid than Kallman's, but a quality of restlessness persists. There is a sense of unquiet motion, once more, around the hands and shoulders, suggesting both a steeling of the self and a letting go.

Two other portraits from the same period, those of Jennifer West and James Baldwin, reflect Bachardy's dual ability to lay bare his subjects and to convey the charisma or intrigue of their presence.[31] Captured in rapid pen-and-ink lines, West stares out from beneath dark lashes with a fixity that offsets (or works against) the implication of motion in her spiraling hair and flexing neck (see p. 94). Her oversize ring, an orb that seems to balance atop her knuckles, anchors the composition in the same way as her dark pupils. Bachardy distills the animate, mercurial character of her glamor, while resisting the temptation to glamorize.

Chester Kallman, 1961 (no. 2)
Graphite and ink on paper, 30 × 20 in. (76.2 × 50.8 cm)
Don Bachardy Papers

In the portrait of Baldwin, as with that of Auden, it is the aversion of the subject's gaze that imbues the image with an intensity. Baldwin appears to focus on someone or something outside the frame, his averted eyes (coupled with the curling of his mouth) conveying a sense of roaming thought (see p. 95). His fingers, too, hint at speculative motion. As in many of Bachardy's drawings, the hand assumes its own character, seeming to condense the sitter's elegance and restiveness. Bachardy's slight magnification of the fingers—his accenting of their gestures—recalls the paintings of Egon Schiele, for example, *Self-Portrait* (1911), in which the artist is seen extending his fingers across his chest in a forking formation, turning the moment of self-exposure into a kind of dance.[32]

The tensions in Bachardy's portraits of the 1960s—the aura versus the physical body, naturalism versus a subtle note of idealization, traceable in the artist's firm, fluid lines—culminated in a set of portraits he made in 1965 of dancers from the New York City Ballet. Each pen-and-ink drawing shows a performer at rest, away from the stage, and yet Bachardy's ultrafine style preserves a sense of their stage presence—their numen. The drawings were commissioned by Lincoln Kirstein, who had founded the company together with the Russian choreographer George Balanchine in 1933. "I got almost all the Balanchine ballet members to sit for me," Bachardy remembers. "But Balanchine himself always refused."[33] Kirstein had failed to tell Balanchine of his plans for an editioned portfolio out of a paranoid fear that Balanchine would suspect an affair with Bachardy; the project was eventually scrapped. But one remark made by the impresario around the same time—recorded by Isherwood—has an oracular ring to it: "Lincoln says that Don will be the [John Singer] Sargent of our time."[34]

IN THE MIRROR

In 1962, when Bachardy and Isherwood redecorated their home at 145 Adelaide Drive, Santa Monica, a full-length mirror was hung in the dining room. As Katherine Bucknell observes in *Christopher Isherwood Inside Out* (2024): "any number of guests were to see themselves reflected in the mirror over the years and to catch the glances of hosts and companions observing one another."[35] In a reversal of the young Bachardy's pursuit of Hollywood stars, his and Isherwood's home (and in particular, his studio) became a magnet for cultural luminaries—actors, writers, directors, producers, choreographers, composers, and so on. Once they were living together more routinely in Santa Monica, the couple were the nucleus of a demimonde,

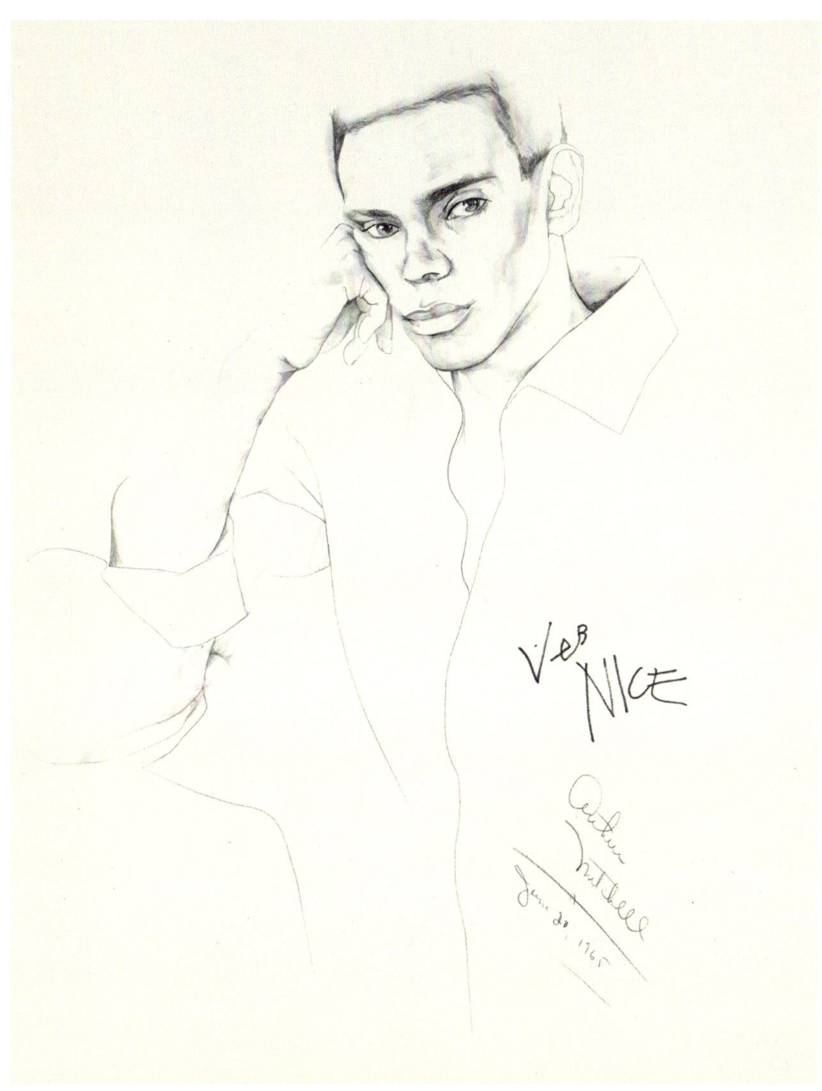

especially from the 1970s onward. In their own undemonstrative way, they conferred glamor on those who entered their orbit.

The awe that had characterized Bachardy's teenage encounters with Hollywood stars transmutes, in his portraits of the 1960s, '70s, and '80s, into an ability to capture a sitter's aura—even to amplify it—and, in the same moment, to distill that aura with a critical eye.[36] Like the mirror in the dining room, his portraits capture and condense the world he and Isherwood inhabited. In its totality, his corpus (numbering some seventeen thousand drawings) constitutes a novelistic portrait of a society—or multiple overlapping societies—even as each work retains an essentially private character, bearing witness to an unrepeatable encounter.

Arthur Mitchell, 1965
Print from the unpublished portfolio *Ballet Portraits,* 1966
with annotations by George Balanchine
Courtesy of Don Bachardy

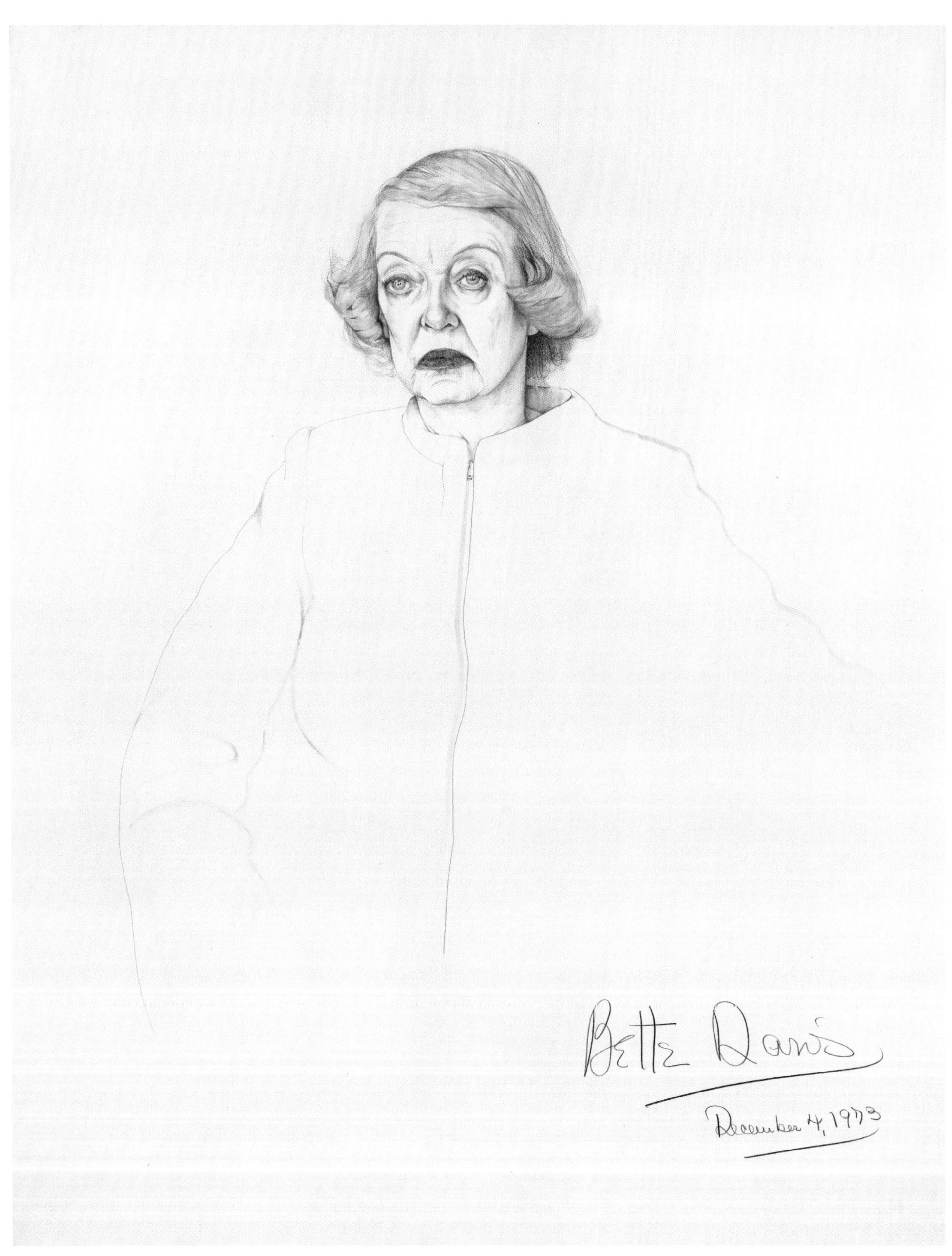

Bette Davis, December 4, 1973
Graphite and ink on paper, 29⅛ × 23⅛ in. (74 × 58.7 cm)
Don Bachardy Papers

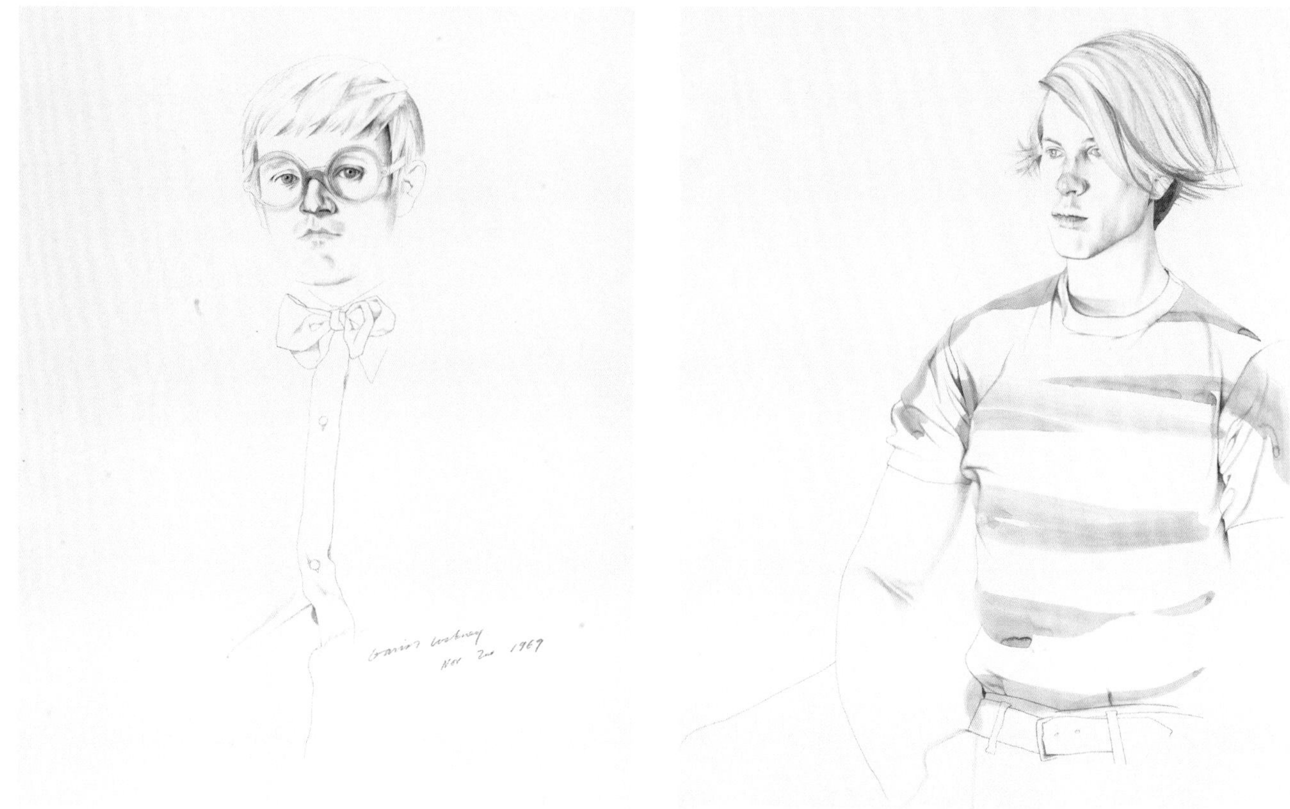

Nowhere is this interlacing of the public and the private more evident than in Bachardy's four portraits of Bette Davis, made over the course of 1973–74. In these, Davis is at once a vestige of Old Hollywood and a solitary woman at the threshold of old age (Bachardy had drawn Davis years earlier, copying a publicity photograph from the 1950 film *All About Eve*).[37] Her verdict upon seeing Bachardy's final portrait of her was withering in its praise: "Yup, that's the old bag."[38] Like so many of Bachardy's subjects, she is resolutely *herself* as well as being a symbol of something larger—her reputation, the lost era of her greatest fame—and yet these actual and symbolic selves are, in the end, impossible to disentangle.

Bachardy has also recorded the art worlds in which he has found himself at various times. Portraits such as those of artist Elaine de Kooning (see p. 99) and critic Harold Rosenberg (see p. 98; both 1966) offer glimpses of the New York scene.[39] But inevitably, many or most of Bachardy's works present the faces he encountered in Los Angeles. Among these were David Hockney and his boyfriend, Peter Schlesinger. The nineteen-year-old Schlesinger, whose relationship with an older, renowned partner was in some ways a mirror image

David Hockney, November 2, 1969
Graphite on paper, 29 × 23⅛ in. (73.7 × 58.7 cm)
Don Bachardy Papers

Peter Schlesinger, October 17, 1967 (no. 1)
Graphite and ink on paper, 29 × 23 in. (73.7 × 58.4 cm)
Don Bachardy Papers

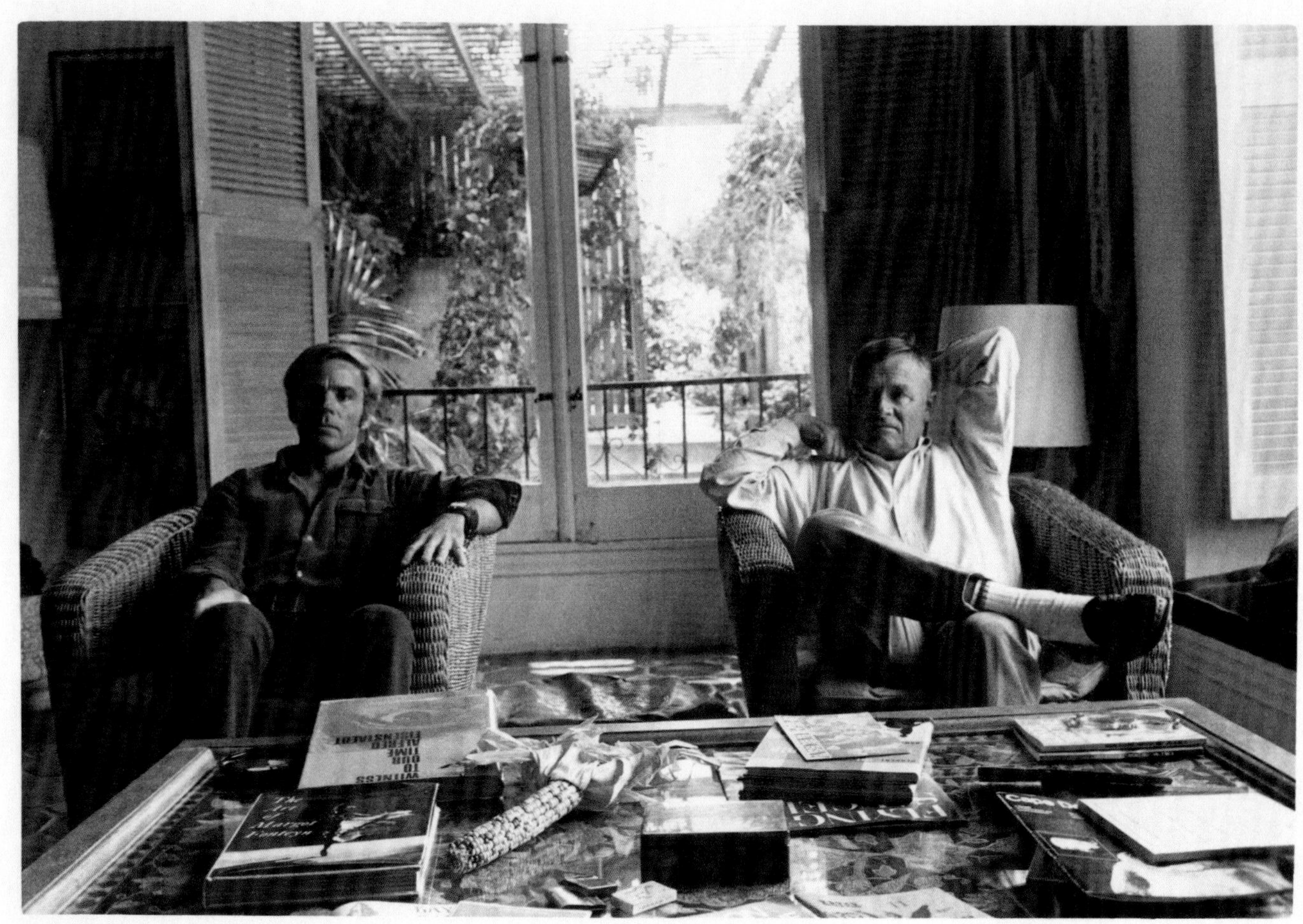

of Bachardy's own, appears in a drawing of 1967. The influences of Neoclassical portraiture and Neue Sachlichkeit realism appear to intersect in this pen-and-ink study; Schlesinger's erect posture and solemnity recall, among other precursors, Ingres's graphite portraits from the 1820s of young aristocrats. In this way, the "here and now" of the portrait's making operates in parallel with a more wide-ranging sense of time and history. Schlesinger's androgynous profile, flowing hair, and striped shirt seem at once to embody his 1960s moment and to lift him out of any given moment, so that he becomes the "timeless" beautiful boy of—say—Thomas Mann's novella *Death in Venice* (1912). Within a narrower historical frame, the portrait might equally be seen to reflect the influence of contemporary British artists, including the quasi-surreal paintings of Lucian Freud and the lyrical, anecdotal watercolors of Patrick Procktor.[40]

Fig. 5 David Hockney (English, b. 1937), *Christopher Isherwood and Don Bachardy (Study)*, March 30, 1968. Photographic print, 3½ × 5 in. (8.9 × 12.7 cm). Private Collection. © David Hockney

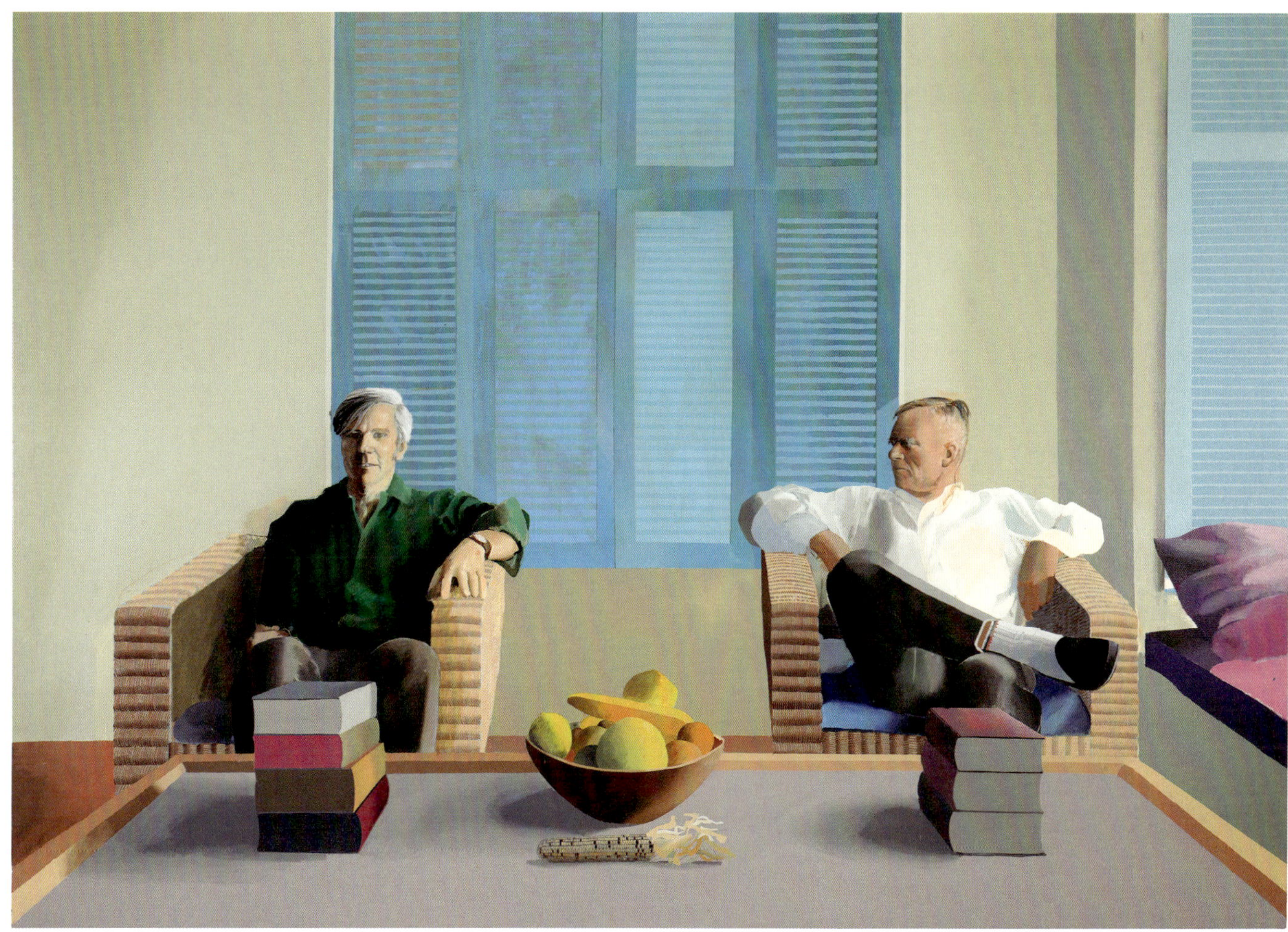

Hockney had met Bachardy and Isherwood in early 1964, soon after arriving in Los Angeles. Bachardy made numerous drawings of the British artist, including a reclining nude in 1966 in which Hockney is even stripped of his trademark owl glasses. In early 1968, Hockney reciprocated by embarking on a large-scale double portrait of Bachardy and Isherwood, a painting that became a defining image of the couple, their relationship, and their era—as well as the first in Hockney's landmark series of double portraits. In many of Hockney's subsequent portraits, notably the pencil drawings he made in Paris in the 1970s, it is possible to discern the influence of Bachardy's lucid, linear style.

Along with Ed Ruscha, Hockney has often been credited with turning Los Angeles into an artistic subject through his evocations of the city's pools, palm trees, architecture, skies, and beautiful

Fig. 6 David Hockney (English, b. 1937), *Christopher Isherwood and Don Bachardy*, 1968. Acrylic on canvas, 83½ × 119½ in. (212 × 303.5 cm). Private Collection. © David Hockney

male bodies. In a different sense, Bachardy's corpus of portraits of L.A. figures may be regarded as a portrait of the city, a cumulative social tapestry. "I have drawings and paintings of just about everybody I have known in the past forty years, including the most casual friends," he has written.[41]

From the late 1960s onward, Bachardy's portraits have reflected his acquaintance with Californian artists, as well as dealers and curators—many of whom he encountered at gallery openings.[42] In 1962, he and Isherwood met the painters Paul Wonner and Bill (Theophilus) Brown, who had recently taken studios in nearby Ocean Park and who would become synonymous with the Bay Area Figuration Group (a reaction against the enduring sway of Abstract Expressionism). The pair might be regarded as the stylistic link between the postwar British artists whom Bachardy had met, or been aware of, in the early 1960s, and the American milieu he came to inhabit. "Their work is influenced by Francis Bacon and (a little bit) Keith Vaughan," Isherwood wrote in December 1962.[43] Bachardy rented a studio in the same building as Wonner and Brown in June 1963, and the pair encouraged his experiments in painting, although for a long while galleries remained averse to showing these works.[44]

In September 1967, *Harper's Bazaar* commissioned Bachardy to draw portraits of leading Los Angeles artists. Among these was Billy Al Bengston, a member of the so-called L.A. Cool School, who would become a close friend. In Bachardy's graphite-and-ink drawing, Bengston's gaze radiates past that of the artist into an unknowable mid-distance, his moustache and tousled hair comprising the two concentrated areas of dark tone in an otherwise virtually shadeless image. Bachardy captures Bengston's signature, showy masculinity—a quality that Bengston played upon in both his life and his work.[45] A motorcycle racer and former stuntman, Bengston had been one of the artists associated with the influential Ferus Gallery, in operation from 1957 to 1961; he worked in a range of media, including heavily lacquered paintings on Formica that referred, in the guise of hard-edge abstraction, to the finishes and motifs of 1960s Americana: motorcycles, sergeant-stripe chevrons, the spray-painted and polished bodywork of automobiles. In September 1970, Bengston included Bachardy's drawings in a group exhibition at his

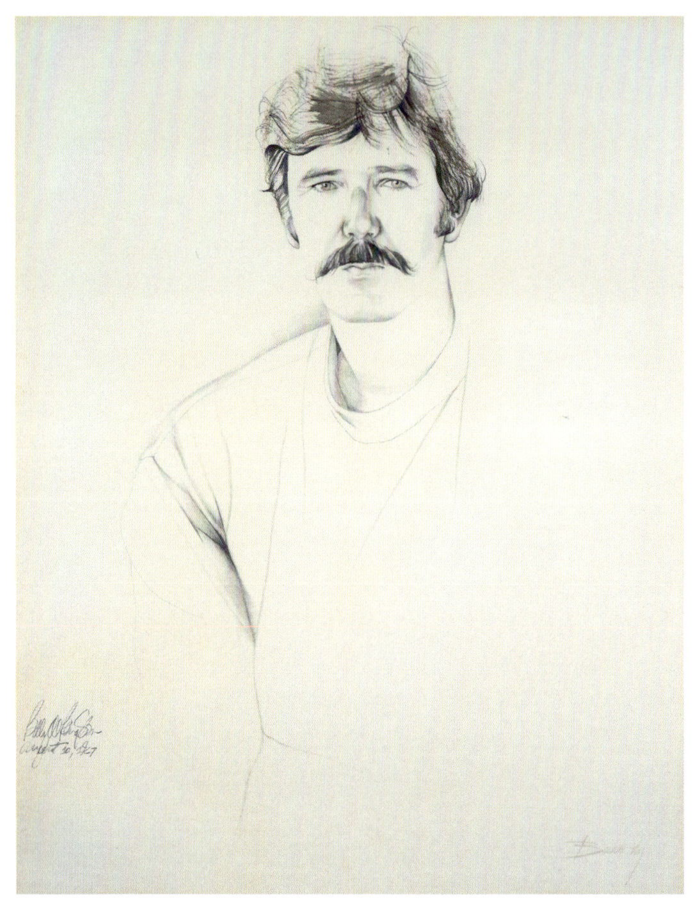

Billy Al Bengston, August 10, 1967
Graphite and ink on paper, 27½ × 22 in. (69.9 × 55.9 cm)
Courtesy of Billy Al Bengston Studio Holdings

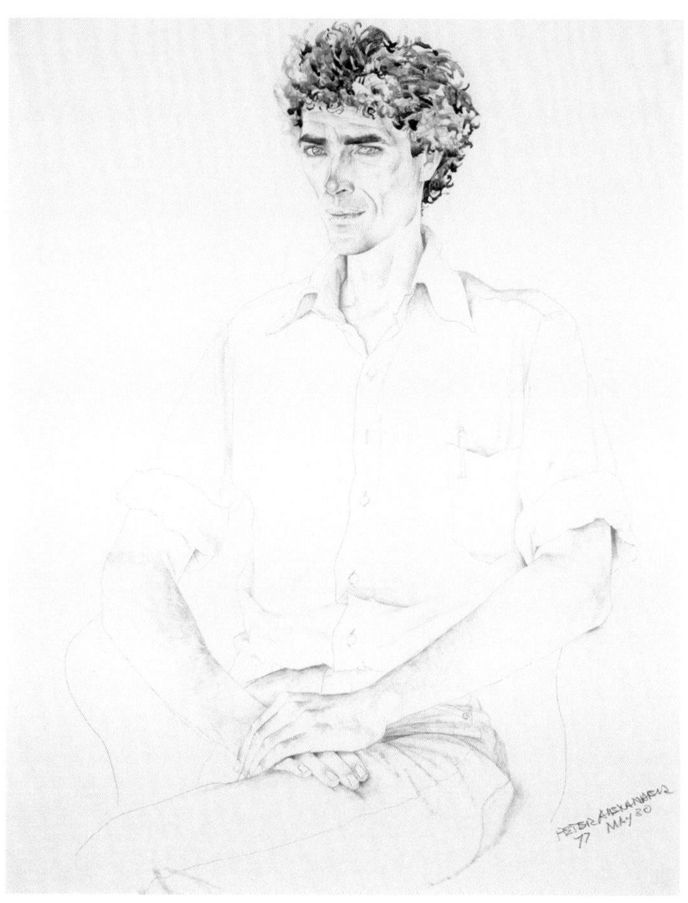

studio—absorbing Bachardy into the nascent (and somewhat macho) Venice art scene—along with Peter Alexander, Larry Bell, Tony Berlant, Ron Davis, Joe Goode, John McCracken, Ed Moses, Ken Price (see p. 103), and Ed Ruscha.[46] In various ways, these artists examined the trappings and veneers of Californian life. Their works offered a vision of Los Angeles that was distinct from, and yet aligned with, Bachardy's humanistic portrait of the city. Peter Alexander, a pioneer of the Light and Space movement (a Californian response to East Coast Minimalism), whose cubes and prisms of translucent resin share with Bachardy's later acrylic works a boldness and ethereality of color, albeit in a radically different idiom, was another close friend.[47] In a portrait of Alexander from 1977, the thirty-eight-year-old artist sits with folded hands, his face intent and searching. Bachardy's customary precision is evident in the faint touches of graphite (sometimes practically invisible) with which he has drawn Alexander's shirt, arms, and legs; the sitter's face is likewise minutely observed. His curly hair, however, is markedly freer—a mass of ink wash and brushed curls that signal the emergence of a more gestural style.[48] A similar contrast between "drawn" and "painted" elements may be observed in contemporaneous portraits of Mark Valen (1977; see p. 110), Natasha Richardson (1978), and Gregory Evans (1979; see p. 72).[49]

"By 1983…I was spending more than half my studio time painting, and by the end of the decade I was working in color exclusively," Bachardy has recalled.[50] A 1980 portrait of the art dealer Nicholas Wilder reflects the artist's growing embrace of acrylic paint (see p. 74). Viewed head-on, Wilder's face coheres out of a luminous assortment of red, pink, ocher, and blue brushstrokes. Alone among dealers in the 1970s, Wilder saw the potential of Bachardy's paintings as well as his drawings; an exhibition at his gallery in 1974 marked the first major showing of the watercolor portraits.

Throughout the 1980s, Bachardy would increasingly turn to this medium, while continuing to favor paper over canvas or any other support—marking a shift away from the cool monochrome and fastidious line of his early style. "Acrylic is ideal for me," he explains. "And I never liked the smell of turpentine, so I didn't want to do oil paintings."[51] While his peers were rejecting established styles in favor of

Peter Alexander, May 30, 1977
Graphite and ink on paper, 24 × 19 in. (61 × 48.3 cm)
Courtesy of Billy Al Bengston Studio Holdings

new (often defiantly "nonart") media, Bachardy rejected the historical baggage of oil paint in favor of the speed, ease, and lightness-
of-touch of acrylics. The brightness of his colors, combined with the
rapidity and simplicity of his method, confirm him—in his later style—
as a distinctly Californian artist.

NOWNESS

The defining relationship of Bachardy's life gave rise, in its final
months, to one of his defining bodies of work. In 1981, Isherwood was
diagnosed with prostate cancer. By 1984, he had ceased to write. As
he succumbed to illness the following year, Bachardy began to draw
him on a near-daily basis, using large sheets of paper, black acrylic
paint, and a Japanese brush—producing as many as ten portraits
a day.

The portraits of Isherwood dying are a tender, merciless marking of time. As Bachardy wrote in his diary, two months prior to the
writer's death: "The thought occurs to me—am I so insistent about
these sittings with Chris as a means of *extending* the time I have
left with him, thereby impressing this time all the more firmly in my
mind?"[52] Across the series, Isherwood's attitudes and expressions
range among resignation, melancholy, alertness, abstraction, and gri-
macing agony. "Sometimes his face seemed to harbour all the world's
pain," according to the critic John Russell, "but there were also times
when one or another of his younger selves made a cameo appearance."[53] As so often in Bachardy's work, the immediate moment of
the portrait's creation gathers up within itself a multitude of
other moments. In each portrait of the dying Isherwood, there
lurks—behind the visceral nowness of the image—a reminder
of the larger, uncontainable life out of which that portrait
has arisen.

In a work from October 19, 1985 (see p. 122), painted in
diluted black, Isherwood appears seated and naked. The sag
of his belly counteracts the erectness of his body and the tight-
ness of his right fist. His determined meeting of Bachardy's
gaze has a similarly paradoxical effect, at once connect-
ing us with the dying (long-dead) subject and confirming his
absence. Two drawings from November 26 (see pp. 122–23)
show him in distinct moods and moments: upright and alert in
the first; slumped against a pillow in the second, with a wince
of pain (or merely of vulnerability) passing over his face. Here,
more strongly than ever, Bachardy's work exhibits a dispas-
sionate empathy—a camera's eye that refutes sentimentality

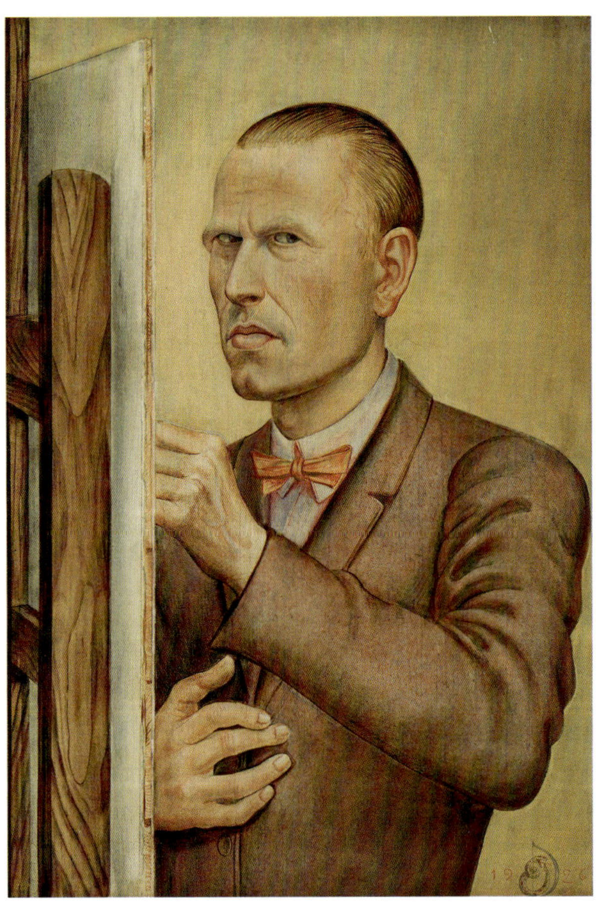

Fig. 7   Otto Dix (German, 1891–1969), *Self-Portrait
with Easel*, 1926. Tempera on panel, 31³⁄₄ × 21⁷⁄₈ in.
(80.5 × 55.5 cm). Leopold-Hoesch-Museum, Düren.
Photo: Peter Hinschläger. © 2019 Artists Rights
Society (ARS), New York / VG Bild-Kunst, Bonn

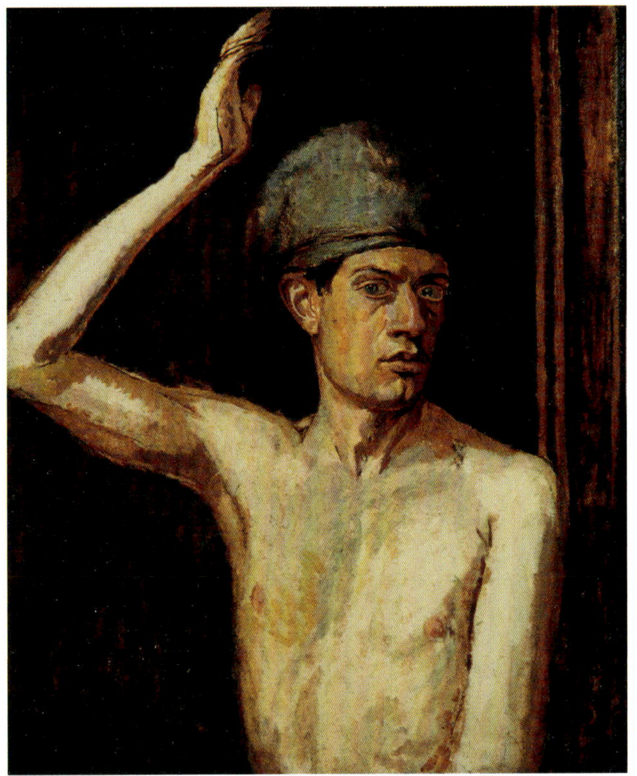

or melodrama in favor of a deeper emotional involvement. "[This] is the most intense way I know of to be with Chris," he wrote in his diary on December 1, 1985. "It is the only situation now in which we are both truly engaged. If I am tormenting him, I suppose it is an extension of something basic in our interaction."[54] Isherwood died on January 4, 1986.

In his portraits of Isherwood dying, Bachardy was also stripping himself bare, acknowledging his own mortality. The self-reflexive impulse that underlies the series becomes explicit in a self-portrait from the following year (see p. 127), made three months after Isherwood's death. In this, the artist—depicted in the same sparse black acrylic wash—stares back at himself, bearing the marks of middle age even as his flowing hair and muscular arms (revealed by his trademark singlet) attest to a residual youthfulness. The intensity of his gaze shares something with that of Otto Dix in a self-portrait of 1926, a ruthless scrutiny that might be regarded either as self-avowal (a declaration, in Gertrude Stein's words, of "Look at me now and here I am") or a scouring-out of the self: the body of the artist voided of thought, of character.[55]

A similar ambiguity pervades many of Bachardy's self-portraits. These works have often come about through the chance absence of a model and have accumulated into a lifelong document of his changing appearance as much as of his stylistic progression. In a 1995 painting in acrylic (see p. 136), Bachardy's pursed and furrowed expression materializes out of graphic strokes of color and looser pools of paint. The ridges of his philtrum and the folds around his throat have been carved out of white paper, by contrast with the impregnable black of his eyes and eyebrows. The segmentation of color and tone into facets aligns his work with that of other modern figurative painters—whether Lucian Freud or modernist forebears such as Wyndham Lewis and Duncan Grant. Grant's *Study for Composition (Self-Portrait in a Turban)* (1910) chimes with Bachardy's self-portraits in terms of their dual character: the artist strips himself bare at the same time as he constructs an image of himself—paints himself into being.[56]

In a self-portrait from 2016 (see p. 157), the use of white space is yet more pronounced, manifesting a tendency in Bachardy's work around that time toward a more sparing application of color. The image has a semblance of hyperbrightness, as if a photographic slide had been laid on a light box. Seen in his eightieth year, Bachardy

Fig. 8 Duncan Grant (Scottish, 1885–1978), *Study for Composition (Self-Portrait in a Turban)*, 1910. Oil on board, 30 × 25 in. (76 × 63.5 cm). Private Collection, Northern Ireland. © Estate of Duncan Grant

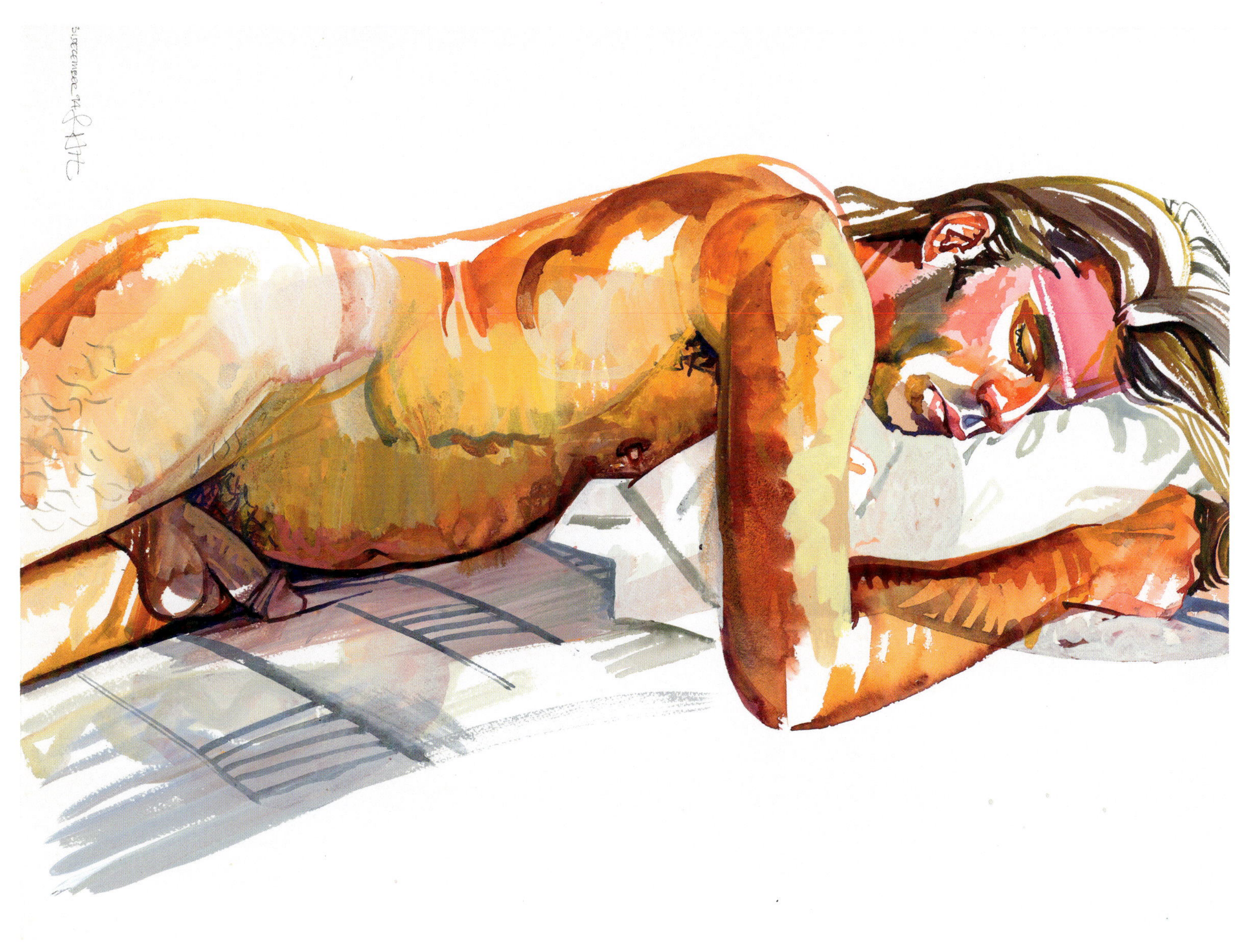

Tim Hilton, December 31, 1994 (no. 2)
Acrylic on paper, 22¼ × 30 in. (56.5 × 76.2 cm)
Don Bachardy Papers

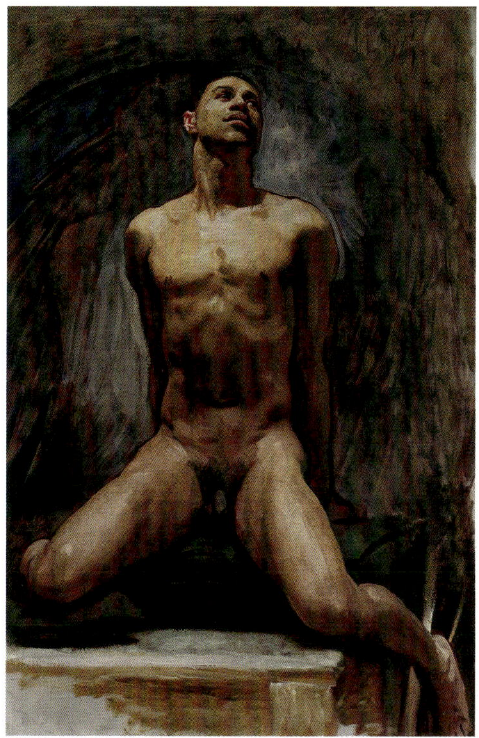

returns his own gaze with no less acuteness than in his 1959 graphite self-portrait, and yet that concentration has seemingly spread to every line in the drawing. Threads of pink wash denote his forehead, eye sockets, cheeks, neck, and clavicles, endowing his image with the forensic, flayed appearance of an écorché.

The desire to anatomize is clear again in the series of male nudes Bachardy painted around the turn of the millennium (see pp. 141, 145, 148).[57] This series finds a close precursor in an acrylic portrait of Tim Hilton from 1994, in which Bachardy's then partner is seen lying against a pillow, his thighs, hips, and torso extending across the picture like a landscape, his head (tinted electric pink) sinking into the pillow as if in sleep. The languor of the pose is countered—complicated—by the scalpel-like accuracy of Bachardy's marks, which invest the planes and contours of the body with a bristling internal tension. These qualities recur throughout the later male nudes, in which the sensual abandon of the model (often supine or reclining) merges with a contrary note of fixity—discernible in the men's arresting gazes as well as in the sharp modulations of color. Bachardy considers each of his nudes a portrait in its own right: "I never wanted them to be anonymous. To me they were all portraits like I'd always wanted to do. I wanted to get the personality of the sitter."[58]

In this quest for personality—and rejection of the anonymity of a "model"—Bachardy channels the intimacy of John Singer Sargent's drawings and watercolors of naked men. In these, classical attitudes reverberate faintly. Antique sculptural models may be glimpsed in Sargent's *Nude Study of Thomas E. McKeller* (ca. 1917–20), but it is the reality of McKeller's animate body that radiates through as he raises himself off a cushion.[59] There is a related, odalisque-like extravagance to many of Bachardy's portraits—that of Jeffrey Kennedy (2003; see p. 148), for example, in which the subject lies on his side, his head angled toward the viewer so that his genitals and unsunned thighs dominate the top half of the picture. In others—especially those of two men together—a more somber note of intimacy prevails. The dynamic poses of several of the subjects also recall the athletic physique and flexing posture of the nude model in *The Marble Polisher* (1882–87) by Henri de Toulouse-Lautrec, a painting Bachardy first saw on his trip to Europe in 1955, on the wall of Somerset Maugham's Villa Mauresque.[60]

CONTEMPORARY PORTRAITURE

Now in the eighth decade of his career, Bachardy has continued to pursue the possibilities of portraiture—its capacity to shadow forth a

Fig. 9 John Singer Sargent (American, 1856–1925), *Nude Study of Thomas E. McKeller*, ca. 1917–20. Oil on canvas, 49½ × 33¼ in. (125.73 × 84.45 cm). Museum of Fine Arts Boston, Henry H. and Zoe Oliver Sherman Fund, 1986.60

personality, to convey the reciprocal (at times, antagonistic) act of looking, or to document the timespan of its own creation while also hinting at the longer, immeasurable time of the sitter's life. Throughout, he has maintained a determined independence from cliques or movements; his art resembles nothing so much as itself. While he has spent decades absorbing historical and modern art, the allusions in his portraits to other art—or to other eras—are rarely explicit.[61]

In the same way, his portraits share loose affinities with those of various modern and contemporary artists, while avoiding direct resemblance. In their totality, his depictions of friends and famous figures mirror the dizzying variety—if not the automated technique—of Andy Warhol's silk-screen portraits of the 1960s to the 1980s. And yet while Warhol's contrastive, colorized images resemble the kind of publicity shots that the young Bachardy copied, Bachardy's own portraits from life have sought, ever since the 1950s, to probe beneath the layers of mediation that flatten a real person into an image. That is, he punctures—with a gentle kind of violence—the fiction of a "public face."

Bachardy's works might again be usefully compared with those of two American artists from the generations preceding and following his own. In their use of saturated color and graphic line, the paintings of Alice Neel closely prefigure his later works in acrylic. Neel's only self-portrait, made in 1980, presents the aging artist seated and naked, the candor of the depiction giving rise to a strange levity of mood; Neel's shapeless, shuffling, unabashed appearance renders her almost childlike. In more recent decades, the painter Elizabeth Peyton has created portraits that evoke Bachardy's both in terms of their technique and their subjects (a wide variety of friends, cultural icons, and historical figures).[62]

Ultimately, though, such affinities serve to highlight Bachardy's difference from, as much as his similarity to, other artists. Within the sprawling terrain of contemporary art, his work is a precise—if defiantly off-center—set of coordinates. Indeed, the white space in his recent portraits is an expression, above all else, of the clarity of vision and singularity of focus that have characterized his art from the outset. In a 2019 portrait of the filmmaker Tina Mascara, the white of the paper suggests a light that dazzles in the same moment as it reveals. That light seems to play across the subject's face, hair, and clothing, almost eclipsing one side of her face. Its glancing movement

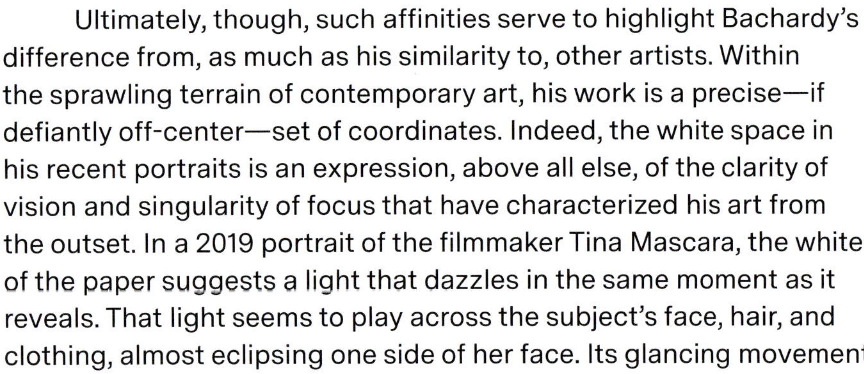

Fig. 10 Alice Neel (American, 1900–1984), *Self-Portrait*, 1980. Oil on canvas, 53¼ × 39¾ in. (135.3 × 101 cm). National Portrait Gallery, Smithsonian Institution, SL.5.2021.56.2. © The Estate of Alice Neel. Courtesy the Estate of Alice Neel and David Zwirner

becomes a double for Mascara's oblique gaze, as well as for the ranging motion of Bachardy's eyes as he depicts her. At once effacing Mascara from view and asserting her presence, the white space expresses a beguiling contradiction of Bachardy's art. He succeeds in fixing a subject even as that subject recedes from reach, and in so doing, he produces a dual sense of what is knowable and unknowable.

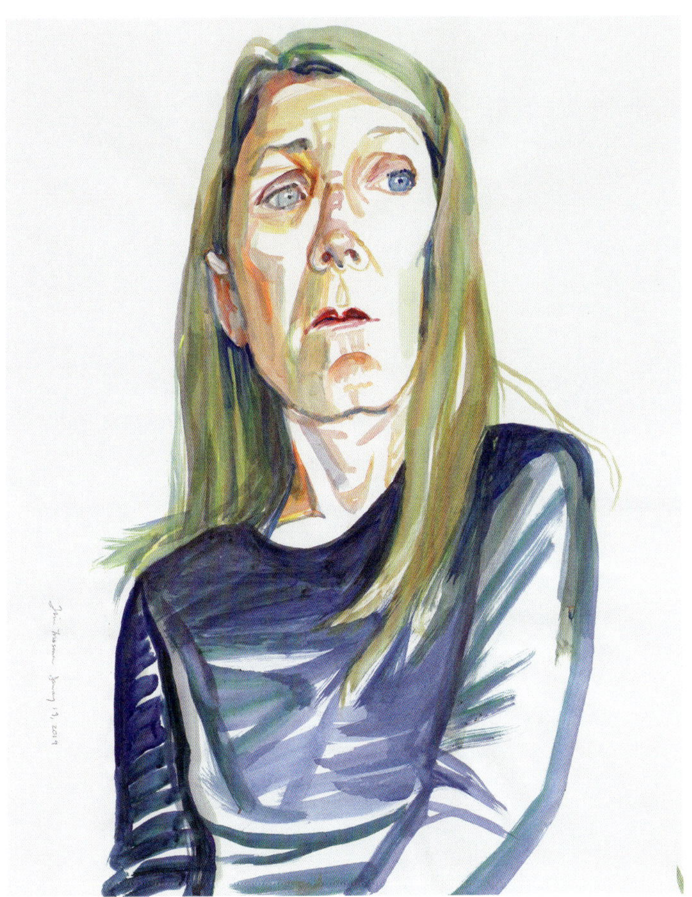

Tina Mascara, January 19, 2019 (no. 2)
Acrylic on paper, 28⅞ × 23 in. (73.3 × 58.4 cm)
Don Bachardy Papers

NOTES

1. This turned out to be Monroe's only Oscars appearance—and as a presenter rather than a nominee.

2. Bachardy recounts the event in the documentary *Chris & Don: A Love Story* (dir. Guido Santi, Tina Mascara, 2007).

3. Don Bachardy, diary entry for September 18, 1985. Don Bachardy, "Introduction," in Don Bachardy, Stephen Spender, and John Russell, *Christopher Isherwood: Last Drawings* (London: Faber & Faber, 1990), xii.

4. Author interview with Don Bachardy, April 23, 2024. He elaborates: "It was Chris who asked, 'Have you ever worked from life?' I said, 'No.' He said, 'I'll sit for you.' And once he did, that was it. I couldn't go back to the photographs." See also Don Bachardy, *Stars in My Eyes* (Madison: University of Wisconsin Press, 2000), 12–13. In Isherwood's diaries, the earliest references to Bachardy drawing occur during their trip to Mexico in 1954, in the company of friends Ben and Jo Masselink. On May 28, 1955, Isherwood recorded a supper with those friends: "Don and Jo drew sketches later. Don's were very good—full of life. He really does have a talent. But they make Jo look so old!" See Christopher Isherwood, *Diaries, Vol. 1: 1939–1960*, ed. Katherine Bucknell (London: Methuen, 1996), 471, 474, 502–3.

5. Jean-Auguste-Dominique Ingres, *Self-Portrait Aged Twenty-Four*, 1804, oil on canvas, Musée Condé, Chantilly.

6. In England, Bachardy met numerous friends of Isherwood's, including Francis Bacon, E. M. Forster, John Gielgud, Stephen and Natasha Spender, and Kenneth Tynan. On January 28, 1956, he and Isherwood visited an exhibition of paintings by Frank Auerbach at the Beaux Arts Gallery. On February 10, they visited Bacon's exhibition at the Hanover Gallery. See Isherwood, *Diaries, Vol. 1*, 569, 580.

7. Christopher Isherwood, diary entry for February 25, 1956. Isherwood, *Diaries, Vol. 1*, 589.

8. Don Bachardy, diary entry for December 19, 1955. Don Bachardy, "So Desperately Alive," *Los Angeles Times*, February 2, 1997.

9. Or, as the philosopher Nelson Goodman put it: "That nature imitates art is too timid a dictum. Nature is a product of art and discourse." Nelson Goodman, *Languages of Art: An Approach to a Theory of Symbols* (Cambridge, MA: Hackett, 1976), 33.

10. In the summer of 1958, Bachardy took additional lessons in painting from Harvey Young, a former lover of Isherwood's, and the following year he obtained a part-time job as a fashion illustrator for the May Company department store. In October 1959, he secured a job drawing hats for Charles LeMaire, who had designed the black gown worn by Marilyn Monroe to the 1951 Oscars.

11. In 1937, Heard had immigrated to California with Aldous Huxley—immediate precedents for Isherwood —and both Heard and Huxley had become disciples of Swami Prabhavananda, a monk of the Ramakrishna Order who later became Isherwood's guru.

12. In 1966, she originated the role of Fräulein Schneider in the first Broadway production of John Kander and Fred Ebb's musical *Cabaret*, directed by Harold Prince—an adaptation of John Van Druten's 1951 play *I Am a Camera*, itself based on Isherwood's Berlin stories.

13. Otto Dix, *Portrait of the Journalist Sylvia von Harden*, 1926, oil and tempera on wood, Musée national d'art moderne, Paris.

14. See Christopher Isherwood, *The Sixties; Diaries, Vol. 2: 1960–1969*, ed. Katherine Bucknell (London: Chatto & Windus, 2010), 3–4, and Hunter Drohojowska-Philp, "Don Bachardy, the Artful Impersonator," *Los Angeles Times*, September 22, 1996. The commission led to other similar jobs— drawing posters for the Broadway productions of Tennessee Williams's *Period of Adjustment* (opened November 1960) and James Costigan's *Little Moon of Alban* (opened December 1960).

15. Author interview with Bachardy, April 23, 2024. Following the display in New York, Isherwood wrote in his diary: "this was relatively speaking the greatest triumph Don will ever have in his life, perhaps— because it was the first and because it's doubtful if the praise of any two people will ever again mean quite as much to him as Beaton's and Bouché's did." Isherwood, *Diaries, Vol. 2*, 16.

16. Bachardy's program of study was funded by Russell and Edna McKinnon, wealthy Californians who had assumed the role of patrons. A job as fashion illustrator for *Women's Wear Daily* also helped to fund the trip.

17. Don Bachardy to Christopher Isherwood, February 6, 1961, and March 5, 1961. Christopher Isherwood and Don Bachardy, *The Animals: Love Letters between Christopher Isherwood and Don Bachardy*, ed. Katherine Bucknell (London: Vintage, 2014), 39, 59.

18. Don Bachardy to Christopher Isherwood, February 12, 1961. Isherwood and Bachardy, *The Animals*, 45. In the same letter, Bachardy requests addresses or phone numbers for figures including Forster, Bacon, Beaton, and Kenneth Tynan and Elaine Dundy.

19. He stayed initially with Stephen and Natasha Spender, before being granted use of Richard and Sybil Burton's house at 11 Squire's Mount, Hampstead.

20. Author interview with Bachardy, April 23, 2024.

21. "I'm at the mercy of good and bad days," he wrote to Isherwood on March 5, 1961, "sometimes feeling I can do it and sometimes not having the faintest idea of what I want to do." Isherwood and Bachardy, *The Animals*, 59.

22. The introduction came about via the stage designer Loudon Sainthill.

23. Christopher Isherwood, diary entry for October 6, 1961. Isherwood, *Diaries, Vol. 2*, 119. Bachardy was subsequently offered a debut exhibition at New York's Sagittarius Gallery for January 1962. Cecil Beaton had made the connection for Bachardy with the gallery's owner, Count Lanfranco Rasponi.

24. Author interview with Bachardy, October 24, 2022. The process wasn't simply one-way, as the novelist Edmund White has observed: "over the years a mysterious personality exchange took place: Don developed an Oxford stutter and Chris became more and more Californian." Edmund White, "Pool in Rocks by the Sea," *Artforum* 30, no. 6 (February 1992): 81. On their first trip together to Europe— while in London in January 1956—Isherwood wrote in his diary: "I notice that, whenever I go into a shop, I'm taken for granted as an American—though my accent seems British to anyone in the States." Christopher Isherwood, diary entry for January 10, 1956. Isherwood, *Diaries, Vol. 1*, 565. Cf. Bachardy's recollection that "On our first trip to England, we were meeting people that he'd known before, and I heard them say again and again, 'You've become so American.' And it wasn't praise. They thought he was putting it on or affecting it." Author interview with Bachardy, October 24, 2022.

25. Christopher Isherwood, *The Berlin Novels* (1935; London: Vintage, 1999), 243.

26. "Profile: Christopher Isherwood; Interview with Clive Jordan," BBC World Service, June 15, 1970.

27. "The confrontation between my sitter and me is the subject of my pictures." Bachardy, *Stars in My Eyes*, 14. Compare the testimony of one of his sitters: "All this work, this whole process, I felt, was almost as much of a confrontation between the two of us as it was a collaboration. And so what, I wondered, must it feel like to be him doing this?" Kevin Kopelson, "All about Me," *London Review of Books* 37, no. 7 (April 9, 2015): 43–45.

28. Don Bachardy quoted in Peter Clothier, "Don Bachardy: Pictures of Christopher," in Don Bachardy and Peter Clothier, *Don Bachardy: Christopher Isherwood Portraits, 1953–1985*, exh. cat. (Fullerton: Main Art Gallery, California State University, 2001), n.p.

29. Author interview with Bachardy, April 23, 2024. Cf. Isherwood's observation that "there are those [sitters] who instinctively resist Don's enquiry into their personalities—by making tiny movements which subtly alter the pose, or by hiding from him (as he calls it), or by forcing their faces into the expression which they think of as their 'best.'" Christopher Isherwood, diary entry for October 20, 1979. Don Bachardy and Christopher Isherwood, *October* (Los Angeles: Twelvetrees, 1981), 58.

30. Don Bachardy, "Introduction," in Don Bachardy, Tom Ford, Douglas Kirkland, and Armistead Maupin, *Hollywood* (New York: Glitterati, 2014), n.p.

31. The same dual quality is found in the portrait photography of Yousuf Karsh, whose 1950 pictures of Somerset Maugham, for example, cast the writer in statuesque attitudes and steely chiaroscuro, and yet shine an unflinching light on his aged, wearied face.

32. Egon Schiele, *Self-Portrait*, 1911, oil on wood panel, Wien Museum Karlsplatz, Vienna. The influence of Schiele, and of the German Expressionists more broadly, is reflected in a letter to Isherwood of June 16, 1964, when Bachardy was visiting Vienna: "[I] saw what I'd really come here for—the Klimts and the Schieles…[Klimt's] Judith with the head of Holofernes is as good as I'd hoped.…the Schiele oils are actually better than any I'd seen—there is one really magic one." Isherwood and Bachardy, *The Animals*, 153. Bachardy wrote of the sitting with Baldwin, which took place in the writer's apartment in New York: "He sat as still and as long as he could, which was neither very still nor very long, but I do like him. There is something silly and adorable about him and his face is marvellous to draw." Don Bachardy to Christopher Isherwood, January 26, 1964. Isherwood and Bachardy, *The Animals*, 142.

33. Author interview with Bachardy, April 23, 2024.

34. Christopher Isherwood, diary entry for February 7, 1965. Isherwood, *Diaries, Vol. 2*, 352.

35. Katherine Bucknell, *Christopher Isherwood Inside Out* (New York: Farrar, Straus & Giroux, 2024), 607.

36. He has referred to the importance of apprehending the "numen" of his live sitters, versus the limitations of using "predigested" photographic imagery. Bachardy, *Stars in My Eyes*, 4.

37. In Don Bachardy's interview with Gregory Evans, Evans states: "Once you said that the first time you can remember being inspired was when you were four years old. It was the movie *Jezebel* [1938]," p. 18 in this volume.

38. Bette Davis, quoted in Bachardy, *Stars in My Eyes*, 26.

39. Elaine was the wife of Willem de Kooning, whom Bachardy held "second only to Bacon." See Isherwood and Bachardy, *The Animals*, 414n4.

40. Procktor also depicted Schlesinger a number of times, including in the watercolor *Peter, Anguillara* (1967).

41. Bachardy, *Stars in My Eyes*, 12.

42. The "Monday Night Art Walk" that took place weekly in Los Angeles was "a cultural imperative" in the 1980s. See William Wilson, "The Fast Life and Artful Times of Nicholas Wilder," *Los Angeles Times*, November 27, 1988. Bachardy's L.A. milieu is reflected in the works that hang at his house in Santa Monica, including those by Billy Al Bengston, Jessie Homer French, Ken Price, and Ed Ruscha.

43. Christopher Isherwood, diary entry for December 4, 1962. Isherwood, *Diaries, Vol. 2*, 248. Comparisons might equally be drawn with American realists such as Edward Hopper, Grant Wood, and Andrew Wyeth.

44. For instance, the Banfer Gallery, New York, in 1964; Rex Evans Gallery, Los Angeles, in 1966; and Irving Blum, Los Angeles, in 1970.

45. "I do like him and all his poses and acts," Isherwood wrote of Bengston in his diary on August 4, 1970, "but I don't feel at ease with him. ('I never feel at ease with any heterosexual man,' I told Don, which rather annoyed him)." Christopher Isherwood, *Liberation; Diaries, Vol. 3: 1970–1983*, ed. Katherine Bucknell (London: Chatto & Windus, 2012), 182.

46. Isherwood, *Diaries, Vol. 3*, 104. In December 1970, Bachardy had a joint show with Ed Ruscha at the Hansen-Fuller Gallery in San Francisco, and the following March, he exhibited in *Drawings '71* at the San Pedro Municipal Gallery alongside Alexander, Bengston, Goode, Price, Ruscha, and others. "Don Bachardy presents suave Ingres-like portraits of artists," wrote William Wilson in the *Los Angeles Times*. "He draws very well but his major talent is in evoking character." William Wilson, "'Drawings '71' at San Pedro Gallery," *Los Angeles Times*, March 22, 1971, part IV, 14. Quoted in Bucknell, *Christopher Isherwood Inside Out*, 694.

47. Other key members of Light and Space were Robert Irwin, Craig Kauffman (who appears in a 1971 portrait by Bachardy; see p. 103), and James Turrell. While still a student at UCLA, Alexander began to experiment with industrial resins, for instance in *Cloud Box* (1966), a ten-inch resin cube whose translucent matter seems to enclose a dramatic cloudscape over an open plain.

48. An Emil Nolde exhibition in the early 1970s had inspired Bachardy to experiment more with color—"working very loose…and still trying to get a likeness," as he has put it—beginning with several watercolor heads of Isherwood. Quoted in Clothier, "Don Bachardy: Pictures of Christopher," n.p.

49. See also "Gregory Evans Talks with Don Bachardy at Ninety," pp. 17–29 in this volume.

50. Bachardy, *Stars in My Eyes*, 11.

51. Author interview with Bachardy, April 23, 2024.

52. Don Bachardy, diary entry for November 6, 1985. "Introduction," xiii.

53. John Russell, "Foreword," in Bachardy, Spender, and Russell, *Christopher Isherwood: Last Drawings*, x.

54. Bachardy, "Introduction," xiii. Cf. Edmund White's remark that "Bachardy's portraits penetrate a face known to a wide public—through book jacket photos, postcards of authors, David Hockney's paintings—and dissolve its exacerbated individuality into a kind of landscape." White, "Pool in Rocks by the Sea," 81.

55. The expression is similar to that found in an earlier self-portrait: Otto Dix, *Self-Portrait*, 1912, oil on paper mounted on poplar panel, Detroit Institute of Arts.

56. According to the art historian Richard Shone, "Grant was rather poor at the time of the painting's creation, and so used himself frequently as a model. He loved headdresses and turbans, but then so did Edward Wadsworth and William Roberts." Conversation with the author, June 4, 2024.

57. See Don Bachardy and Edmund White, *Nudes*, exh. cat. (2017).

58. Author interview with Bachardy, April 23, 2024.

59. McKeller was a young African American man (born in 1890) who had been working as an elevator operator at the Hotel Vendome, Boston, when Sargent met him. The painting was likely not exhibited in Sargent's lifetime. See Nathaniel Silver, ed., *Boston's Apollo: Thomas McKeller and John Singer Sargent*, exh. cat. (New Haven and London: Yale University Press, 2020).

60. Henri de Toulouse-Lautrec, *The Marble Polisher*, 1882–87, oil on canvas, Princeton University Art Museum.

61. Bachardy's shelves contain volumes on artists and movements as diverse as Art Nouveau, Francis Bacon, Agnolo Bronzino, Bruce Conner, Gustave Doré, Lucian Freud, Henri Fantin-Latour, Duncan Grant and Bloomsbury, Greek sculpture, David Hockney, Jean-Auguste-Dominique Ingres, Mexican masks, Alice Neel, Patrick Procktor, Ed Ruscha, John Singer Sargent, Egon Schiele, Chaim Soutine, and Keith Vaughan.

62. See, for example, *Portrait at the Opera (Elizabeth)*, 2016, oil on board, The Brant Foundation, Greenwich, Connecticut; *Klara (Klara Liden), 10 October 2009, Berlin*, 2000, colored pencil on paper, private collection; *Piotr on Couch*, 1996, oil on board, Seattle Art Museum.

Max Hoff, July 17, 1982 (no. 2)
Pen and ink on paper, 24 × 19 in. (61 × 48.3 cm)
Don Bachardy Papers

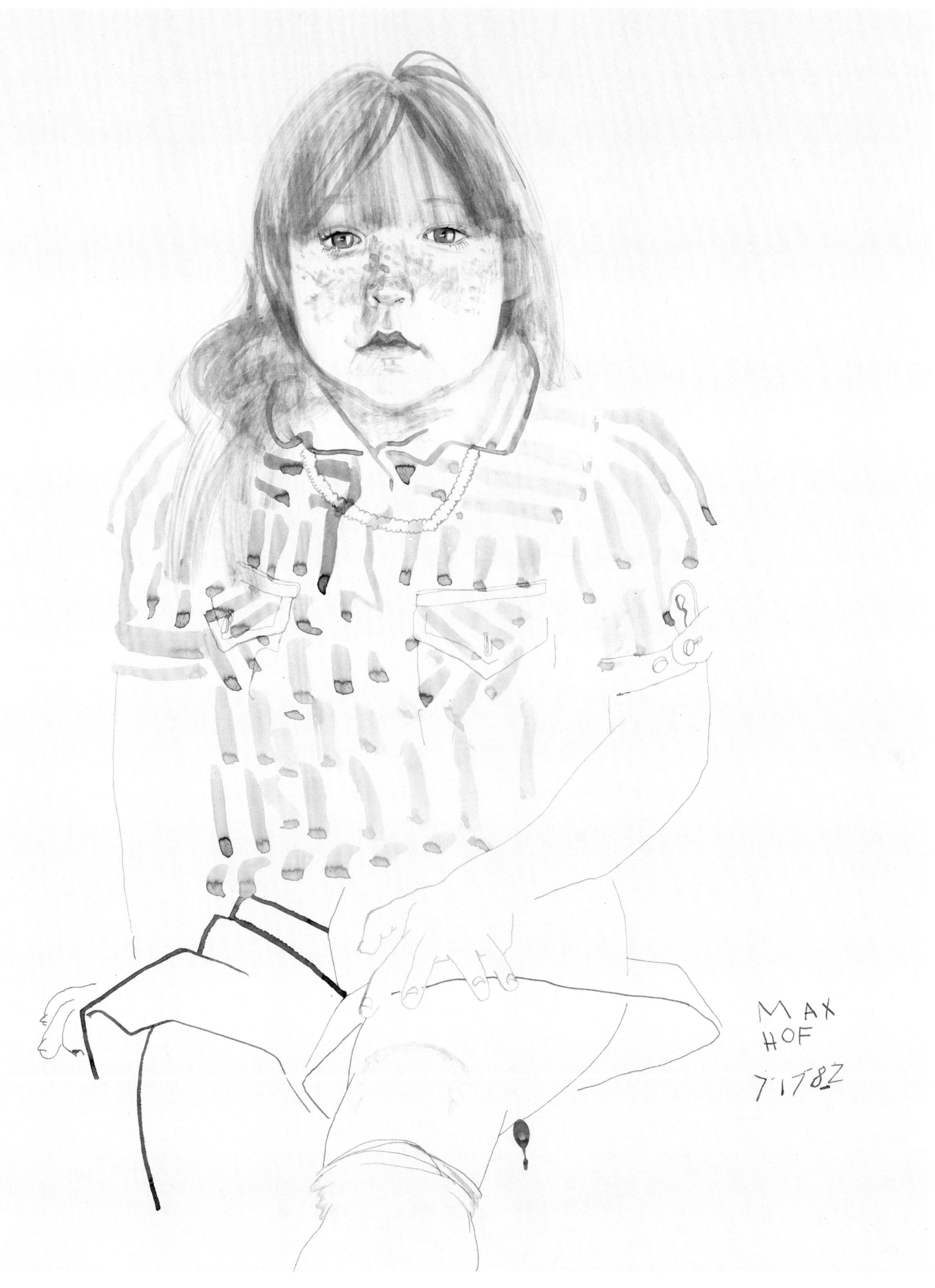
MAX
HOF
7·17·82

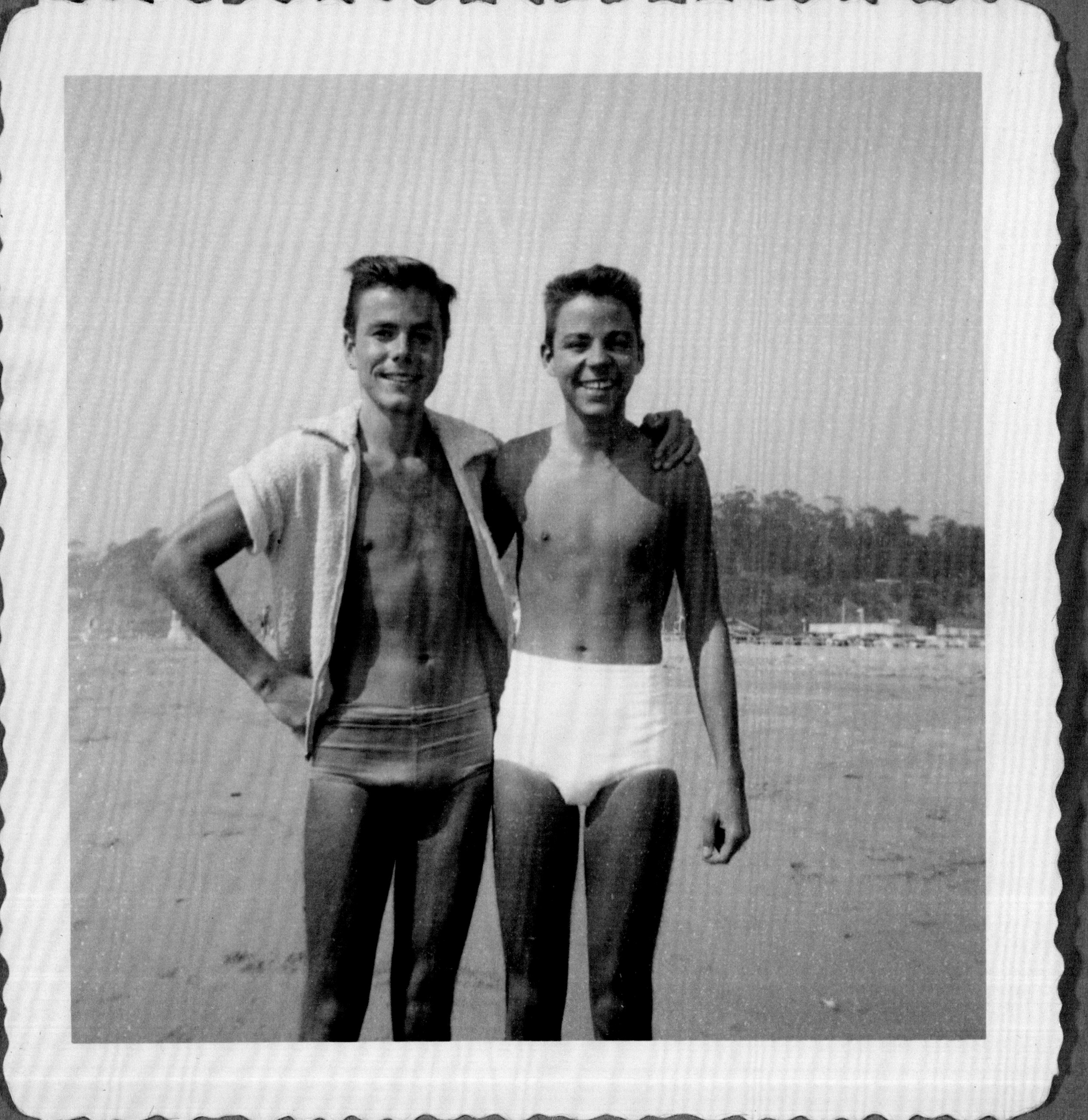

CHRISTOPHER ISHERWOOD AND DON BACHARDY

Katherine Bucknell

At age eighteen, Don Bachardy met the man who was destined to love and to mentor him for the next thirty-three years—British-American writer Christopher Isherwood, three decades his senior. Isherwood encouraged Bachardy to attend art school, asked every evening to see his work, believed in his talent, and steadfastly supported his career, including sitting for hundreds of portraits. More than that, he shaped Bachardy's sensibility and moral outlook and nurtured his confidence as a gay man.

Remembered nowadays as the originator of *Cabaret* and *A Single Man*, Isherwood in his youth had intentionally flunked out of Cambridge University, spurned the sixteenth-century family estate to which he was heir, found sexual liberation in Berlin during the last years of the Weimar Republic, and achieved fame in the 1930s as the leading novelist of the literary left. After his German boyfriend was arrested by Hitler's Gestapo in 1937, he immigrated to New York with his friend and stage collaborator, the poet W. H. Auden, then relocated to Hollywood, where he adopted a new religion, Vedanta, and fulfilled his lifelong dream of writing for the movie studios. He became famous all over again when his story "Sally Bowles" was adapted as the hit Broadway play *I Am a Camera* (1951), and later the musical *Cabaret* (1966).

In the late 1940s and early '50s, Bachardy accompanied his brother, Ted, to the beach in Santa Monica, a scene of sexual opportunity for Ted, four years older, who made a conquest of Isherwood. So began a nodding acquaintance between Isherwood and Don Bachardy, followed by an interrupted kiss at a Hollywood sex party during Bachardy's freshman semester at UCLA as he began his own sexual experimentation. One Sunday morning in February 1953, the brothers stopped by Isherwood's studio-house in a Brentwood garden; Isherwood cooked them breakfast, and all three drove off in Ted's seafoam-green Pontiac to meet friends at beach houses on the Pacific Coast Highway and a barbecue in the mountains above Malibu. The partying continued the next weekend, and Bachardy spent Saturday night, Valentine's Day, with Isherwood.

Fig. 1 Don Bachardy (right) on the beach with his brother, Ted, photograph attributed to Christopher Isherwood, ca. 1953. Christopher Isherwood Papers

Bachardy's parents were separated, and his brother, Ted, experienced breakdowns precipitated by bipolar disorder and schizophrenia; these breakdowns destabilized the whole family. That February, Ted was dragged off by the police after assaulting their father, and Don broke down in tears reporting the incident to Isherwood. Over the following weeks, Isherwood drove him to visit Ted in the state hospital in Camarillo and took up Ted's case with his psychiatrists.

Sensing Don's uniquely eager intelligence, Isherwood had already begun taking him to foreign films and the ballet, and giving him novels to read. He also accepted Bachardy's offer to type from dictation the novel he was then writing, *The World in the Evening* (1954), "a supreme act of intimacy," as Isherwood was later to describe such collaborations.[1] Bachardy's aesthetic education, powered by eros as in the ideal of Socratic love in fifth-century BC Athens, had begun. There would soon be a honeymoon trip to Monument Valley and Las Vegas, a first airplane trip to New York, and later, setting off by ship, a Grand Tour of Europe.

Six months into their romance, Isherwood was evicted from his garden house because his landlords feared that harboring overnight visits between a middle-aged man and a teenaged boy might lead to scandal and even cost them their jobs. This was the first of numerous challenges to the Isherwood-Bachardy ménage as the conformism of the period laid siege to their domestic routine and peace of mind.

Bachardy was more of a risk-taker than Isherwood. In adolescence, he sometimes drove his brother's car without permission and without a license. Occasionally, he shoplifted. Once, he climbed the wall around the beach house of William Randolph Hearst's showgirl mistress Marion Davies and dove into her pool. He liked to dress in drag, and at age thirteen, with a friend, both in dresses, wigs, high heels, and makeup, took the streetcar to the movies on Halloween. He and Ted learned to sneak into film premieres, wearing suits and carrying a Brownie camera. They would ask stars for autographs and photographs together (see p. 32), early selfies. In 1954, Bachardy had to register for the draft; with Isherwood's encouragement, he defiantly told the draft board he was homosexual, suffered their sneering disgust, and was classified 4-F, unfit for military service.

Isherwood was more circumspect by nature and also as a result of painful and frightening experiences not only with the Nazis but also with the British authorities, who had deported his German

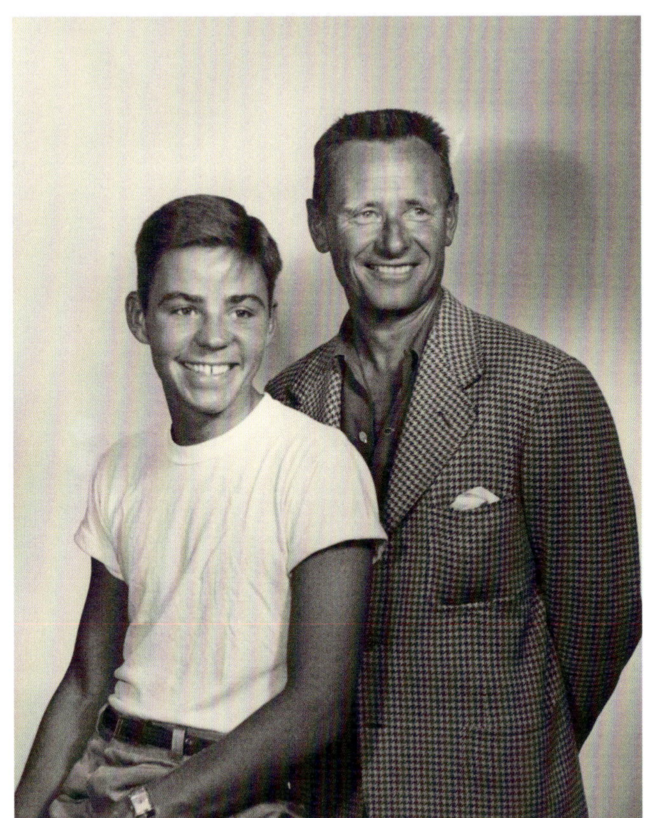

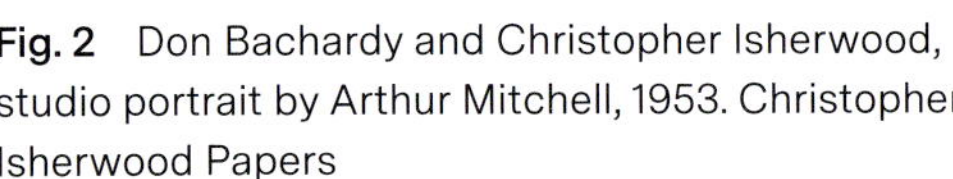

Fig. 2 Don Bachardy and Christopher Isherwood, studio portrait by Arthur Mitchell, 1953. Christopher Isherwood Papers

boyfriend in 1934. In 1951, he was questioned by the FBI about the defection of the British spies Guy Burgess and Donald Maclean to Moscow; their reports show he evinced candor about his youthful leftism while concealing the more dangerous fact that he and Burgess had shared a boyfriend. In 1954, he was cross-examined at MGM about his communist affiliations; again, he responded strategically, anxious to conceal his homosexuality, which was an equal threat to employment at the studios. At first, to be safe, he excluded Bachardy from his professional screenwriting life and from the star parties they were to attend openly together in later years. Nevertheless, by 1959, they settled in a canyonside property in Santa Monica that was to become the center of their shared artistic lives, Isherwood writing in his workroom at one end of the house (fig. 4), Bachardy drawing and painting in the studio they built at the other end of the property.

The thirty-year age gap that scandalized many was one key to the success of their relationship. Isherwood had long sought a younger-brother figure he could mold and protect. Bachardy was the first person in his family to attend college—transferring from UCLA to L.A. City College, then back to UCLA before dropping out—and he wanted someone to guide him, someone he could look up to and emulate. Though he was a risk-taker, he suffered crises of self-confidence and even feared he might go mad like his brother; he required constant reassurance.

Another key to the bond was their shared decision to have an open sexual relationship. Isherwood had had countless lovers prior to meeting Bachardy. "Was he going to deny me the adventures he had had? Never," Bachardy later said.[2] But sometimes the outside relationships became deeper and ruptured their domestic harmony. This was painful to navigate. Isherwood ballasted himself with his religion, Vedanta, and worked to love Bachardy without being possessive or controlling. Eventually, Bachardy, too, took up Vedanta; he was initiated by Isherwood's guru, Swami Prabhavananda, in December 1962, occasionally attended the temple, and meditated at the same time as Isherwood in a different room. But years later he told Isherwood, "If anybody's my guru, you are."[3]

Isherwood and Bachardy also had a secret world in which they thought of themselves as The Animals, creatures rather than humans, with creaturely needs for warmth, for play, for love without judgment, for acceptance including whatever faults were part of their natural identity. Isherwood was a horse, Dobbin, loyal,

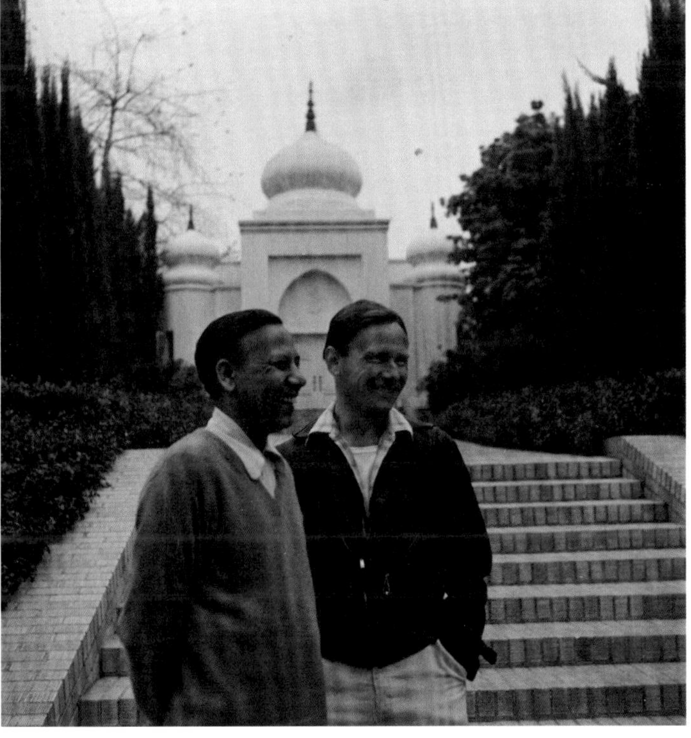

Fig. 3 Swami Prabhavananda and Christopher Isherwood in front of the Hollywood Temple, 1943. Christopher Isherwood Papers

strong, sometimes clumsy; Bachardy was Kitty, white as snow, shy, skittish, and subject to unpredictable Black Cat fury and despair. Their Animal identities, referred to in the third person, allowed Isherwood and Bachardy to distance themselves from unmanageable emotions and avoid conflict. As The Animals, hidden away in their Basket, they felt themselves in league against outsiders, especially straight people who did not understand or accept their homosexual life, and whom they called The Others.

Art was another key to the relationship. They supported one another unstintingly in their individual work, promoting ever-growing mutual understanding. From the time he took dictation at age eighteen, Bachardy was infiltrating Isherwood's writerly imagination; he became Isherwood's most valued first reader, offering sometimes startling advice that pushed Isherwood in unexpected creative directions. He came up with the titles for many of Isherwood's later books.

For his part, Isherwood drew on their relationship in hidden ways, offering private messages to Bachardy in his fiction. For instance, "Mr. Lancaster," the first story in *Down There on a Visit* (1962), reimagines an episode from Isherwood's youth, when he struggled to deal with the established older generation, and it also obliquely addresses Bachardy's predicament. Some of Isherwood's friends looked down on and even ignored Bachardy, a humiliation toward which Isherwood felt keen empathy. "Mr. Lancaster" recalls of a condescending elder cousin, "You had to study him, like lessons."[4] This was secretly advice for Bachardy, and Bachardy took it. His portraits, like the portraits Isherwood created in prose, were to become "psychological studies," as one critic noticed.[5] Bachardy got under the skin, portraying personality, in all its evanescence, rather than an idealized external image.

In 1961, after nearly eight years together, Bachardy went to London to study at the Slade School of Fine Art, where he was awarded temporary, non-degree status. In London, he earned money outside school, drawing fashion illustrations and portraits, but he struggled to paint in oils. His debut show of portrait drawings at the Redfern Gallery in October 1961 was a knockout, bringing both sales and commissions. Next came debuts in New York and Los Angeles. But he wanted to paint as well as draw, and he suffered constant anxiety that his success was partly based on Isherwood's address book. Isherwood knew many of the creative stars of the day—writers, composers, actors, directors, spiritual trailblazers. Bachardy shared his friendships with

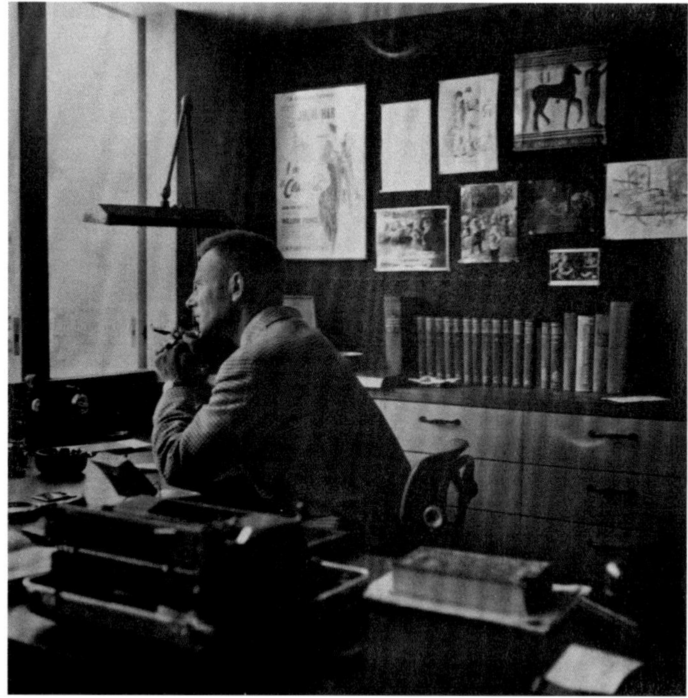

Fig. 4 Christopher Isherwood in the garden house, photograph attributed to Jim Charlton, 1952 or 1953. Christopher Isherwood Papers

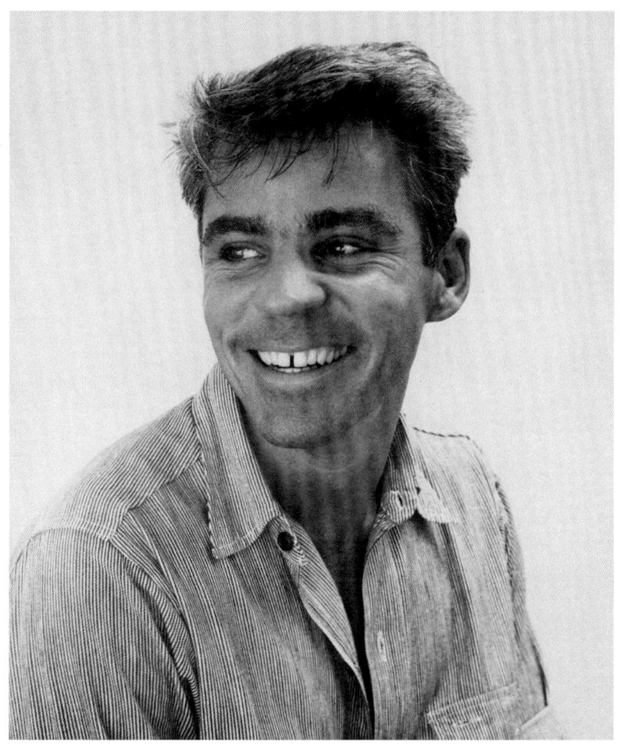

Francis Bacon (see p. 88), Truman Capote (see p. 91), Leslie Caron, John Gielgud, Julie Harris, Aldous and Maria Huxley (see p. 93), Somerset Maugham, David Selznick and Jennifer Jones, Igor and Vera Stravinsky (see p. 89), Gore Vidal, Tennessee Williams (see p. 100), and many more, but he was determined to develop independently and to establish himself as an artist in his own right. He insisted on having his own studio and his own set of friends. Isherwood acceded, up to a point, but friction escalated. In 1963, they split for a few months. Thereafter, they spent important and constructive spells apart, but always in touch by phone and letter.

In 1968, there was another serious rupture, closely observed by David Hockney (see p. 43), who was fascinated by their bond and trying for a similar partnership with his young boyfriend, Peter Schlesinger (see p. 43). While Bachardy was in London conducting a turbulent affair, Hockney painted his seminal double portrait, *Christopher Isherwood and Don Bachardy* (see p. 45), showing the couple in matching chairs in their Santa Monica living room. The balanced, seemingly stable domestic scene featuring two men was revolutionary. It was a portrait, in fact, of a modus vivendi being carved out through painful give-and-take, a struggle for both love and freedom during which Isherwood suffered a minor breakdown.

He and Bachardy renewed their bond partly by becoming collaborators on screenplays and scripts, reanimating the mood of their playful early work sessions on *The World in the Evening*, but now as two professionals. Among their scripts was the cult classic *Frankenstein: The True Story* (1973), drawing on Pygmalion as much as on Mary Shelley and camping one version of their own story, in which the artist's beautiful creation turns into a monster.

Isherwood publicly criticized marriage as a fetish of bourgeois straight people. He adopted Bachardy in 1977, formalizing the father-son dynamic between them. It was tempting for Isherwood, as for Hockney, to offer an ideally harmonious public image of a love relationship between two men. As early as 1947, he had admonished Gore Vidal that they must cease subscribing in their work to "the Tragic Homosexual myth" and instead, with self-conscious political intent, portray homosexuals (his preferred term at the time) in a positive light: "There are laws which could be changed. There are public prejudices which could be removed. Anything an author writes on these subjects is bound, therefore, to have a certain propaganda value, whether he likes it or not."[6]

Fig. 5 Don Bachardy, photograph by Dale Laster, 1964. Christopher Isherwood Papers

Indeed, he had worked since the 1920s to make the idea of the homosexual acceptable and, moreover, attractive to mainstream audiences. In Berlin, he had learned about propaganda while employed as a translator for a communist front; when Hitler scourged the communists, Isherwood observed how they worked from underground and abroad, and he studied how they coded their writing, substituting in one pamphlet the word "Christian" for the word "communist," a technique he adopted later in *A Single Man* (1964), where he has his professor character, George, silently substitute one minority for another, thereby introducing a then-unrecognized minority, homosexuals, into the reader's mind without using the word. The novel serves its propagandistic aim by presenting the same-sex bonds—between George and Jim, between George and Kenny—as more truly romantic and profound than the heterosexual bonds—between Jim and Doris, between George and Charley—but this is balanced when George admonishes his students that "minorities are people; *people*, not angels."[7] Even if imperfect, even if disliked, nobody should be persecuted.

Isherwood had lived as a Vedanta monk for more than two years during World War II and learned that celibacy was not for him. He needed an intimate domestic relationship, and he could not live without sex. Yet he continued to be a devoted Hindu, even if not a spiritually perfect one. His guru, Swami Prabhavananda, taught him that "Purity is telling the truth."[8] Telling the truth became the motivating theme of his life and of his art. In his last three books, published in the age of gay liberation, he conjured his past with fresh willingness to shock. He came out explicitly in 1971 in his family memoir, *Kathleen and Frank*, and he revealed his sexual life in 1930s Berlin and elsewhere in *Christopher and His Kind* (1976). In *My Guru and His Disciple* (1980), he outed himself as a Hindu and described how his sexuality fit into his spiritual life. *Christopher and His Kind* made him a hero of the gay liberation movement when he was in his seventies. Bachardy was by his side during book tours, supporting him on and off the stage and sometimes answering questions in front of enormous audiences and the press. Though their sexual relationship was mostly over, they still slept in the same bed, and they discovered when using a tape recorder in their script-writing sessions that they could no longer tell their voices apart when they spoke, so closely had Bachardy studied, even impersonated, Isherwood.

Bachardy also came to share Isherwood's commitment to truth-telling. As a child, he had learned from his mother and elder brother how to deceive his overworked, undereducated father so

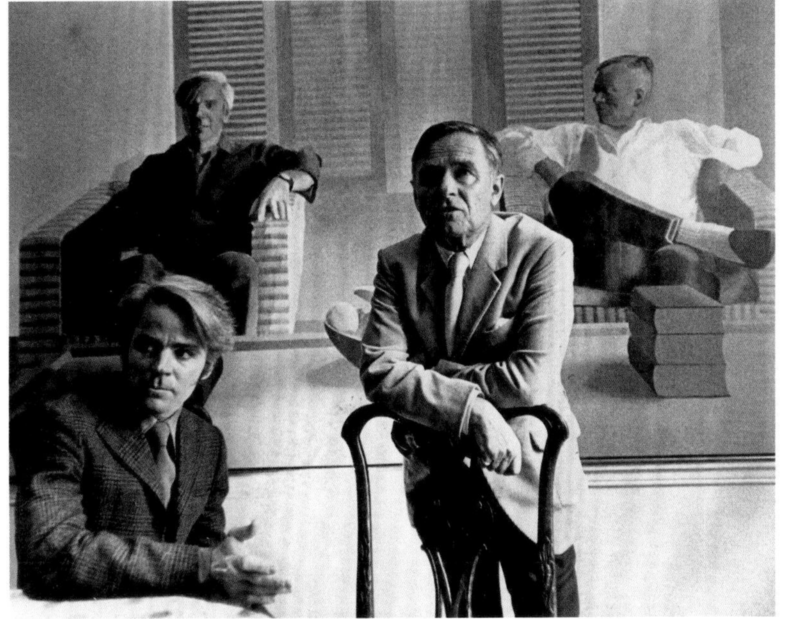

they could spend the family's scant money on movies; this had led to other deceptions. When Isherwood replaced Bachardy's disapproving father, he nevertheless admonished Bachardy to stop sneaking into movie premieres and to refrain from any lawbreaking that could attract police attention. For years, off and on, Bachardy deceived Isherwood about such things and also about his love life. Yet he was ruthlessly truthful in his portraits, and as he grew older, he became more forthright about himself. He saw to it that Isherwood's diaries were published unexpurgated, apart from passages that might attract libel suits, that Isherwood's papers were preserved at The Huntington for long-term study, and that his own correspondence with Isherwood was published.

As Bachardy's career developed in the 1960s and '70s, Isherwood was carried into the heart of the newly developing L.A. art scene.[9] He was fascinated by Bachardy's closest artist friends, Peter Alexander (see p. 47) and Billy Al Bengston (see p. 46), as well as by the Brits, Hockney and Patrick Procktor. He relished the success of Bachardy's 1973 show at the L.A. Municipal Art Gallery in Barnsdall Park and the first acquisition of his work by the National Portrait Gallery in London (a 1967 drawing of Auden), which coincided with a commission to portray a cousin of Queen Elizabeth II, the Earl of Harewood, and his second countess. In 1974, with a rising young dealer, Nicholas Wilder (see p. 74), who was the first to fully recognize his talent, Bachardy finally showed his paintings. The *Los Angeles Times* critic William Wilson told Isherwood these completely changed his view of Bachardy as an artist.[10] Wilson's colleague Henry Seldis, who reviewed the show, compared the portraits of anonymous friends and acquaintances to Egon Schiele (a Bachardy favorite) and Oskar Kokoschka.[11] Isherwood copied this, as he had copied earlier reviews, into his diary, interpolating his thoughts on the motivation of the reviewers, and the quality of their observations, and expressing his immense pride in Bachardy.

Their life together was a work of art in itself, exemplified by their shared 1979 diary, *October* (published 1980), for which Bachardy made at least one drawing each day of the month and Isherwood made diary entries. The Isherwood-Bachardy style was spare, forthright, and intense; the book positioned their aesthetic at the center of

Fig. 6 Don Bachardy and Christopher Isherwood in front of David Hockney's double portrait in Marguerite Littman's dining room, Chester Square, London, 1970. Photograph by Kelvin Brodie, *Sunday Times* (London), Everett Collection, Alamy

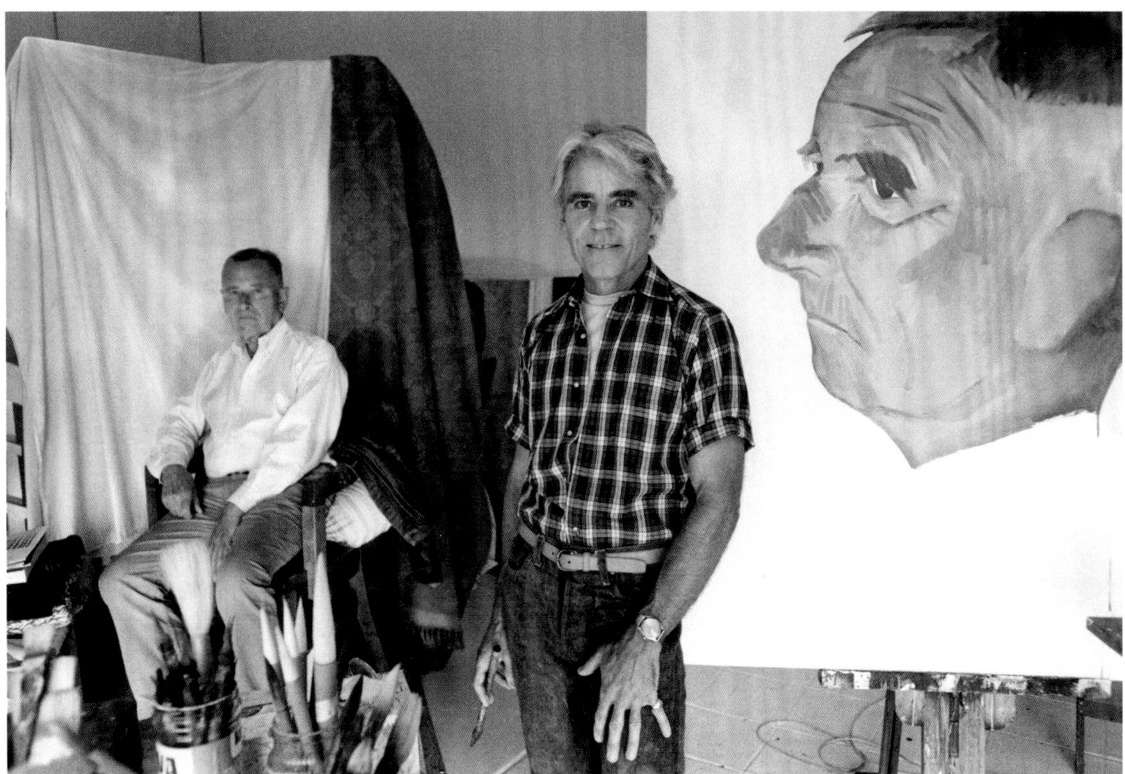

highbrow gay culture a few years prior to the widespread outbreak of AIDS. During Isherwood's subsequent decline and death from cancer, Bachardy embraced and extended their aesthetic in a final collaboration, drawing Isherwood every day with a Japanese brush and black acrylic paint as Isherwood approached the last great threshold (see pp. 122–24). "It began to seem that dying was something which we were doing together," Bachardy wrote in his diary.[12]

After Isherwood's death, Bachardy put away the black of mourning and developed his signature palette of jewel and marine colors, applied in minimal amounts with masterful control, cutting with a paintbrush the bold, economical line that he had first practiced with scissors around the outline of adored movie stars in his childhood fan magazines. As Isherwood noted in 1974, his individual style was unmistakable: "They are so absolutely Bachardy and no one else."[13] Gregory Evans's acute selection in the exhibition associated with this book, eschewing celebrity for intimacy and artistry, reveals the long trajectory of this style, instantly recognizable, yet always changing and ever more powerful. And it foregrounds Bachardy's tenacious poise on the tightrope, where wild energies run between artist and sitter, and his mighty determination makes the turbulence resemble a face.

Fig. 7 Michael Childers (American, b. 1944), Christopher Isherwood and Don Bachardy at work on large portrait, 1983. Christopher Isherwood Papers

NOTES

1. Christopher Isherwood, *Christopher and His Kind, 1929–1939* (New York: Farrar, Straus & Giroux, 1976), 108.

2. Don Bachardy, conversation with the author, April 19, 2018.

3. Christopher Isherwood, diary entry for December 25, 1973. Christopher Isherwood, *Liberation; Diaries, Vol. 3: 1970–1983*, ed. Katherine Bucknell (New York: HarperCollins, 2012), 412.

4. Christopher Isherwood, *Down There on a Visit* (New York: Simon & Schuster, 1962), 40.

5. Unsigned review [William Wilson and Henry J. Seldis], "Art Walk: A Critical Guide to the Galleries," *Los Angeles Times*, March 13, 1970, part IV, 8.

6. Christopher Isherwood to Gore Vidal, December 19, 1947, Houghton Library, Harvard University, Cambridge, Massachusetts.

7. Christopher Isherwood, *A Single Man* (New York: Simon & Schuster, 1964), 57.

8. Christopher Isherwood, diary entry for November 19, 1943. Christopher Isherwood, *Diaries, Vol. 1: 1939–1960*, ed. Katherine Bucknell (New York: HarperCollins; London: Chatto & Windus, 2000), 328.

9. Coalescing around Americans including Billy Al Bengston, Ed Ruscha, Peter Alexander, Joe Goode, Ken Price, Ed Moses, Robert Graham, Laddie John Dill, and others.

10. Christopher Isherwood, diary entry for October 30, 1974. Isherwood, *Diaries, Vol. 3*, 460.

11. Henry J. Seldis, "Art Walk," *Los Angeles Times*, November 15, 1974, part IV, 86, and Christopher Isherwood, diary entry for November 15, 1974, Isherwood, *Diaries, Vol. 3*, 460.

12. Don Bachardy, diary entry for January 3, 1986. "Introduction," in Don Bachardy, Stephen Spender, and John Russell, *Last Drawings of Christopher Isherwood* (London: Faber & Faber, 1990), xviii.

13. Christopher Isherwood, diary entry for November 15, 1974. Isherwood, *Diaries, Vol. 3*, 461.

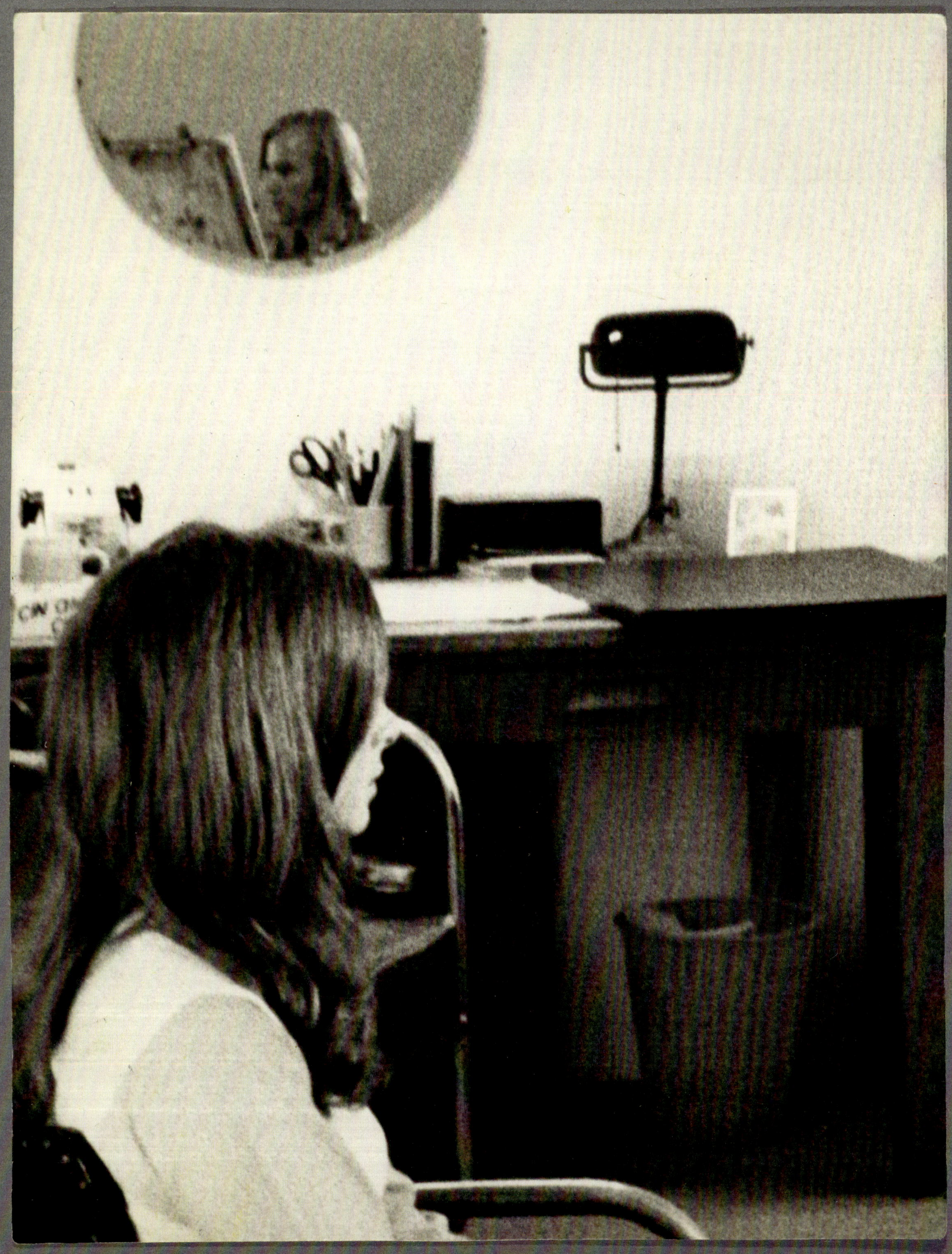

Don Bachardy wasn't part of the group of artists who transformed the Los Angeles art world into an international force in the 1960s. He drew portraits. The work of those artists was as far from figurative as you could get. It was dominated by the unconventional use of materials, light, and space, infused with a sense of the absurd stemming from Pop Art. Images were used only as icons.

But Don's portraits are never simply figurative. They were never drawn to please or flatter the sitter, or to capture a photographic image. Don always looked for what was behind the mask and drew what he saw. And his portraits are always about the drawing, not the sitter, which, in a sense, turned the sitter into an ever-changing icon. For an artist who was hammering dents into fiberglass, to understand that was close to impossible. But Billy Al Bengston did.

Don and Chris Isherwood were fans of Billy's work, and even though they didn't know him, they invited him to dinner. On his own. Flattered, Billy went to what turned out to be a meeting of like minds rather than a dinner party, and by the end of the evening not only had they become fast friends, but Billy had become a great champion of Don's work. And, of course, he sat for a portrait (see p. 46). And, of course, he made sure everybody he knew saw that portrait and, soon after, every artist who knew Billy wanted to be drawn by Don. Eventually, if you hadn't been drawn by Don Bachardy at least once, you felt as if you didn't matter. At the same time, Don was also drawing every star that had ever glittered in the Hollywood firmament, but what he was doing in the art world was different. It was as if he was becoming a visual Vasari, drawing not only all the important Los Angeles artists of the time, but the people surrounding them as well. His drawings became a record of those times.

I was first drawn by Don in 1970. I had arrived in Los Angeles only a year earlier and was living with the artist Joe Goode. Joe asked Don to draw me. No one had ever drawn me. The idea of anyone drawing me was unimaginable. Los Angeles isn't a reading town, so although many of the people I'd met in the art world pretended

A FEW STORIES

Mary Agnes Donoghue

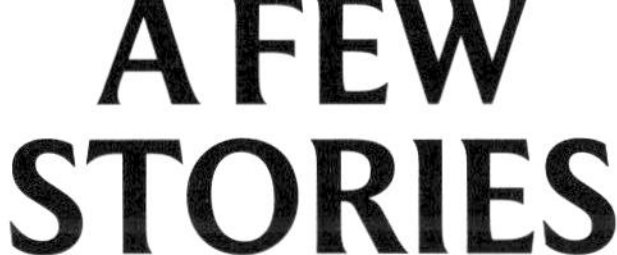

Fig. 1 Don Bachardy sketching Mary Agnes Donoghue, photograph by Joe Goode, 1970. Collection of Mary Agnes Donoghue

to have read all of Christopher Isherwood's books, which they could fake a little having all seen *Cabaret*, they hadn't. I had, which was intimidating enough, but I had also seen enough of Don's work to be paralyzed by fear at the thought of being drawn by him. I barely spoke to him when he arrived, and during the sitting became so still and expressionless I thought I had managed to somehow become invisible. I was hiding. Over the years, Don has done many drawings and paintings of me, but I particularly love that one. Along with the beauty of the drawing itself, he drew me hiding. When you are sitting for Don Bachardy, it is impossible to evade detection.

That portrait led to many dinners at the Isherwood-Bachardy house, a bungalow sitting on the edge of a hillside in Santa Monica Canyon with a wide, sweeping view across the canyon all the way out to the sea and beyond. Don told me when he and Chris were looking for a house to buy in the late 1950s and visited this one it was a filthy, decaying teardown. When Chris asked him what he thought, Don immediately said, "This is it. This is our house." Chris said, "You can't be serious." Don said, "I am," and Don was right. They restored the house and gardens and filled it with art, so much art that along with every other wall, a large mirrored wall was eventually also covered with paintings, and as you made your way to the dining-room table you tripped over the sculptures on the floor.

Things are quieter now, but in those days, there were many dinner parties. The guests were a mix of artists, actors, filmmakers, and writers. The conversation was quick and bright, wit and laughter dominated even the darkest subjects, their housekeeper Natalie served delicious food which was often cooked by Don, the wine flowed, and you left feeling a glow from being in such good company that it lasted for days.

My first dinner there was the beginning of my fifty-three-year-long friendship with Don. It followed soon after that first sitting. Shyness fled when I came across a photograph of Don as a young teenager with Marilyn Monroe (see p. 32), propped up against a wall in the kitchen. Their faces are very close together, and, if I remember correctly, her lush, red lips are pursed, and he is dressed in a suit and tie, smiling like the cat that ate the canary. When I asked if he knew her, he said no, but as teenagers he and his brother, Ted, both of whom had seen every movie ever made with their mother, would dress up in their finest,

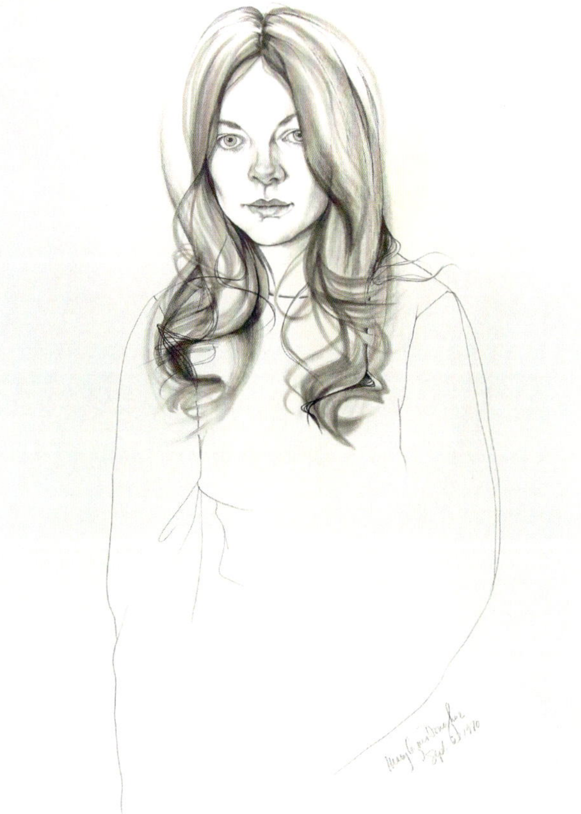

Fig. 2 *Mary Agnes Donoghue*, September 27, 1970 (no. 1). Graphite and ink on paper, 29⅛ × 23¼ in. (74 × 59.1 cm). Courtesy of Don Bachardy

complete with tie and pocket handkerchief, and join the crowds outside any theater where a movie premiere was being held. Stars would go by, but Don and Ted were looking for an unknown couple to use as parents. When they finally spotted them, they would quickly slip under the ropes holding back the hoi polloi and join them as if they were invited guests, chatting a little with the strangers so they would appear to be a family. They attended some of the biggest premieres in Hollywood on the arms of their fake parents.

If I had to choose a single quality that bound Don and myself to one another over the years, it would be laughter. Don's wit is never cruel but it is sharp, astute, and very mischievous. His book *Stars in My Eyes* (2000), a collection of portraits of Hollywood stars, each one accompanied by a mercilessly witty commentary on the sittings by Don, was published at the same time as a nonfiction book about the Vietnam War written by my husband, Chris Robbins, which, like most histories of war, was not flying off the shelves. Don's book was. At his book-signing party, as Don walked past us, he turned sideways to Chris with that same cat-that-ate-the-canary grin on his face and softly sang, "I'm the tops, I'm the Mona Lisa, I'm the tops, I'm the tower of Pisa, baby you're the bottom, I'm the tops," before sauntering off with unabashed delight toward the crowd waiting for him to sign his book. It was wicked, it was playful, it was lovable and irresistibly funny.

Many years ago, Don told me he always started a portrait with the eyes. Recently, driven by a romantic impulse, I asked if it was because he found the person's soul in their eyes. He answered in a slightly impatient voice that, well, yes, he did, but the real reason he drew the eyes first was because if he drew all the other stuff first and got the eyes wrong, he would have wasted his time. Art does not exist without a sharp streak of pragmatism running through it, and his honesty made me laugh.

Because of that conversation, I was going to call this essay "A Portrait of Don Bachardy by a Sitter," which would have been ridiculous. Had I started with the eyes, by now what I've written would have barely outlined their shape. Instead, I've had to settle for just telling a few stories, some told to me by Don, some drawn from observation, the rest taken from firsthand experience. But fifty-three years is a very long time, and I am forced by space to leave out a vast wealth of good stories I could tell about Don. When I vanish they will vanish with me, but still, lucky me to have lived them. What larks.

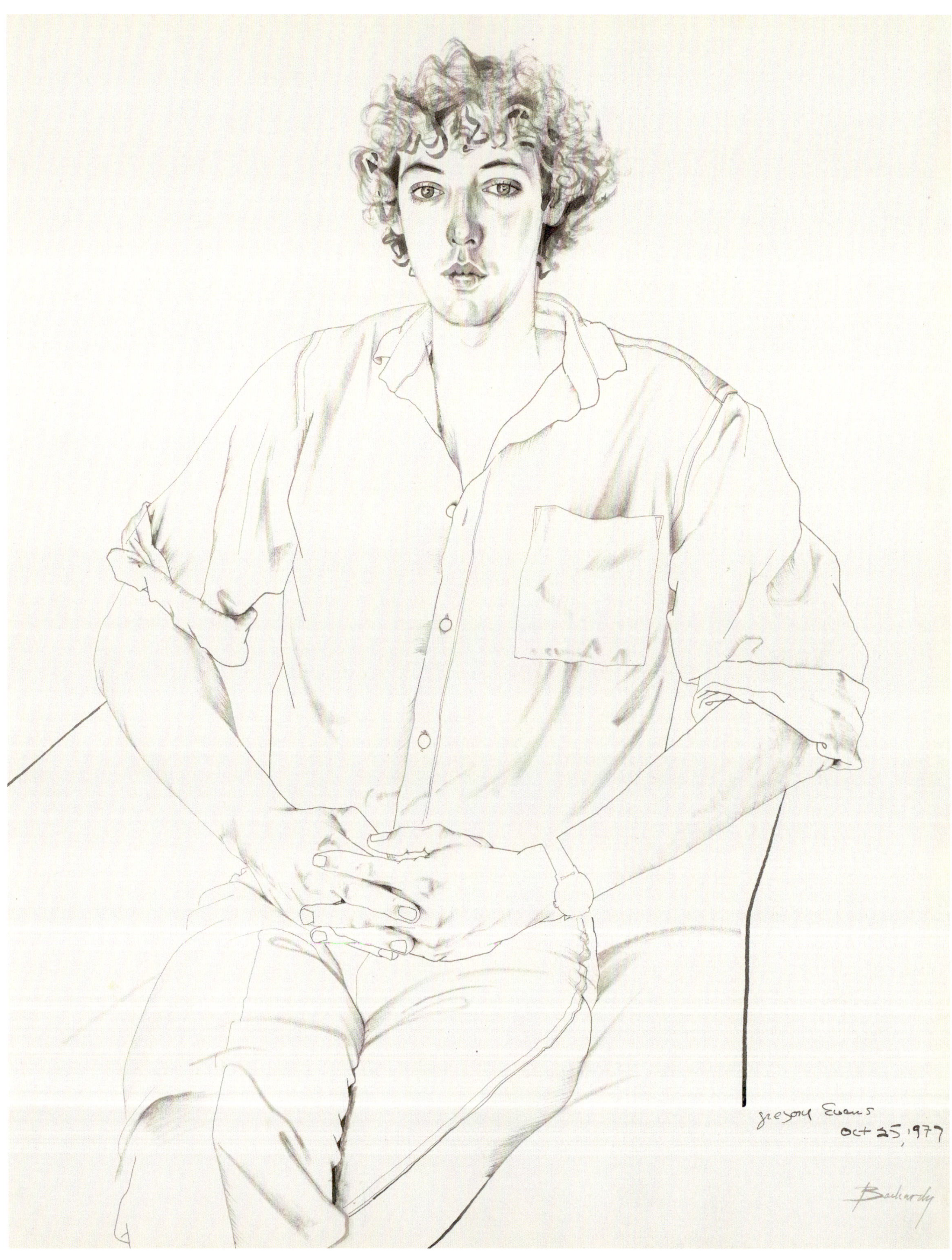

Gregory Evans
Oct 25, 1977
Bachardy

AN
INTERVIEW
WITH GUEST
CURATOR
GREGORY
EVANS

Christina Nielsen

Christina Nielsen Hello, Gregory Evans. Thank you for coming in today to talk to us about this project of looking at art produced by a friend of yours over many, many decades. I want to go back and start at the beginning. Really going to dig into the relationship, the deep, deep friendship that you have, but taking it back to the very first recollection you have of meeting Don and Chris.

Gregory Evans The first memory I have of meeting them was in 1970. And I was then in a relationship with art dealer Nicholas Wilder (see p. 74). He said, "We're going to go have dinner tonight. We're going to meet this…I had no idea who Christopher Isherwood was, or Don Bachardy. So, I really just met them in the raw. Nick had said it was an artist that he was interested in. They may have met before, maybe at openings or something, but I think this was a first-time sort of one-on-one gathering for everybody. But I still remember the evening, and it was at [the Hollywood restaurant] Musso and Frank's, and it was in the big dining room in the corner, in the far corner table.

CN The star corner.

GE And you know, I was just a kid in those days, and I had been plopped suddenly into this world of artists and museum openings and important people and directors, and I always felt so out of my depth. Meeting Don and Chris was magical. It was like love at first sight. It was so comfortable being with them. I remember especially Christopher, because you always had his full attention, and anyway they were just both so warm and friendly, and it remained like that forever. So, it was quick friends and uncomplicated and a good sense of humor. I always felt so welcomed around them, and just enjoyed being with them so much. A fascinating couple and interesting, both of them, to listen to them and learn so much from them—

Gregory Evans, October 25, 1979
Pen and ink on paper, 29 × 23 in. (73.7 × 58.4 cm)
Don Bachardy Papers

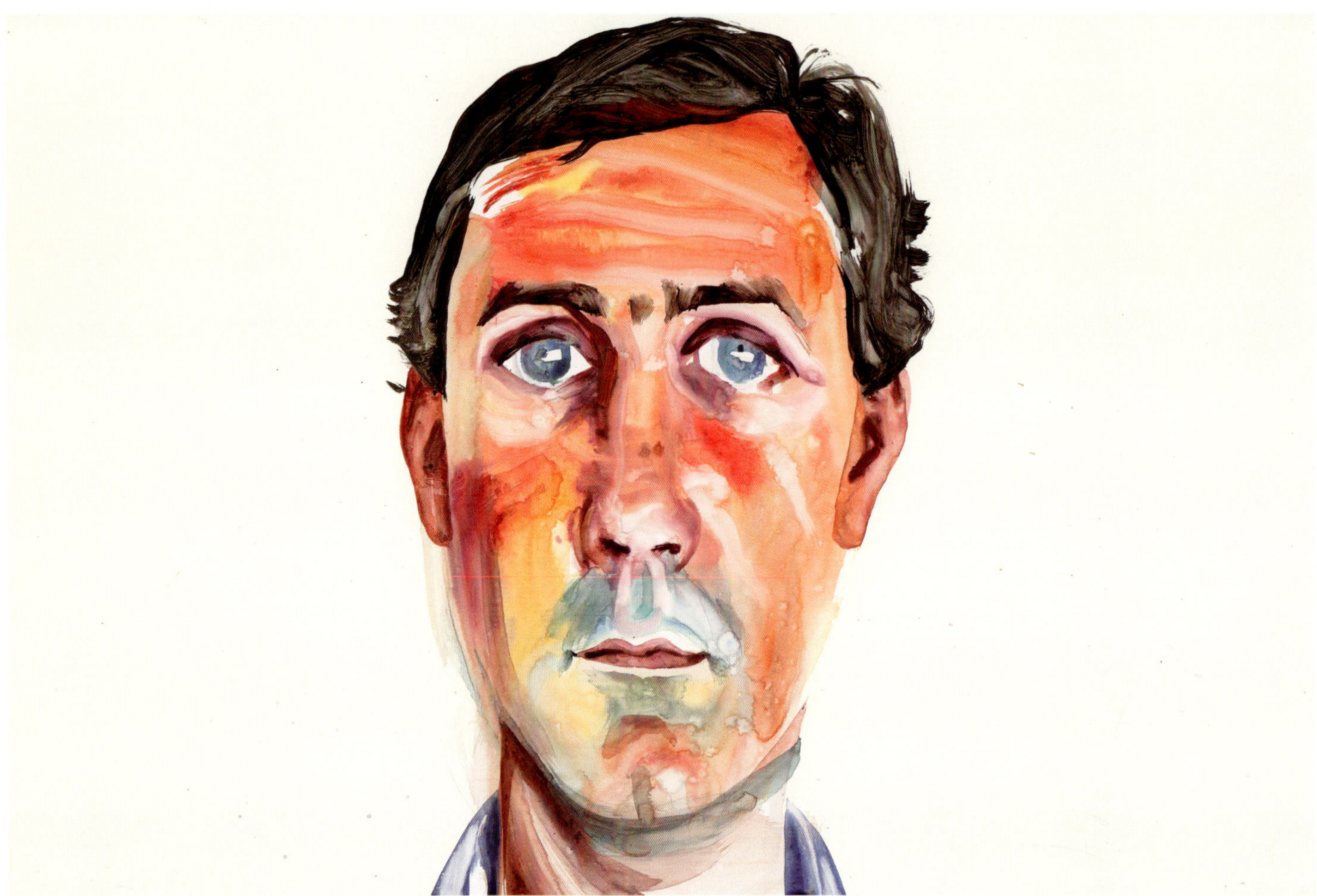

CN Are they recounting stories the whole time, or are they bouncing off of each other?

GE —and conversations with Nick, but also Christopher had a lot of curiosity. I realized as I was working on this project—I don't know where I've been all these years—but I thought, there were two portraitists living in the same house, because Christopher did literary portraits. So, of course he had as much interest in people as Don did, his painting people. So, Christopher wanted to know as much as he could about somebody, looking in hindsight.

CN He's an observer.

GE He's an observer and he wants to know about you. So, he was always great fun to talk with. I could talk to him. I think Don was

Nick Wilder, August 12, 1980
Acrylic on paper, 26 × 40 in. (66 × 101.6 cm)

always maybe a little bit quieter, because he was a listener. But the two of them together, I could feel they were *very* connected to one another, and that there was a real warmth between them that they shared with others.

CN Amazing.

GE Yeah, it came through. That was my first impression.

CN That's fantastic, and in the big dining room—I love that. Tell me about your first encounter with Don's art in general.

GE My first encounter was that Don asked if he could draw me. And in those days, he made house calls. So, he came up to Nick's and my house, up in Laurel Canyon, and I sat for several portraits. So *that* was my first encounter. I had no idea prior to that what his art was. I hadn't seen it. It was from that time that I then became more exposed to it through exhibitions. And there weren't a lot of exhibitions happening at that time. And I think he was—I might be wrong about this—but I think at that time he may have been between galleries. I think he was with Irving Blum for, like, one exhibition, and I think really that was the whole reason for Nick wanting to meet Don, because Nick had an interest in Don's art. So, I started sitting for him (see p. 72), and then I believe after that, he did quite a few over the decades that I've known him, but then I was invited to his studio, and so that exposed me to a bit more; you know, he had works pinned up on the walls. But I learned about Don as the relationship developed.

CN Your friendship.

GE Yes. I was exposed to Don before I was exposed to his art, so I had no opinion of him before I met him. It wasn't like, "Oh my God, I'm going to meet the artist who drew Bette Davis [see pp. 19, 42]." Through the years, all the works of his that I was exposed to in exhibitions and publications were always works done; it's just that I happened to have this friend Don Bachardy, who happened to be an artist. This, now, having this project was the first time that I was looking at the artist Don Bachardy, who happens to have been a friend of mine for the past fifty years.

CN How hard is it to separate friend from artist? Do you have to?

GE It happened early on. I remember making a conscious decision when I became aware of that—OK, now, I'm looking at the work of an artist. I'm not looking at my friend's latest exhibition. And the amount of works that I was looking at—and I think I was able to separate myself from that—like he was almost this person I didn't know. I became detached from my friend Don Bachardy, and now I was researching this artist, Don Bachardy.

CN Are you talking about now, or like in the '70s or '80s or…

GE No, I'm talking about now, looking through the work in his studio. Suddenly, it had nothing to do with my friend. Now, I'm looking at the life's work of an artist.

CN Which must be a very singular experience for you. And you've been close and had long-standing relationships of all kinds with many different types of artists. You know the people. And then you look at the art. I don't know that I've ever encountered anything like it, where suddenly somebody, in retrospect, is looking back over such a huge oeuvre and so many decades.

GE I met Don in 1970, so there's, as we've discovered, work that goes back to 1940 [see p. 20]. He's been drawing since he was four years old. But up until that time, these were all portraits of people, some of whom I met later on. But it's a period that I was not involved in, and I didn't know Don or Chris or any of these people. And so then in the '70s, it's like *my* life. I'm starting to see *my* life and the people that I met through Don and Chris, through dinner parties at their house. I start to see old friends of *mine* that Don met through me that I didn't know he had drawn. So, it was a very emotional journey. I knew so much from his drawings of—that he was Don Bachardy, Christopher Isherwood's partner. And I know him because he's done these por-traits of Christopher and Hollywood celebrities and movie stars, and this famous person and that famous person. But I started discovering something much deeper than that, and that there was so much more to his work than this, than what he had been known for. And so, I felt like I was looking at something that had perhaps been just hidden away for, like I said, years and decades, or maybe works that nobody had ever seen. Or maybe Don didn't have the courage or the confi-dence in his work, or the people were always demanding, "We want to see the Hollywood pictures." He got pigeonholed into a certain style, but he was doing so much more than that. And that's what was excit-ing, and really thrilling and emotional for me. At the same time, there were so many personal moments in there that had been recorded that were a lot of people I didn't know, or they were just friends of Don or maybe a friend of a friend, finding some of my friends in there that Don had met through me. And so, it was really a rich experience, a very profound experience.

CN I can imagine, which is why I think it's so extraordinary. We talked about that moment where you said, "I'd love to do a show," and I said, "Let's do it." Because you are the perfect one to help us sort of decode this body of work. I'm going to come back to the totality of the oeuvre, but first I want to telescope in. Talk to us about a dinner party at Chris and Don's.

GE Well, they were always small. They always said they were very strict about keeping it—I think at most, they would only allow six guests because that's what the table held. And so, if ever you said, "Oh, I have so-and-so in town, can I bring…?" "No." They were always very strict about not overcrowding. You never knew who was going to be there. I was just this green teenager. I mean, when I first met them, I was seventeen years old.

CN Wow.

GE So, I met a lot of important writers and directors and Hollywood people or visitors, literary people. Or just friends or—I don't want to say unimportant—but good friends that were not accomplished artists. It was always very mixed. And then I think it was always people that they *liked* and that they knew. I don't ever recall being to a dinner there that somebody was there, a guest they didn't know. I certainly didn't know a lot of them, but came to know them. But they were always very entertaining. I think Christopher really held court, and he could banter with people, and a lot of opinions were shared, strong opinions. And Christopher could always knock them down. So, it was always entertaining. And it was always fun. And there was always plenty to drink and eat.

CN Tell me about the experience of sitting for Don. That first time he comes to your home in Laurel Canyon, you sit. Do you remember that, or are there particular moments?

GE Well, I do remember that. I do remember him coming. I had sat for an artist before, but they were always very quick sketches, and so they were quite fast drawings. But with Don, it was different. Drawings took a couple of hours. To be quite honest, they're very *painful*, because he always, like many artists, starts with the eyes. "Just hold the eyes." And, of course, your leg's going numb and your elbow's going numb. It's like the minute you sit down to pose for somebody you want to drop off to sleep. "Can you just open your eyes?" I was honored and flattered that he was interested enough in me that he wanted to draw me. But at the same time, it wasn't fun sitting, but not because of him. I've posed a lot, and it's never fun; it's hard work to sit for two hours in a chair and not move.

CN And, did you talk? Were you talking?

GE No, he doesn't. Rarely, no. He's pretty focused on his work. But it was interesting to watch him maneuver, and how he had this portable stool and easel where he had his paper, and to watch him move back and forth between brushes or pens or different-size brushes, and he'd hold one in his mouth and be working with another. And so, I would watch him, his hands moving. And of course, the curiosity of what's going on, what's going on, on the other side that you can't see.

CN When does he show you?

GE Well, you knew when it was finished.

CN At the end, what did you think when you saw it?

GE You know, I don't recall. I can look at the drawing now and I recall the moment. I do absolutely remember the day and the feelings and the nervousness. Being uncomfortable. I don't think it shows in the drawing that I'm uncomfortable. I would never say, "I can't do this. When do I get to move?" So, I think I was a good participant [*laughter*].

CN Absolutely. Tell us a little bit about the Los Angeles art world in the 1970s. You had a very unique perspective on it.

GE Gosh, there's a lot. As I said, when I came to Los Angeles, and I was in a relationship—I was seventeen years old, just about to go on eighteen—with Nicholas Wilder, who had one of the top art galleries at that time, so that was my introduction. Boom. I was just kerplunked right into it. I was always interested in art and artists, and I always hung out in this bohemian world of actors and writers and poets, but nobody was really a great success. But now, I was being introduced into what was the Los Angeles art world and the New York art world at the same time. Because many of the artists that Nick showed came from New York. So, I got to know artists by being in the gallery, and some I became friends with because Nick was friends with them, and we socialized and went to dinner. I mean, that's how I know Mary Agnes [Donoghue; see pp. 68–71]. She was living with Joe Goode at the time, and Joe Goode was at the Nicholas Wilder Gallery, and we spent a lot of time together. So, friendships were made and some not; artists come and go. But it was a small world. It seemed like the Los Angeles art world in the '70s was much more of a family; everybody knew each other—the collectors and the artists and the galleries. Everybody knew each other and supported one another.

CN What a special time. Let's go back to the long arc of this career, from an artist you're now looking at—and you and I were talking before we turned on the recorder about a somewhat obsessive quality to it. I mean, the output is *prolific*. So, as you look back over tens of thousands of images, do you see a development decade by decade? Are there a couple of critical pivots that you see? Talk to us about the maturation or points of inflection?

GE Well, I see this drive, and what's consistent over the years is this determination, this perfectionism. I think that Don worked really *hard.* You don't see it, I don't think, in the drawings—because his works don't look overworked. Not all drawings are successful. But I don't think he can ever be accused of *overworking* a portrait; I've never come across one. He may have given up on a lot of them, and not every one can be a hit, but I think he had this perfectionism that drove him to really capture the person's likeness. So, it was this literal

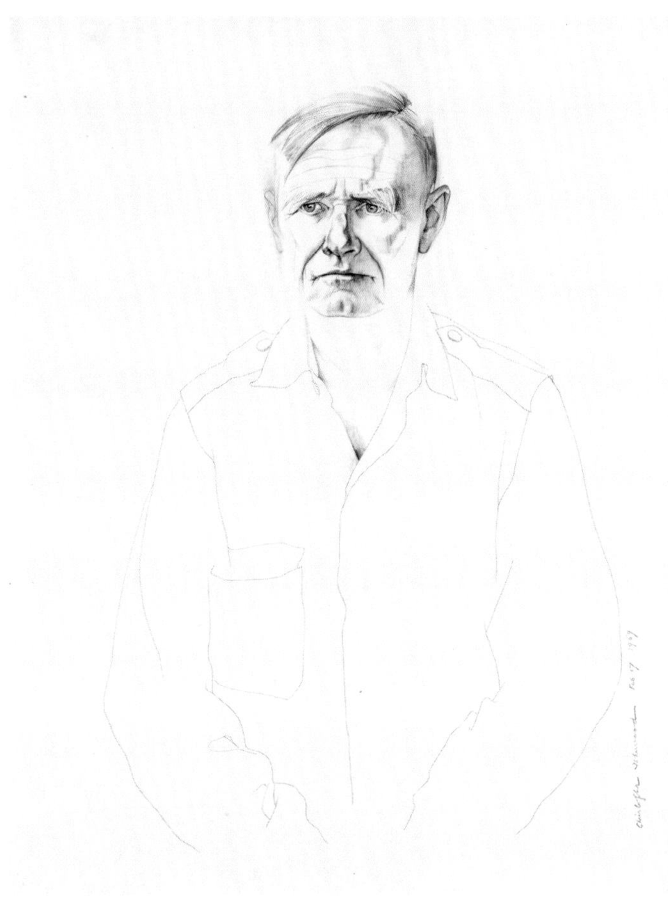

representation that drove him. He was obsessed with that for the first couple of decades, probably well into the mid-'70s, even the late '70s. I think that was the most important thing. But he did have this unique ability at a very young age—even though he got the eyes perfect or the hands perfect—to reach beneath the surface and pull that forward as well. And I think as far as the development, it came from drawing a literal representation of eyes or of an eye; later on, he was able to go *into* the eye and *through* the eye.

And later on, especially when he starts working in watercolors or washes, what becomes evident to me is that we have multiple masks, and he had this uncanny ability to move through them. And I think that really started happening for him in the '80s. So, I saw that sort of development, and then the drawings become looser, as he probably felt that he had mastered being able to go as far as he could go with his literal representation of a person.

When I saw him after Christopher's death, I saw him struggling with color; he was experimenting. I think he was obviously trying to find a new way and struggling to find something. He developed a new approach to color over the decades after Christopher's death. I could see that he was having a hard time being interested in the sitter and then he catches his stride. And I think from that period, the works become much looser, much more expressionistic, and colorful and faster. I think he starts having *fun*. Not that he stops working. I think up to that time, he worked very hard at it. I think he was very hard on himself with getting this exact representation of somebody. And then I think it became much more experiential for him with the color. He may disagree with me on that, but that was my impression looking in.

CN Let's talk a little bit about artist and model. Tell us about faces and bodies and eyes and limbs as you're looking across all these images he's made.

GE Well, I can't help but create my own narrative. When you're looking at all these images forward, backward, and back again, and over and over, and through, and wondering. My selection initially, not for the exhibition, was for a whole other purpose. The exhibition came out

Christopher Isherwood, February 17, 1969
Graphite on paper, 29 × 23⅛ in. (73.7 × 58.7 cm)
Don Bachardy Papers

of it. The portraits I most connected with were those where I could see there was a really strong connection between the sitter and the artist, where I felt that they merged, or the person gave themselves to Don or let their guard down.

CN How often does that happen?

GE That's a tough question, because you can also say that a drawing is—I don't like to say "good" or "bad," but I do say that. But it's basically drawings that I liked and didn't like, because there are certainly a lot of drawings that—I think some people would argue with me, and I'll probably hear blowback—they'll say, "Why didn't you include that, or why didn't you include this? That was a very important drawing, or that was a very important person." And I said that it's not my criteria; if I do this, it's going to be what I respond to, and what *I* like, and I felt that really strongly. So, some people are very rigid because they're uncomfortable. Now that's a good picture, that's a good representation of somebody who's uptight or scared or nervous of somebody looking at them, or they don't want to be looked at in the eye, which Don talks about, because he would always say, "Look at me in the eyes. I want to look at the eye." Well, that's very uncomfortable for a lot of us to have somebody look at your eyes for an hour. So, I found that interesting. It's hard for me to really articulate. But then there were just these wonderful moments where you could tell the real art and the magic, where really the sitter was totally open and uninhibited, and Don just went with that, and that's the beauty of art, isn't it?

CN Are there any misconceptions about Don or his practice or his output that you'd want to address?

GE Don has a large following. I mean, Don knows hundreds of people—well, thousands of people, apparently—that he's met over the years, not that they've all been his friends, and some people that he's drawn, he doesn't even know. But I think I always felt that Don had been sort of pigeonholed: "Don Bachardy. Oh yes, he's the one who, you know, drew Hollywood stars. Oh, yes, Christopher Isherwood's partner. Oh yes, the one who does the nudes, you know? Oh yes, the gay artist." I think what I discovered in his work is, no, Don's an artist who *happened* to live with Christopher Isherwood, and just *happens* to be homosexual, and was *fortunate* enough to draw these movie stars that he had idolized as a child in movie magazines, who he had done drawings of as a child. And that he couldn't believe it when he met Christopher, that he got *introduced* to these people and then he was actually…There they *were* in front of him— his *idols*—and he was drawing them. But there's so much more to him than that. What I feel like I discovered was his art and not his reputation.

CN When did you discover that?

GE Early, early on, starting a couple of years ago, when I started going through this archive, which I realized that there's *so* much here that I've never seen. I've never seen it reproduced. I've never seen it exhibited. Because I think the demand has always been, "We want to see Bette, we want to see Hollywood, or we want to see the nudes." But Don had never shared this other work with anyone other than Christopher, up until his death. Because they did share with each other their daily work at the end of the day. Christopher would share his with Don, and Don would share his with Chris. And they would both critique each other and weigh in. I really wanted to show the unfamiliar, or certainly what I was unfamiliar with. And it wasn't that that was the criteria. Again, I go back to, the criteria were really the art, and what I personally connected with, had a strong connection with, and felt that magic moment that the sitter and the artist were allowing me to enter this very private, intimate moment, and that's really all I chose.

CN Well, I think the misconception question is sort of like, he had *such* access that it's almost a liability, but I think future generations won't judge him that way. They'll see it with a remove.

GE See the art.

CN You're a good friend. And we're really lucky to have you as the guest curator for the show.

GE I am grateful for the opportunity.

This interview was conducted at The Huntington on June 5, 2024.

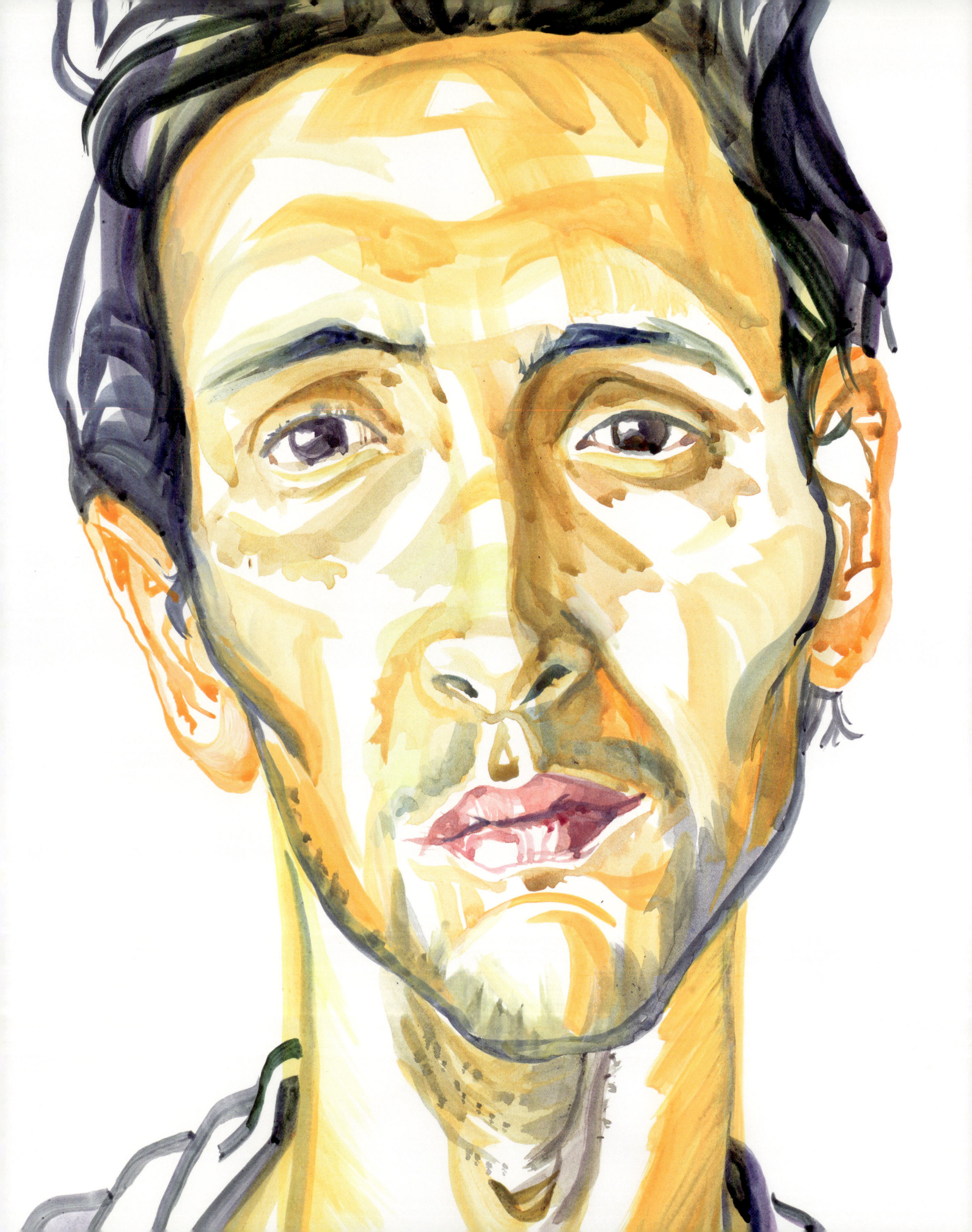

PLATES

Christopher Isherwood, 1959
Graphite and acrylic on paper, 22 × 14¼ in. (55.9 × 36.2 cm)
Don Bachardy Papers

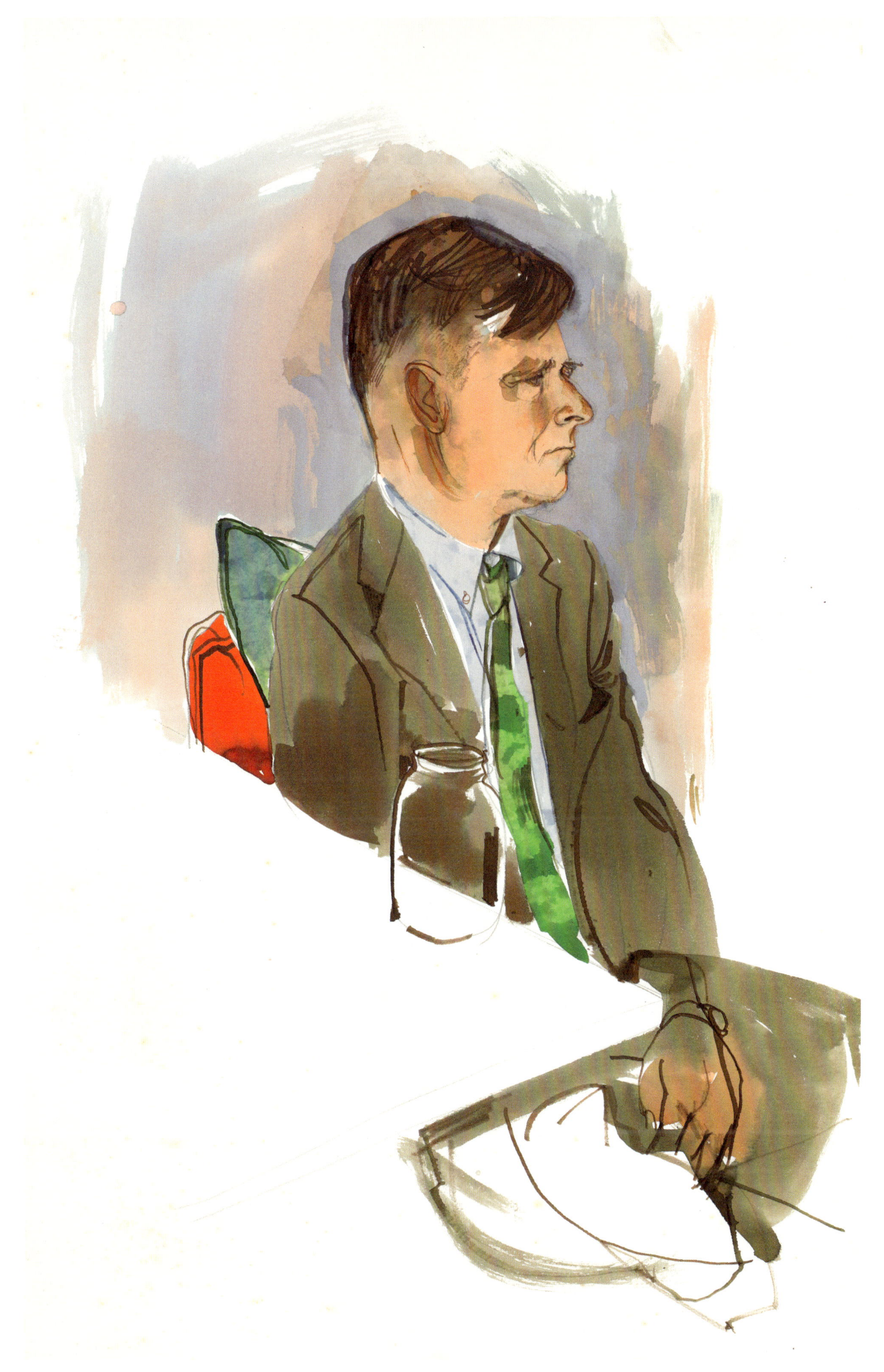

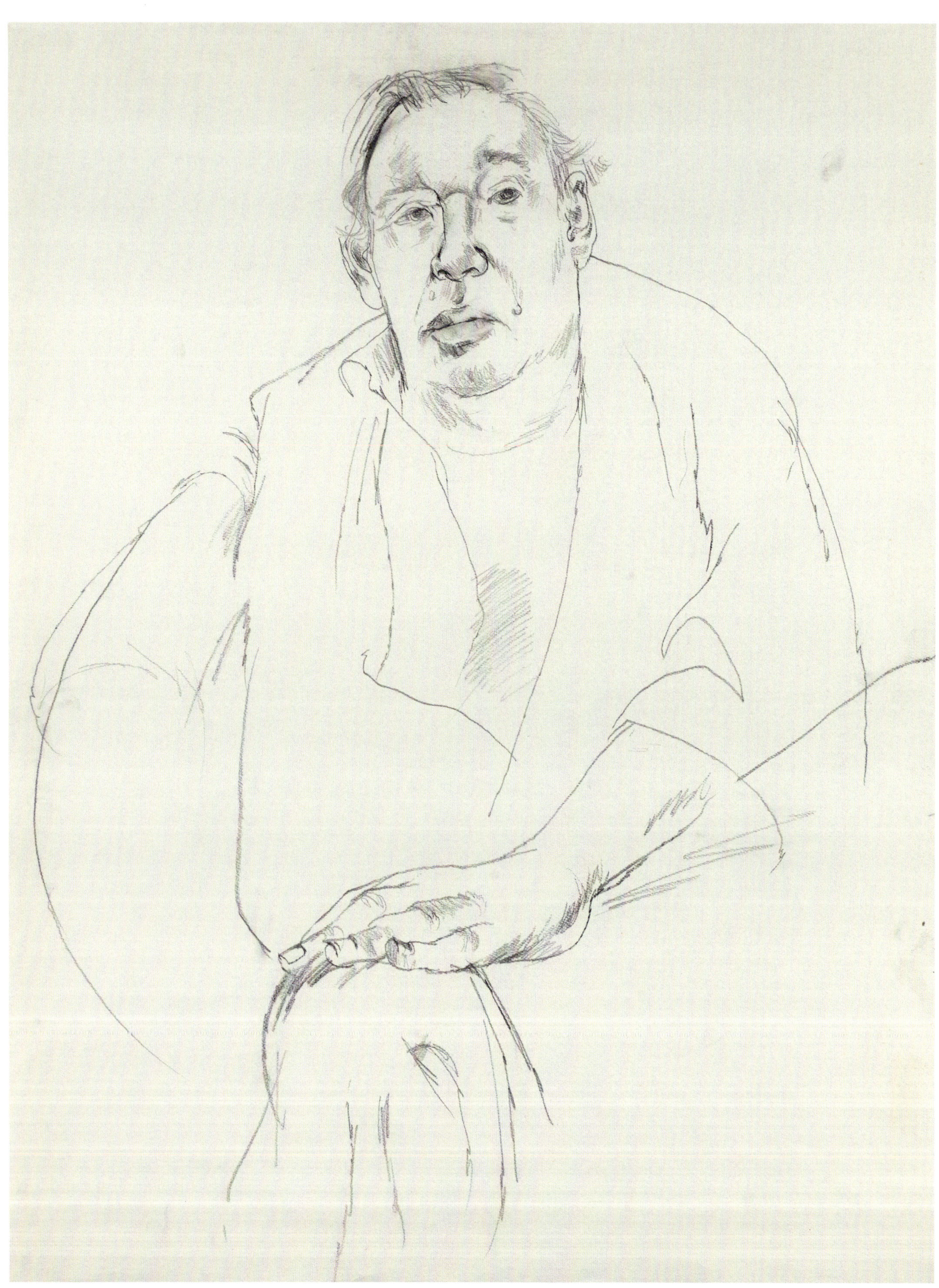

Charles Laughton, 1959 (no. 2)
Graphite on paper, 26 × 20 in. (66 × 50.8 cm)
Don Bachardy Papers

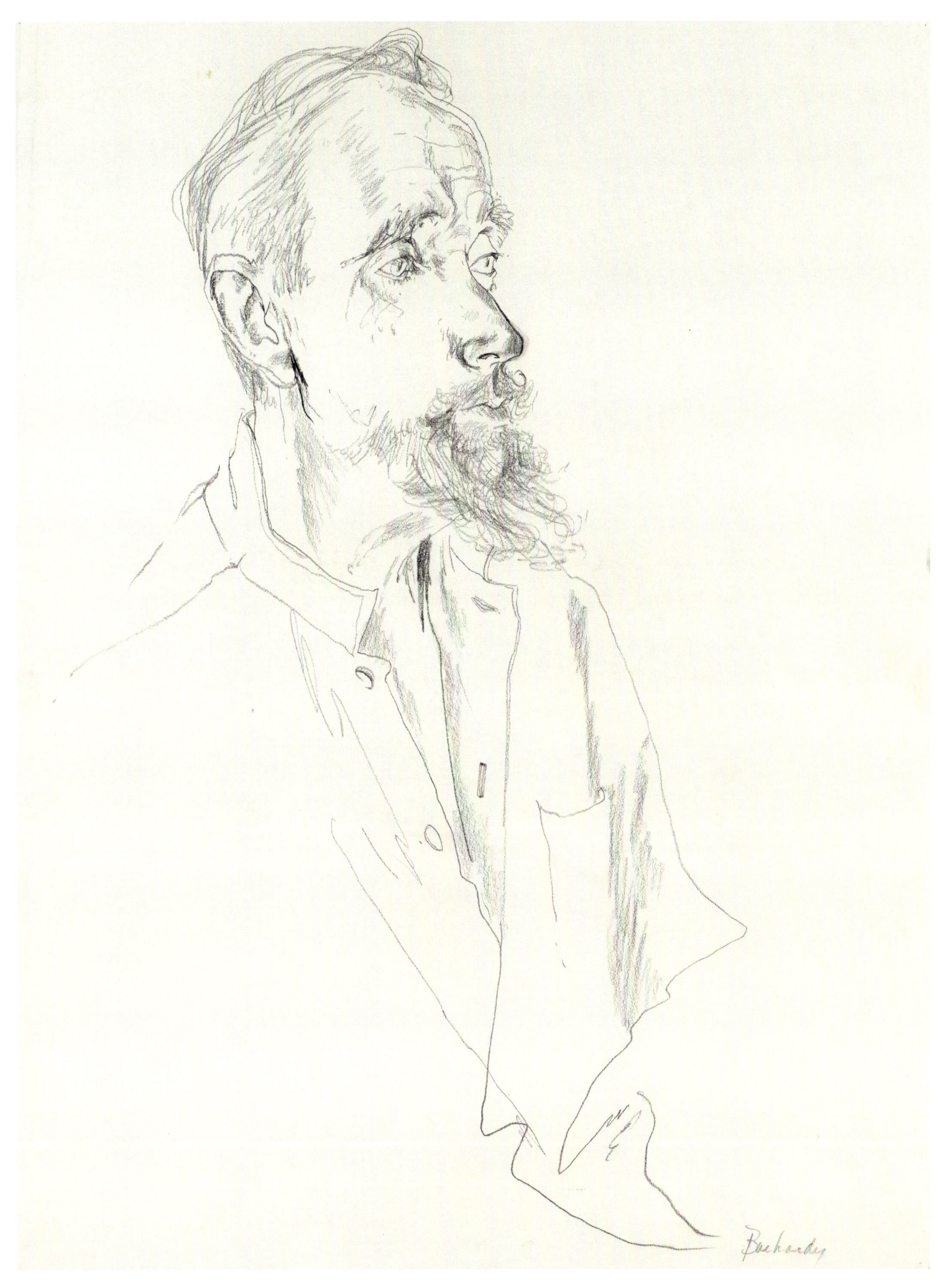

Gerald Heard, 1960
Graphite on paper, 24 × 18 in. (61 × 45.7 cm)
Don Bachardy Papers

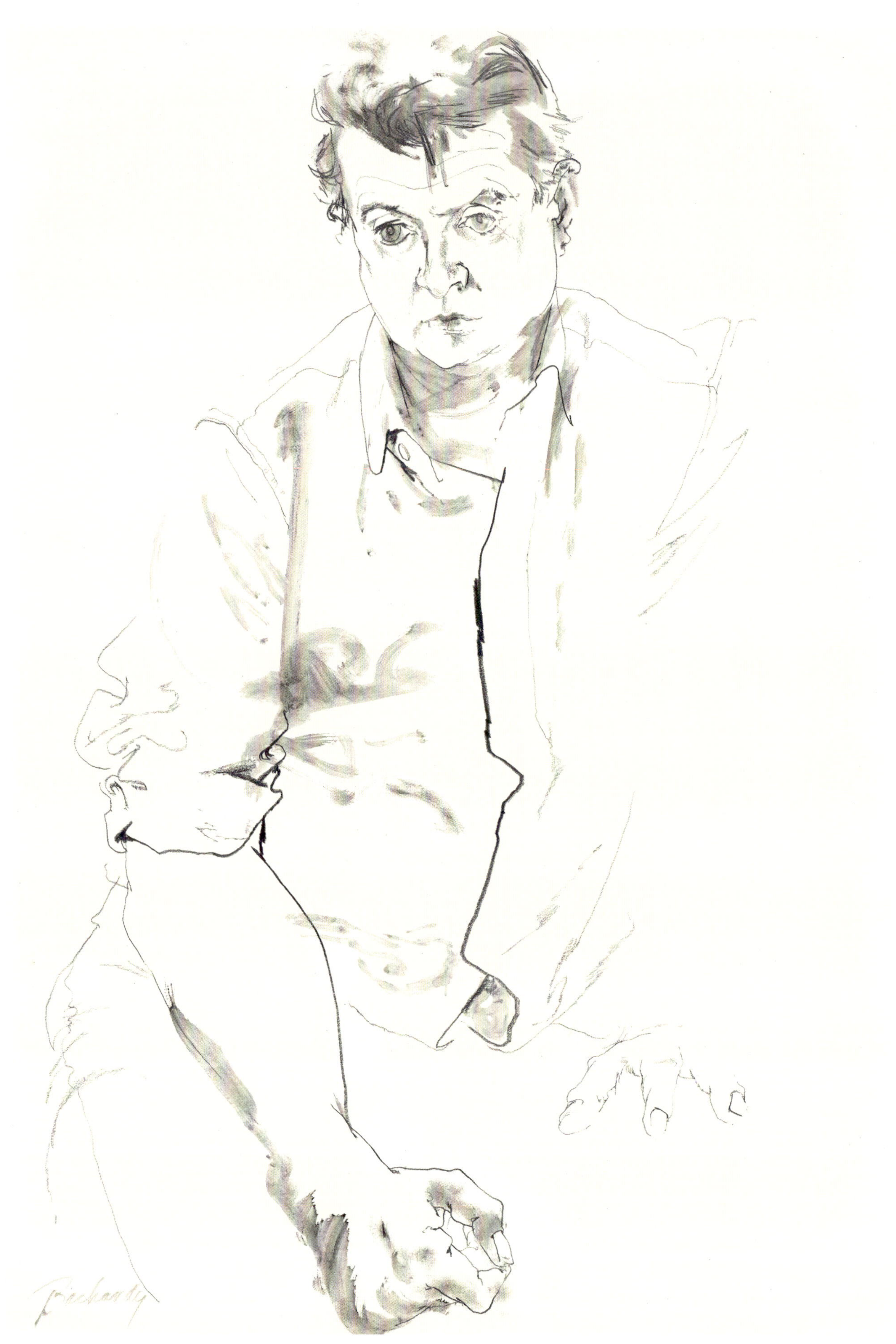

Francis Bacon, 1961
Graphite and ink on paper, 30½ × 20½ in. (77.5 × 52.1 cm)
Courtesy of the Christopher Isherwood Foundation

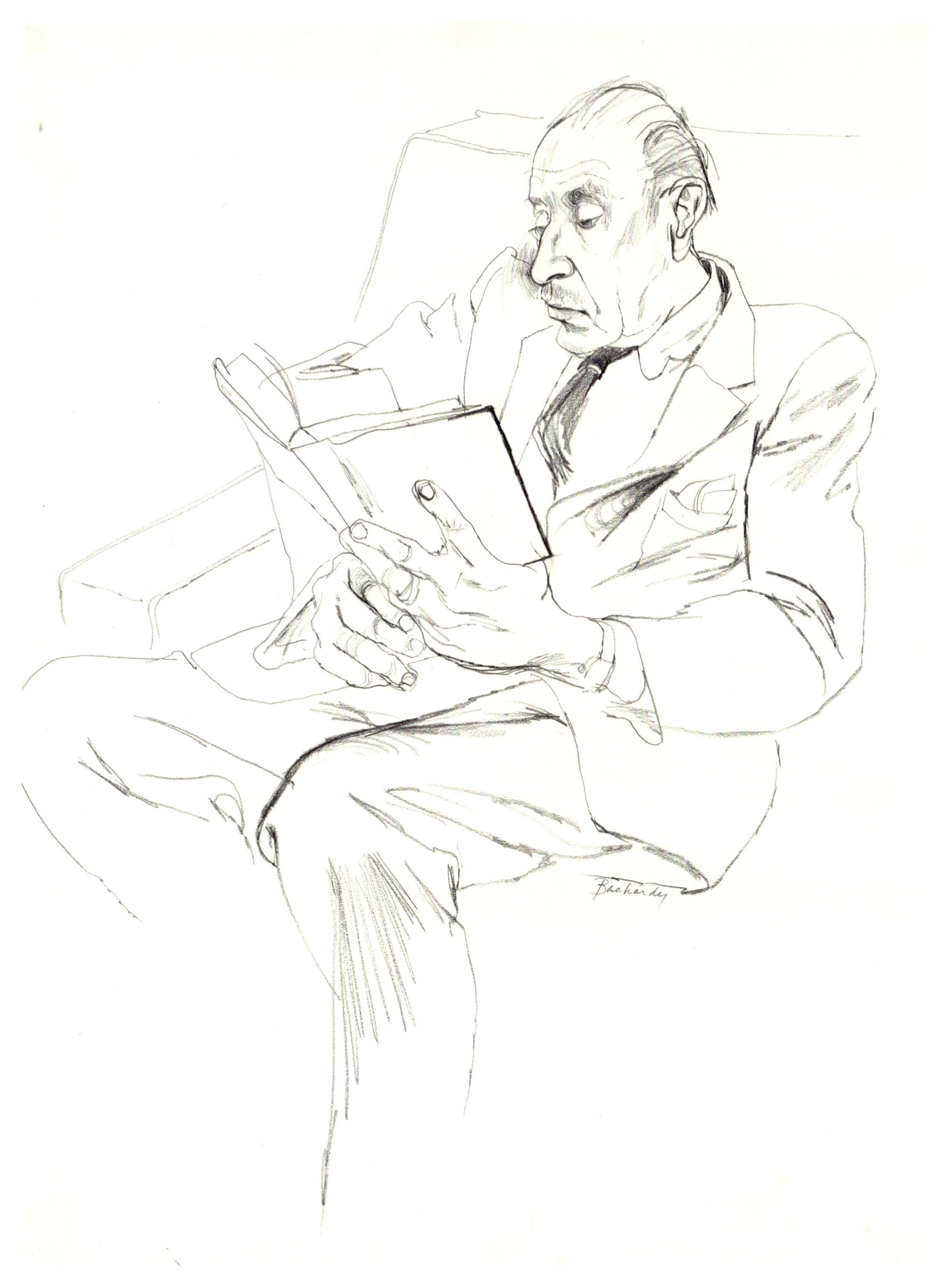

Igor Stravinsky, March 24, 1960 (no. 4)
Graphite on paper, 23½ × 18 in. (59.7 × 45.7 cm)
Don Bachardy Papers

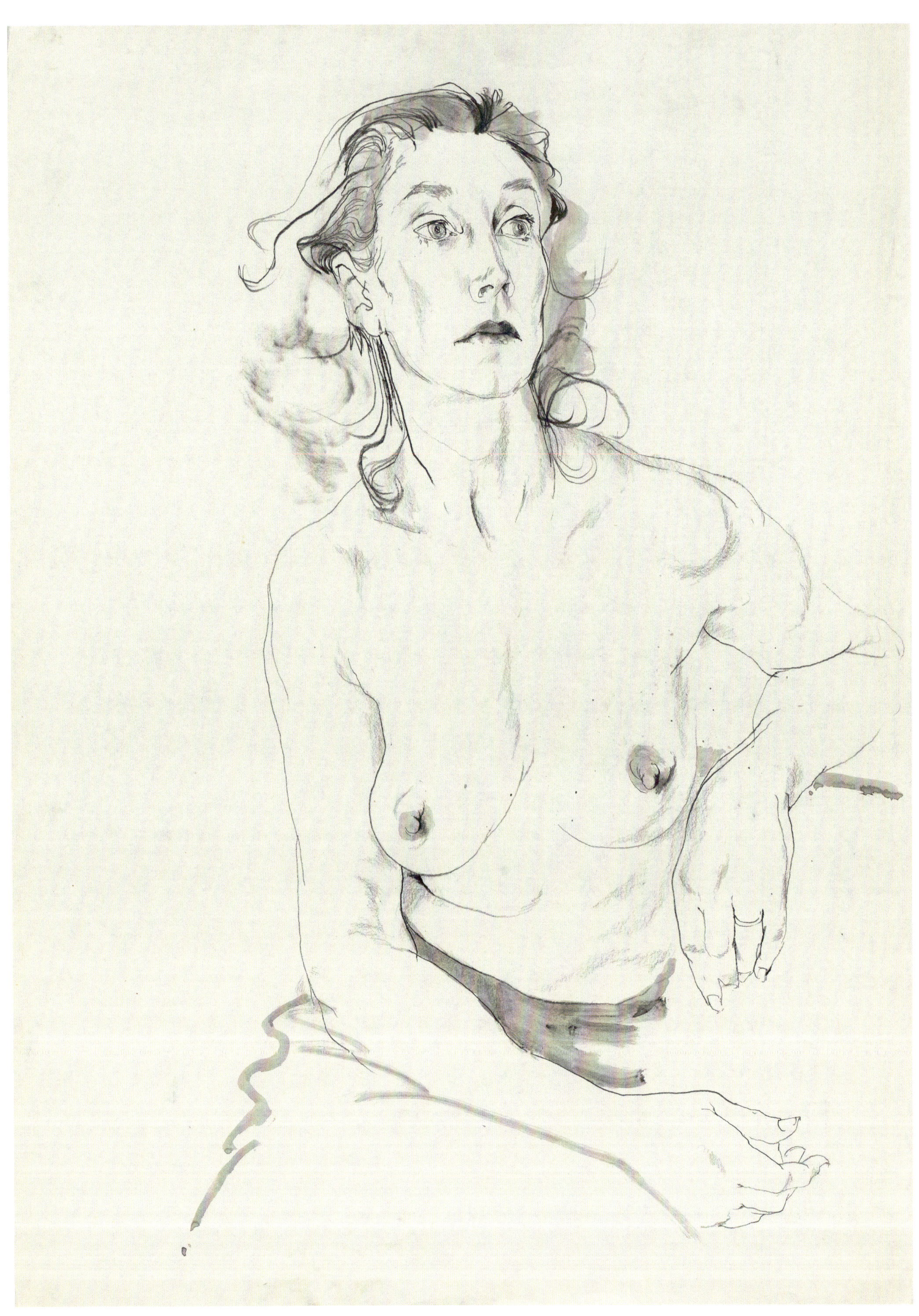

Mrs. Cyriax, 1961
Graphite and ink on paper, 30 × 22 in. (76.2 × 55.9 cm)
Don Bachardy Papers

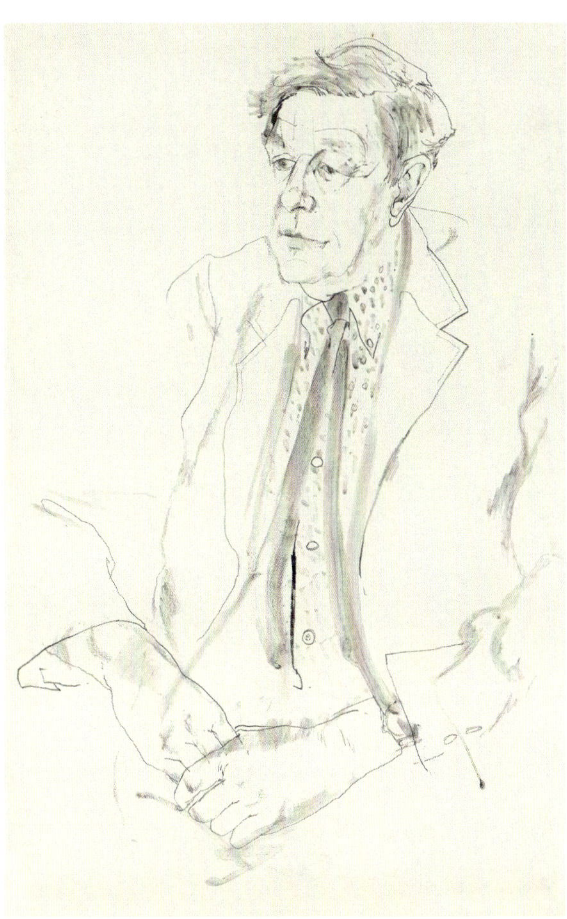

Wystan Auden, 1961
Graphite and ink on paper, 30 × 22 in.
(76.2 × 55.9 cm)
Don Bachardy Papers

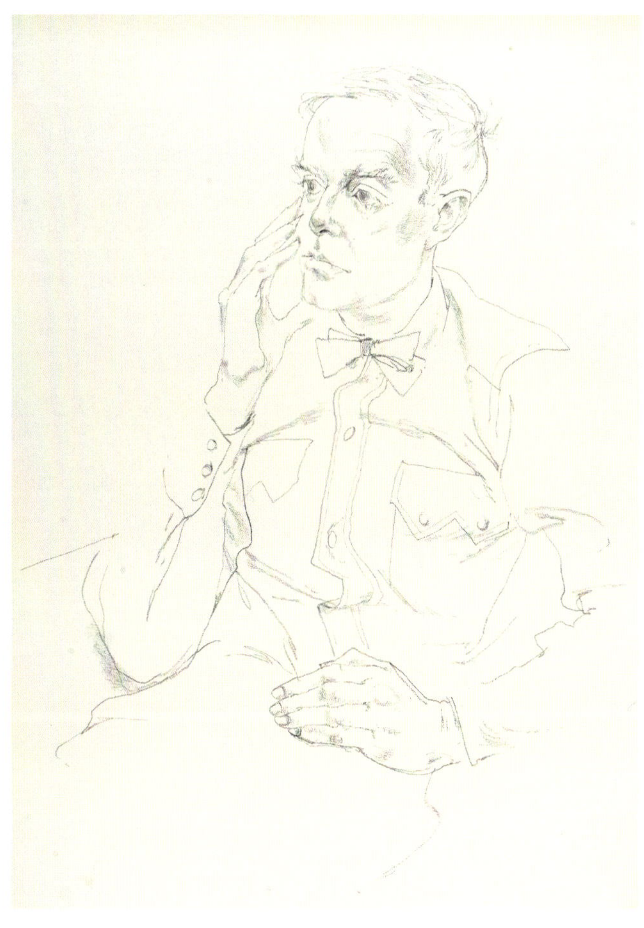

Truman Capote, June 26, 1961 (no. 1)
Graphite on paper, 27 × 20 in. (68.6 × 50.8 cm)
Don Bachardy Papers

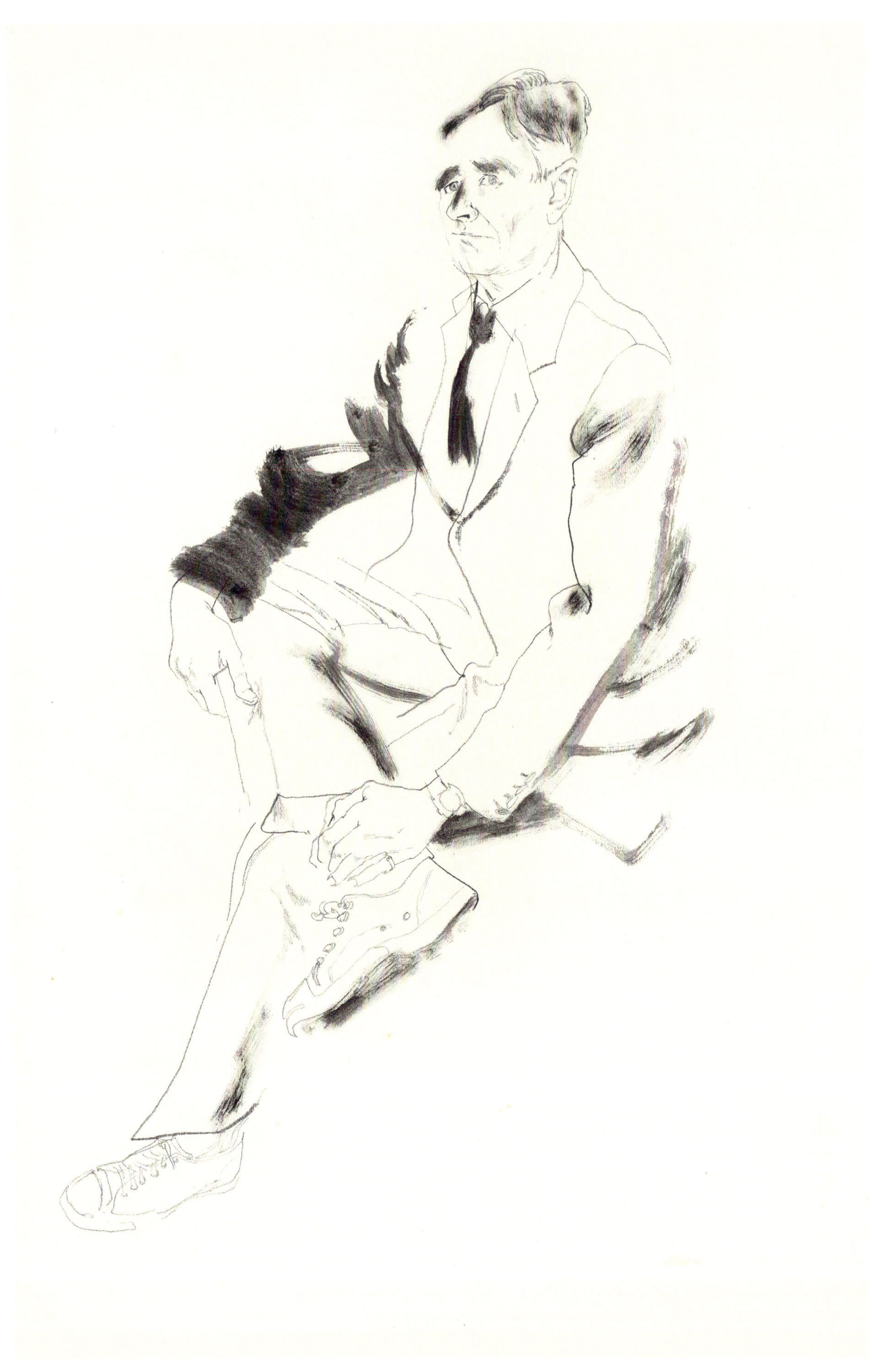

Christopher Isherwood, 1961
Graphite, pen, and ink on paper, 29⅞ × 19⅞ in. (75.9 × 50.5 cm)
Don Bachardy Papers

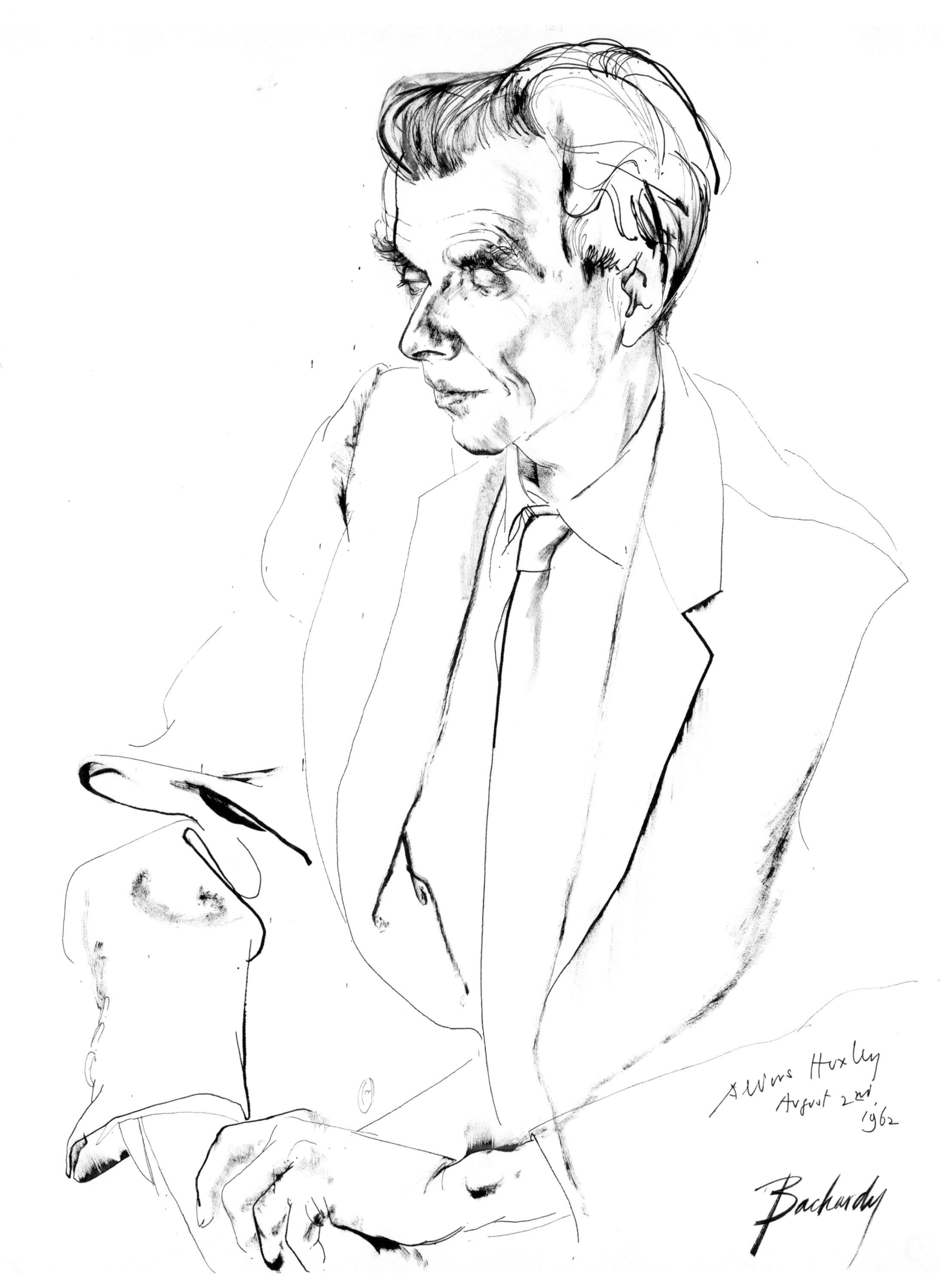

Aldous Huxley, August 2, 1962
Pen and ink on paper, 34⅛ × 28¼ in. (86.7 × 71.8 cm)
Don Bachardy Papers

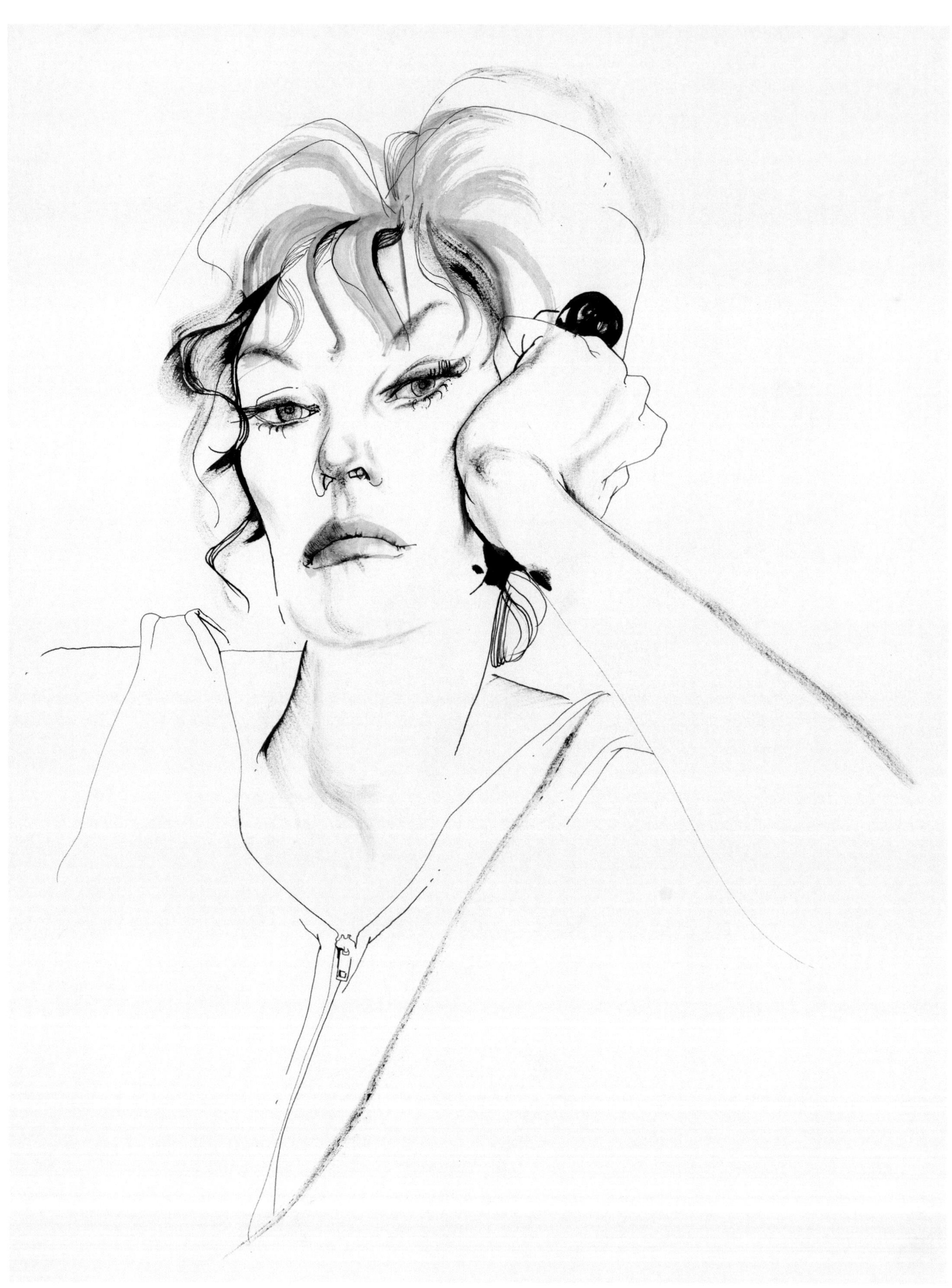

Jennifer West, 1963 (no. 1)
Pen and ink on paper, 22½ × 17½ in. (57.2 × 44.5 cm)
Don Bachardy Papers

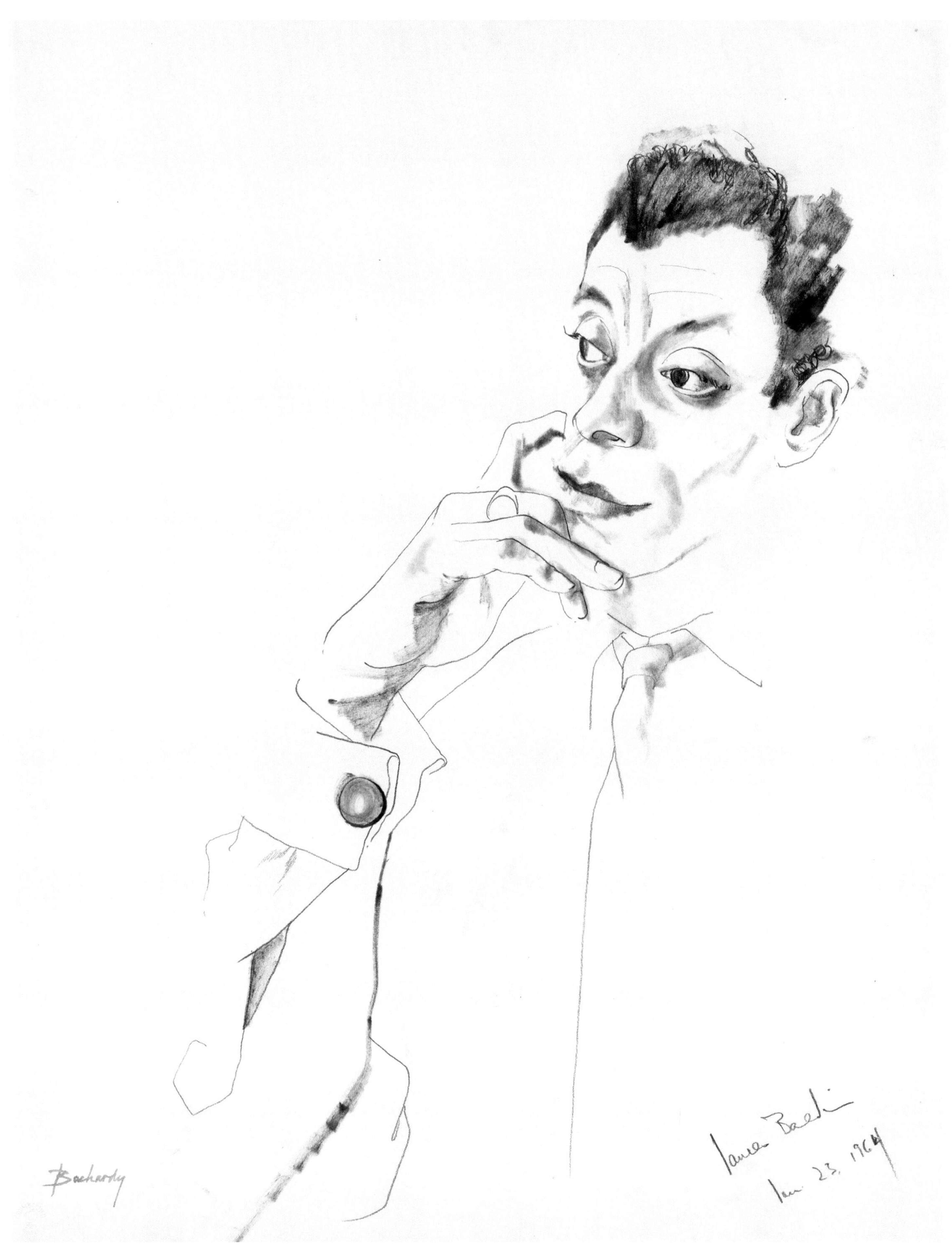

James Baldwin, January 23, 1964 (no. 2)
Graphite and ink on paper, 29 × 23 in. (73.7 × 58.4 cm)
Don Bachardy Papers

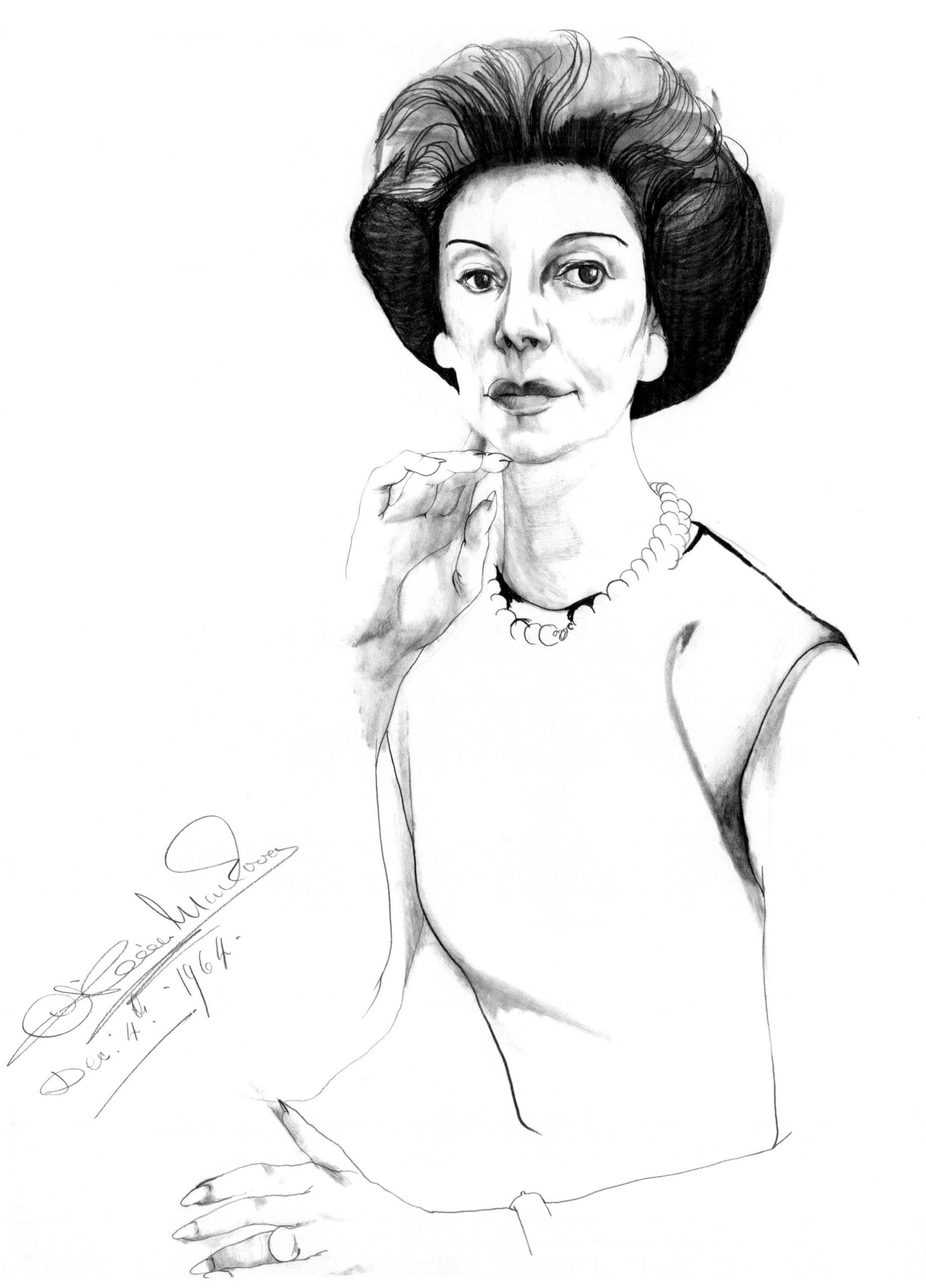

Alicia Markova, December 4, 1964 (no. 3)
Graphite and ink on paper, 29 × 23 in. (73.7 × 58.4 cm)

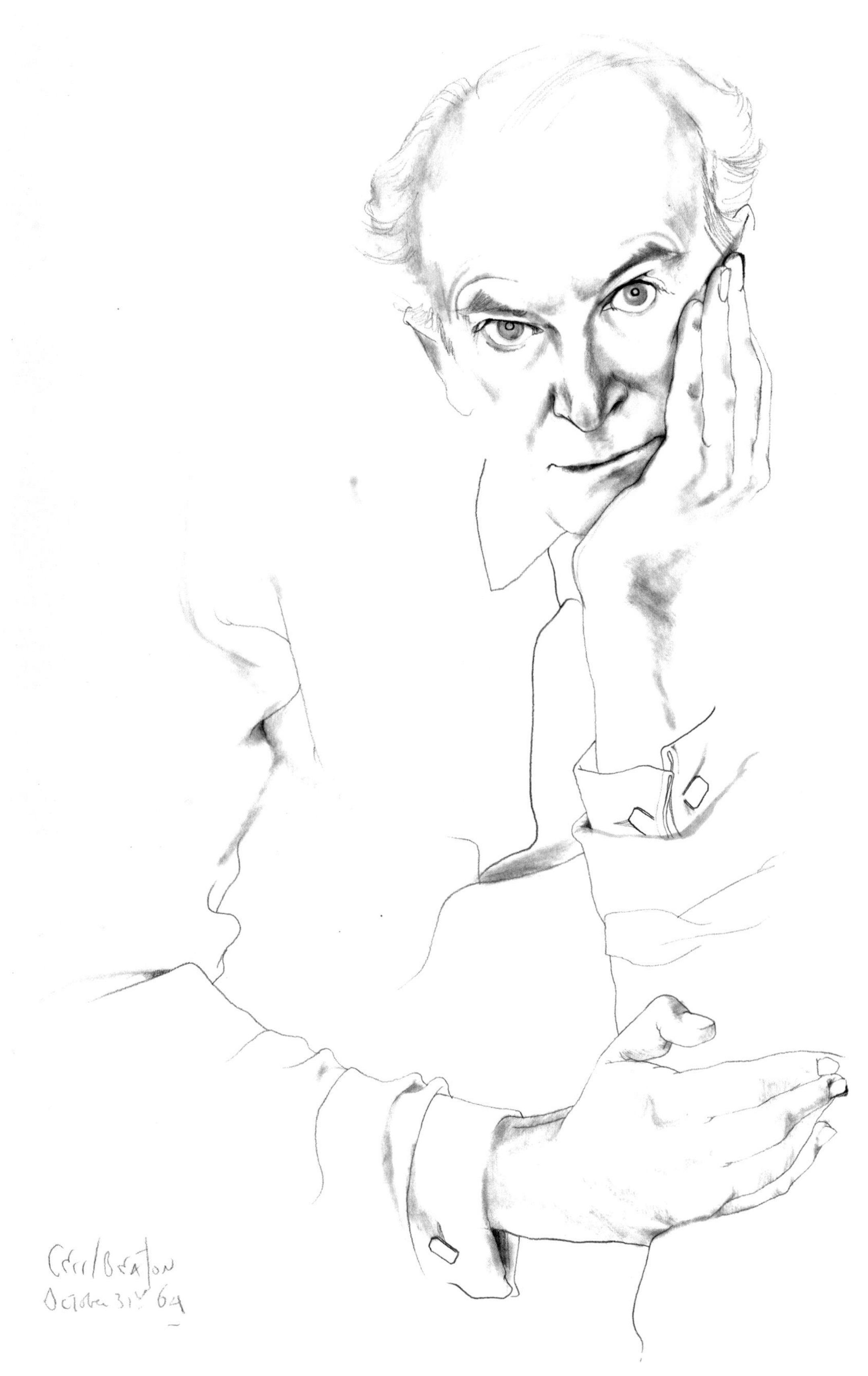

Cecil Beaton, October 31, 1964
Graphite and ink on paper, 29 × 23⅛ in. (73.7 × 58.7 cm)
Don Bachardy Papers

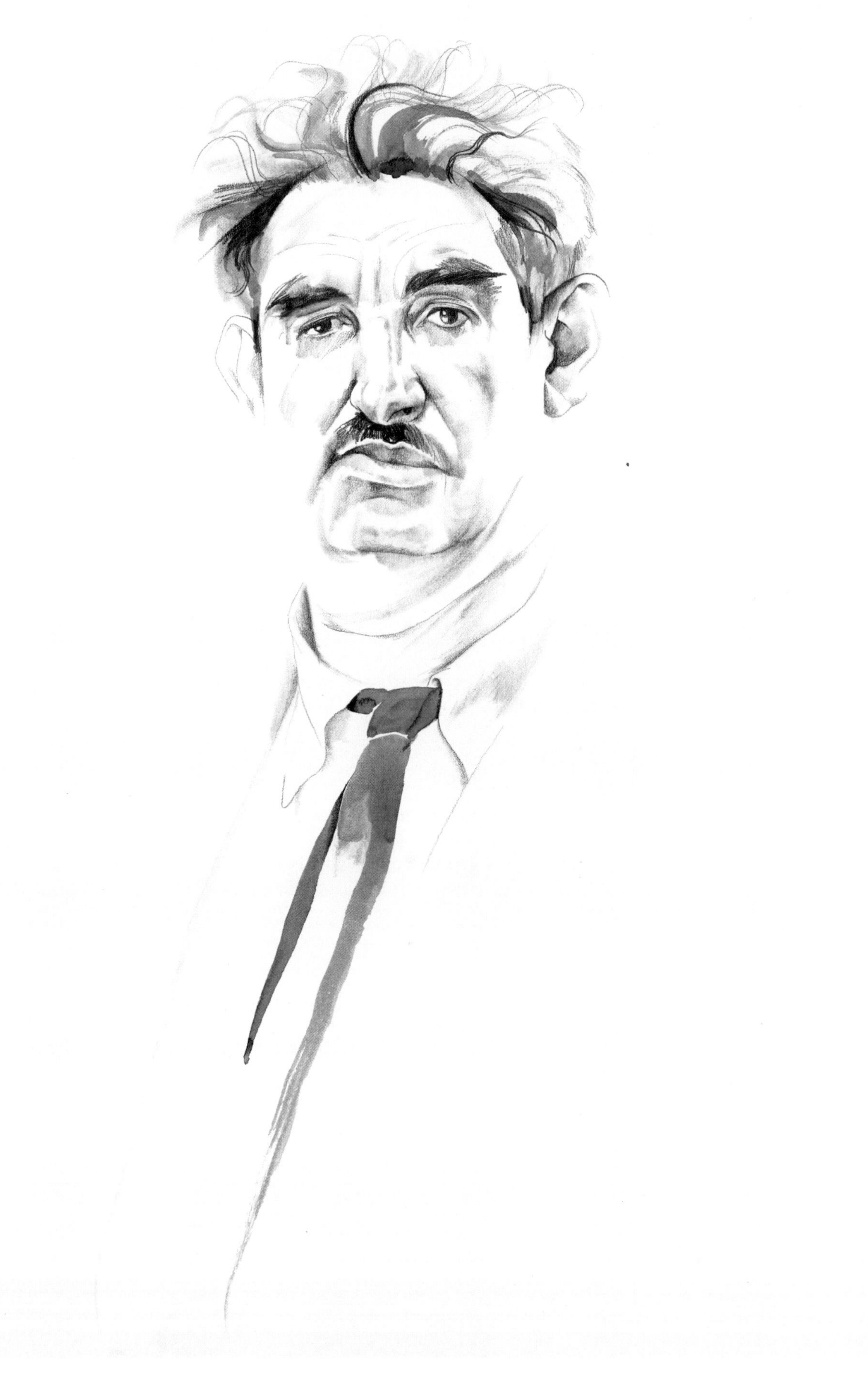

Harold Rosenberg, March 24, 1966 (no. 2)
Graphite and ink on paper, 29 × 23 in. (73.7 × 58.4 cm)
Don Bachardy Papers

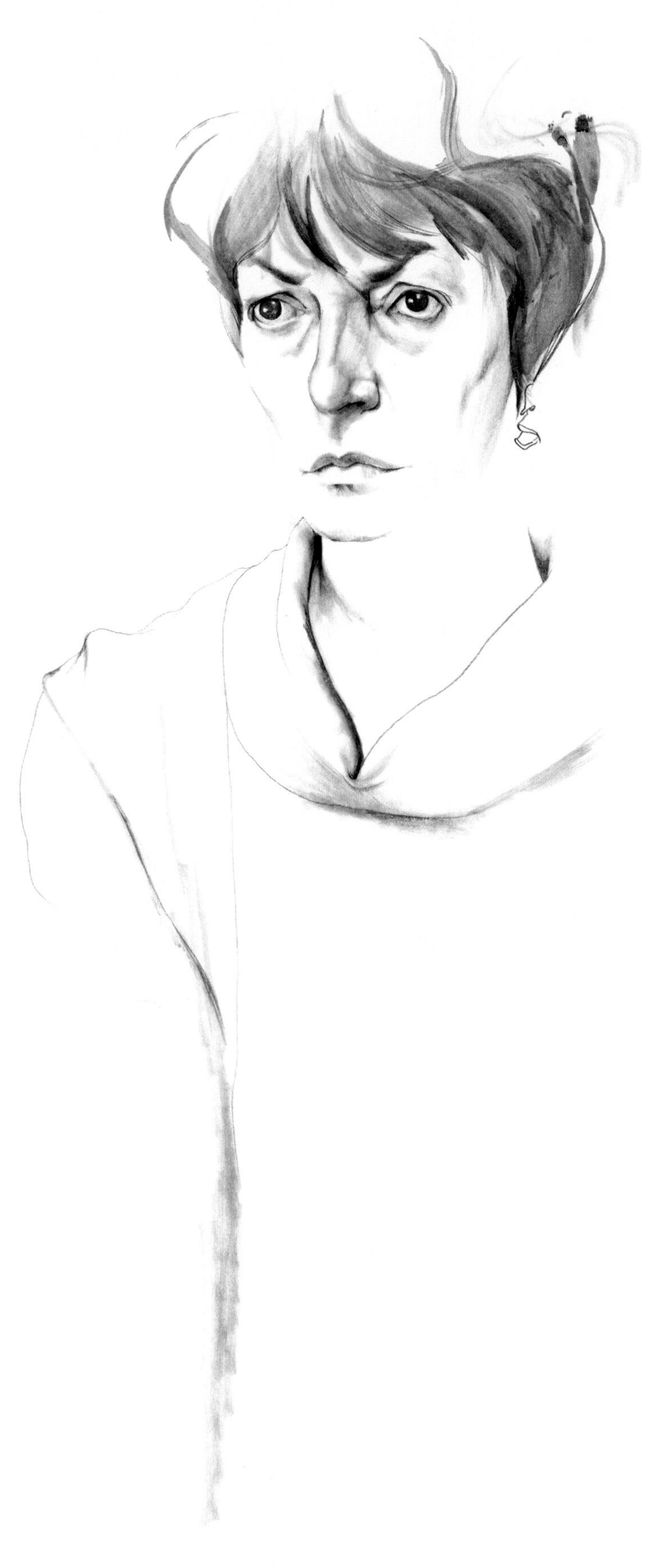

Elaine de Kooning, March 20, 1966
Graphite and ink on paper, 29 × 23 in. (73.7 × 58.4 cm)
Don Bachardy Papers

99

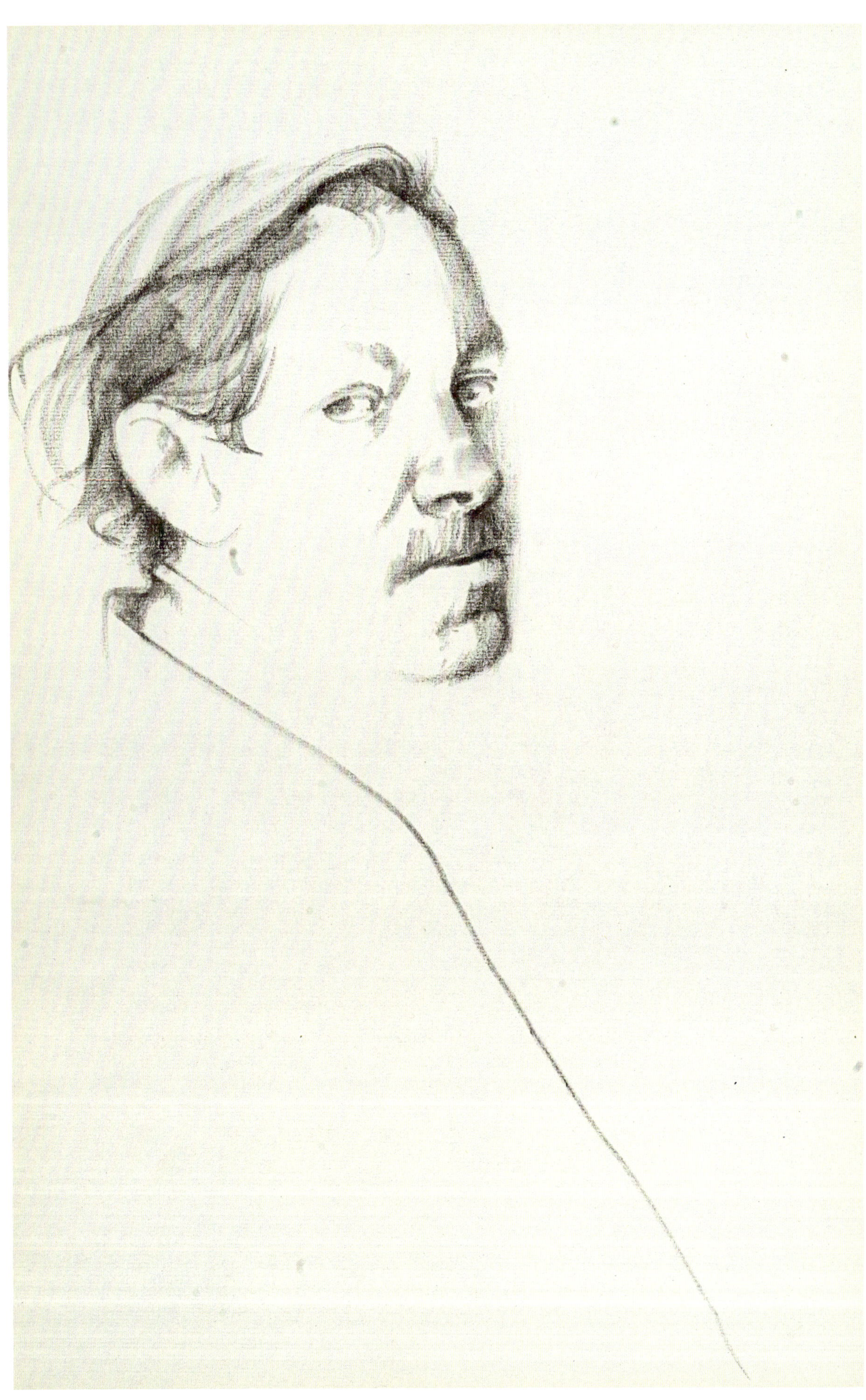

Tennessee Williams, September 7, 1968 (no. 2)
Graphite on paper, 20 × 13⅛ in. (50.8 × 33.3 cm)
Don Bachardy Papers

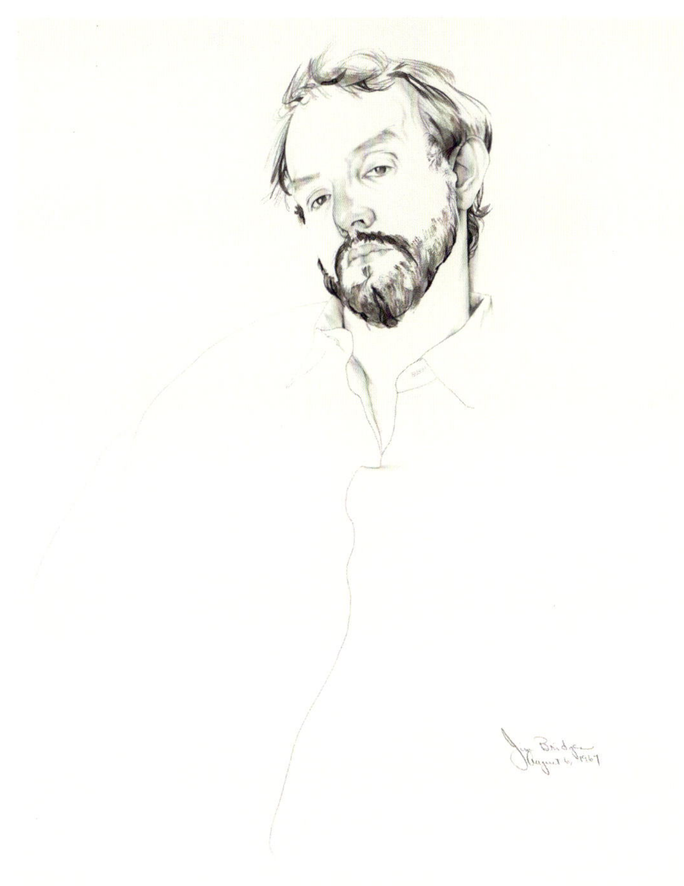

Jim Bridges, August 6, 1967 (no. 1)
Graphite and ink on paper, 29 × 23 in.
(73.7 × 58.4 cm)
Don Bachardy Papers

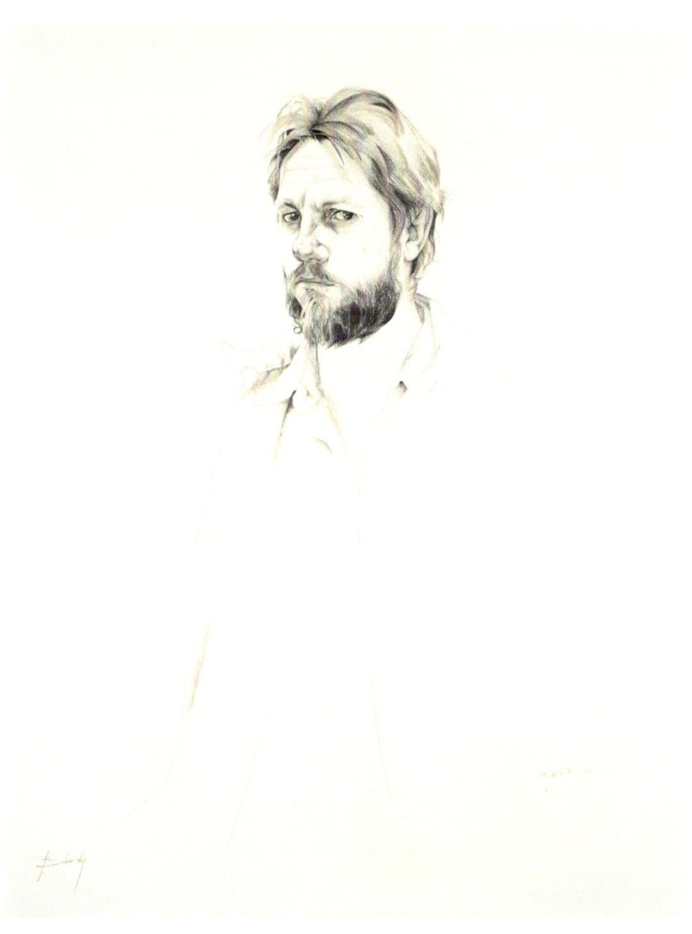

Ed Moses, July 2, 1969
Graphite and ink on paper, 28½ × 23 in. (72.4 × 58.4 cm)
Courtesy of Billy Al Bengston Studio Holdings

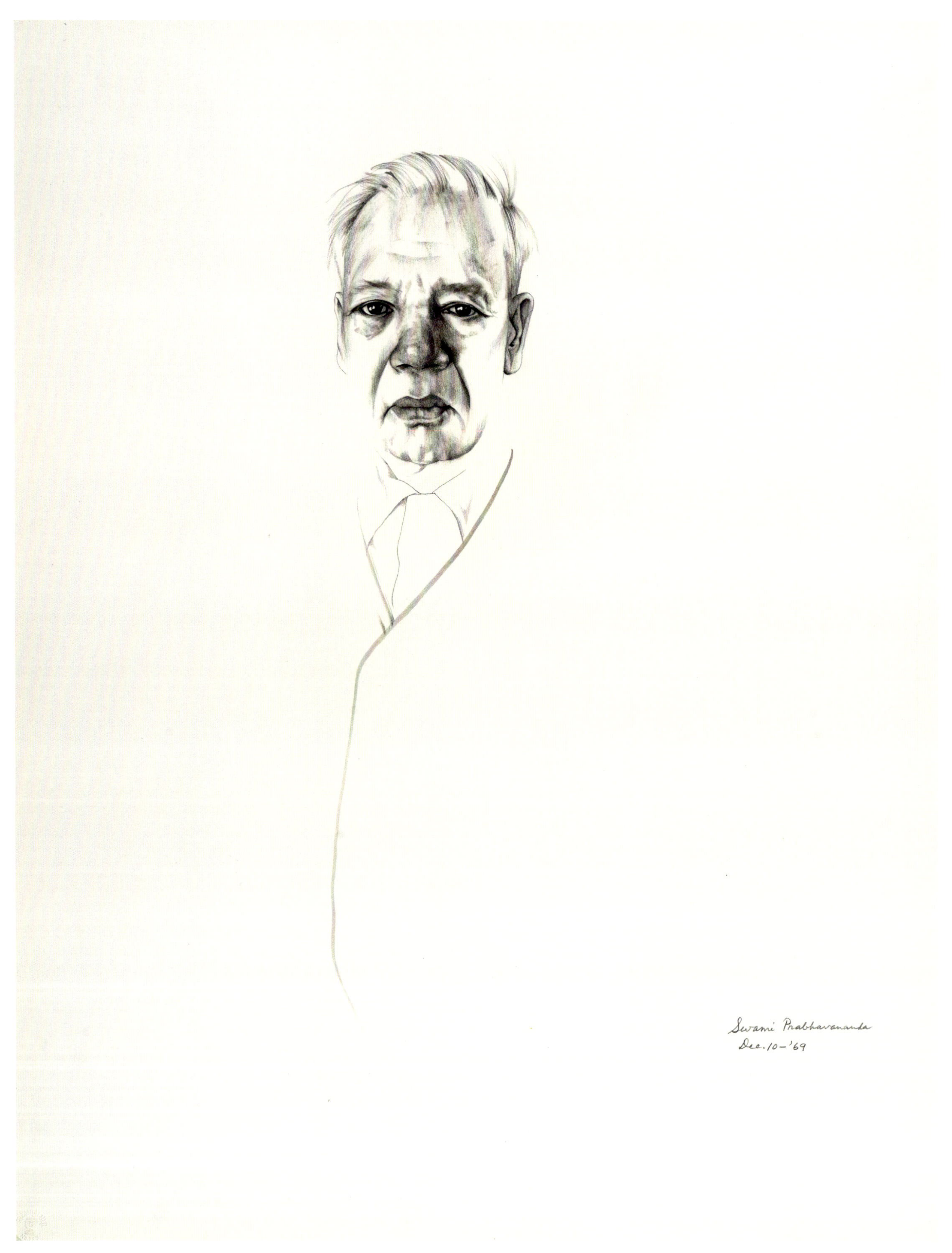

Swami Prabhavananda, December 10, 1969
Graphite and ink on paper, 26¼ × 20 in. (66.7 × 51 cm)
Don Bachardy Papers

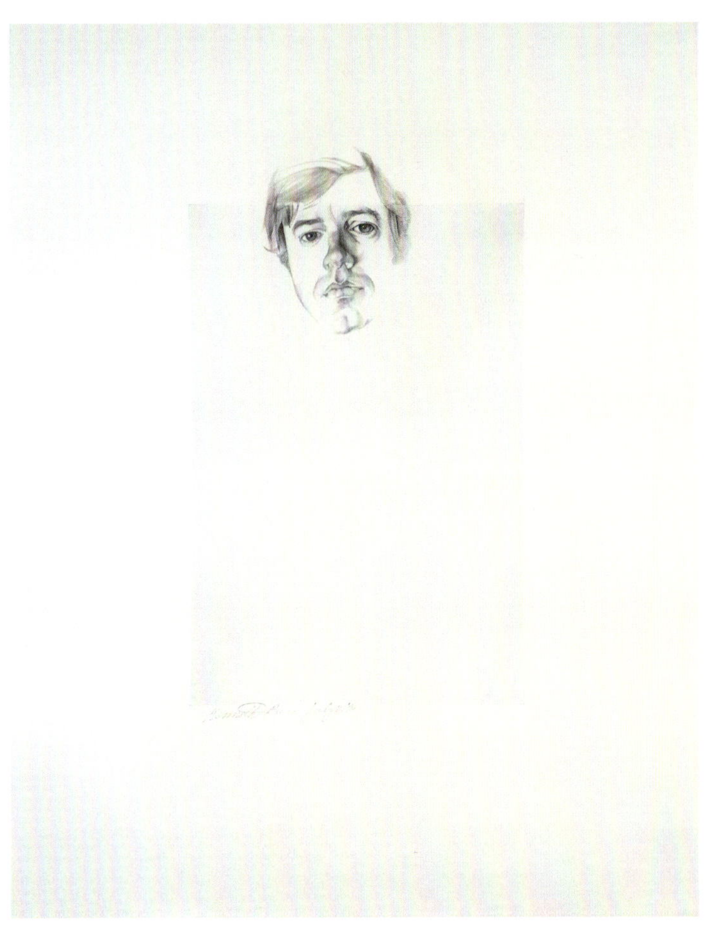

Kenneth Price, July 2, 1970
Graphite and ink on paper, 29 × 23 in.
(73.7 × 58.4 cm)
Courtesy of Billy Al Bengston Studio Holdings

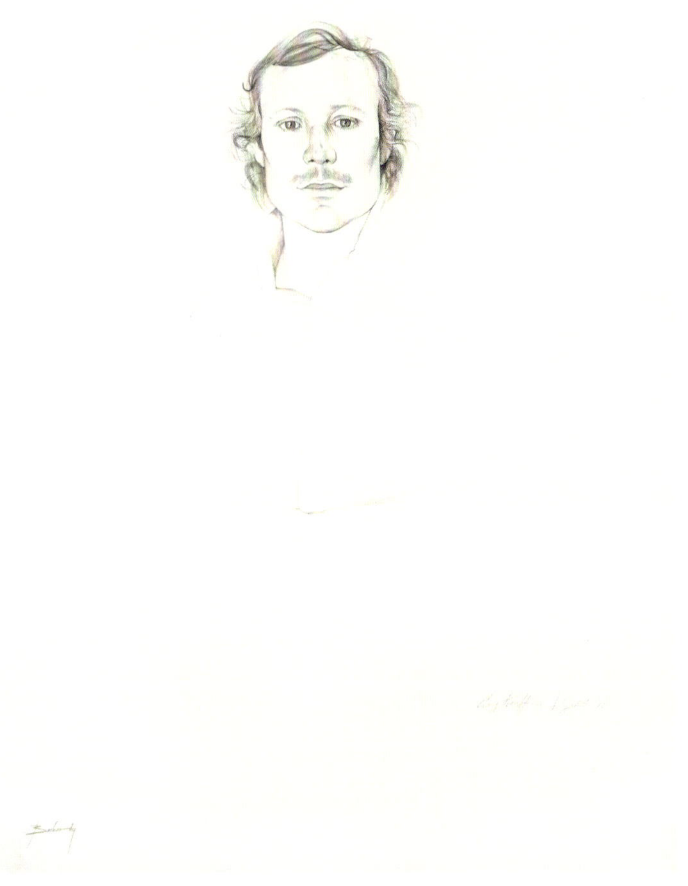

Craig Kauffman, July 24, 1971
Graphite and ink on paper, 28½ × 23 in. (72.4 × 58.4 cm)
Courtesy of Billy Al Bengston Studio Holdings

Robert Graham, January 19, 1972 (no. 1)
Graphite and ink on paper, 29 × 23 in.
(73.7 × 58.4 cm)
Don Bachardy Papers

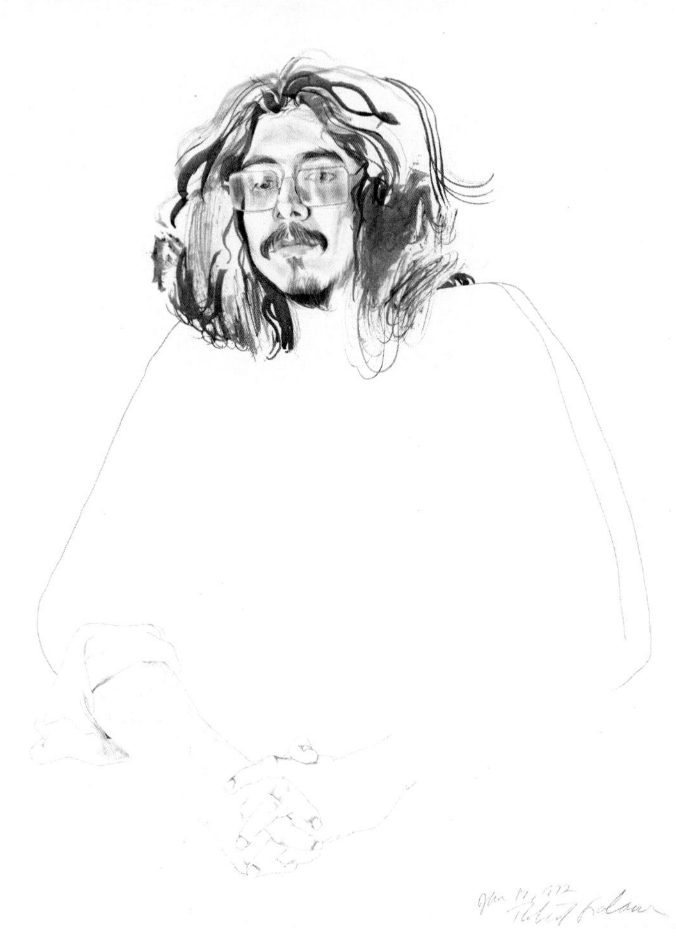

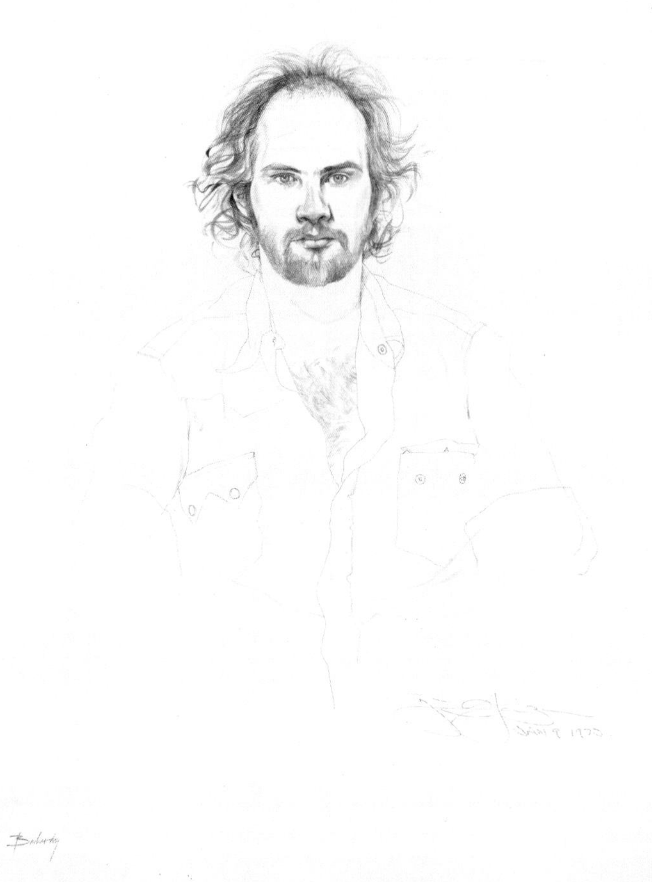

Jim Ganzer, January 9, 1973 (no. 1)
Graphite and ink on paper, 29 × 23 in. (73.7 × 58.4 cm)
Don Bachardy Papers

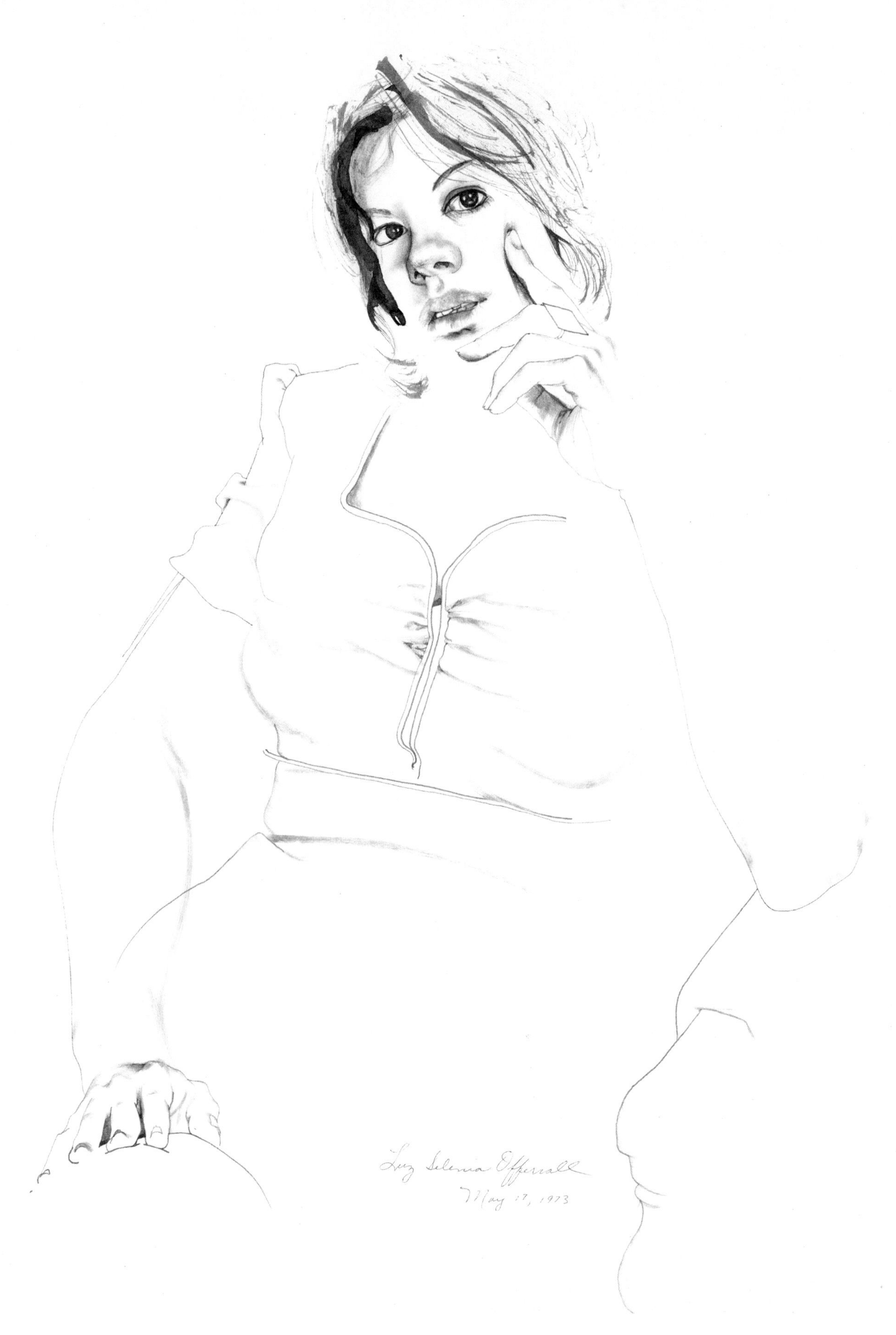

Luz Offerrall, May 17, 1973
Graphite and ink on paper, 24 × 18¾ in. (61 × 47.6 cm)
Don Bachardy Papers

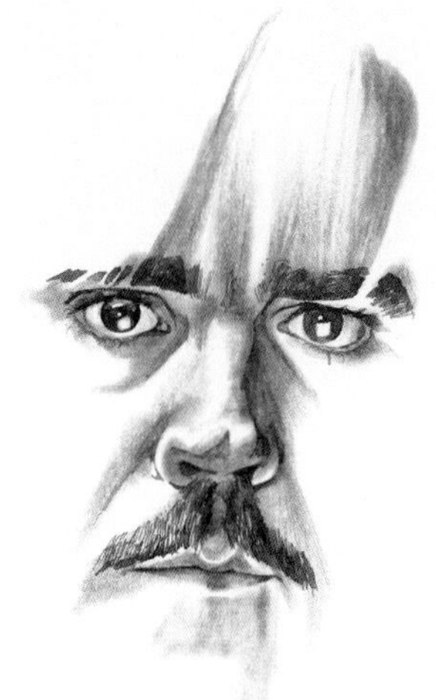

Self-Portrait, January 27, 1974
Pen and ink on paper, 24 × 19 in.
(61 × 48.3 cm)
Don Bachardy Papers

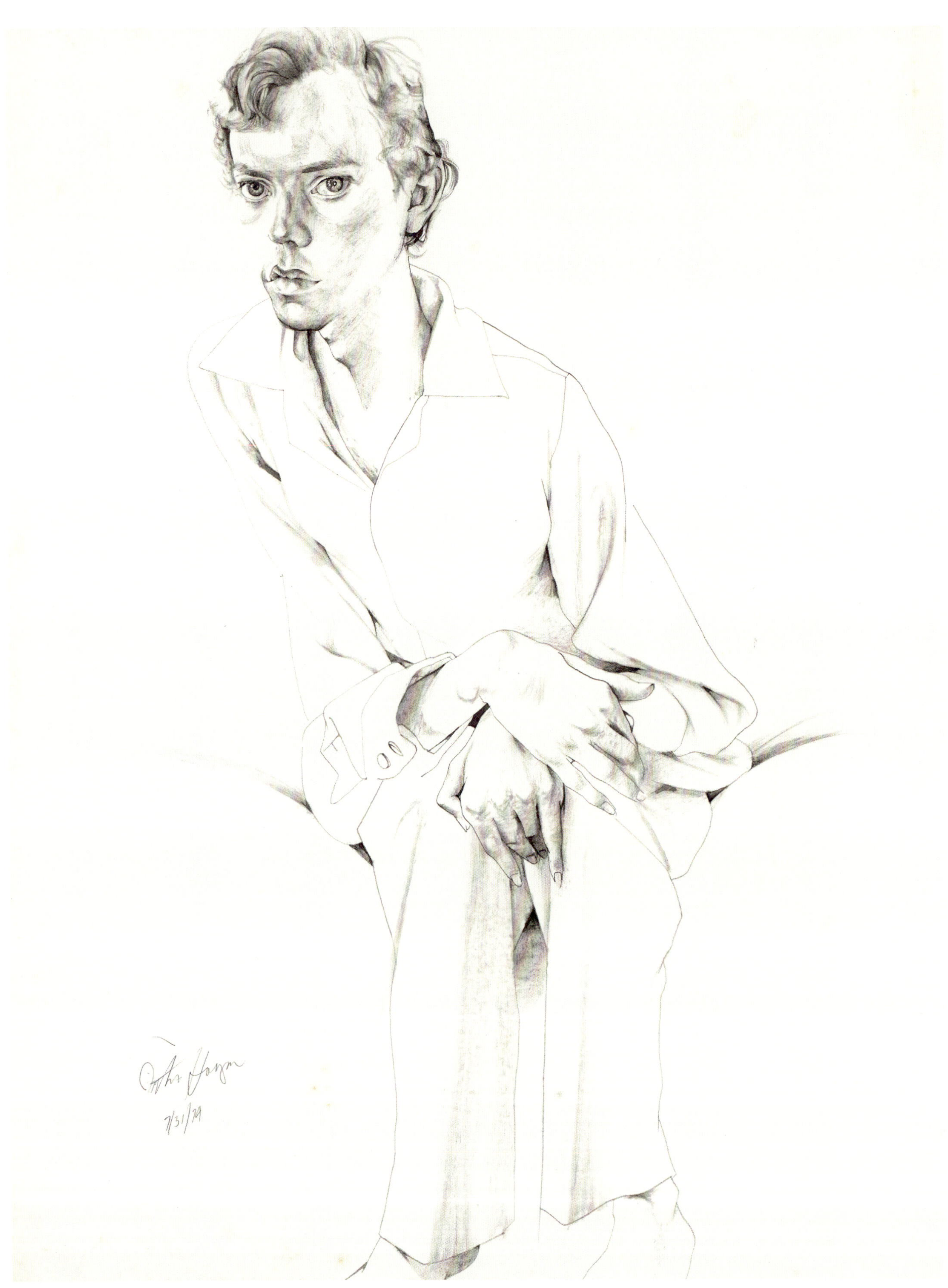

Patrick Hogan, July 31, 1974 (no. 2)
Pen and ink on paper, 24 × 19 in. (61 × 48.3 cm)
Don Bachardy Papers

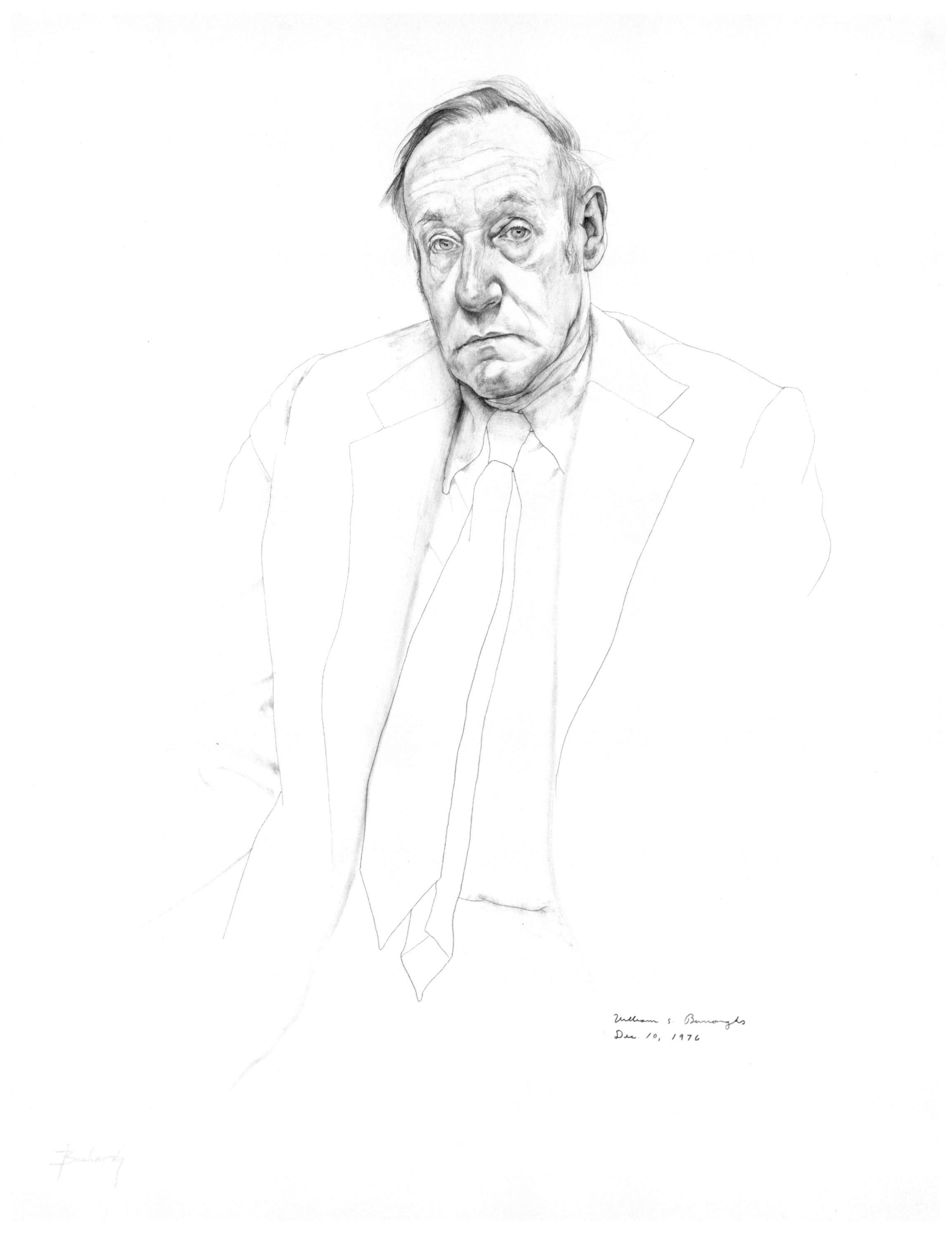

William S. Burroughs, December 10, 1976
Graphite and ink on paper, 29 × 23 in. (73.7 × 58.4 cm)
Don Bachardy Papers

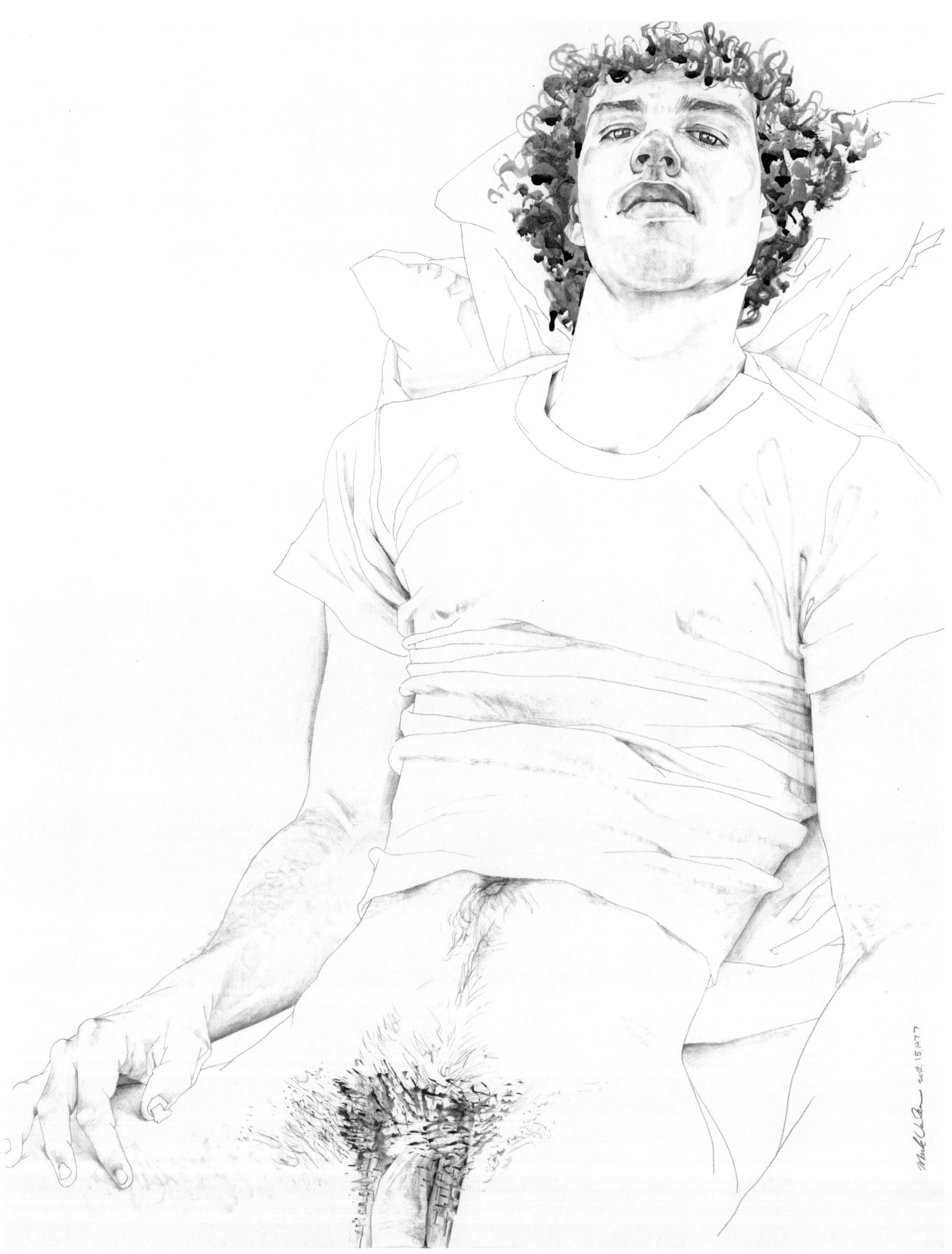

Mark Valen, September 15, 1977 (no. 1)
Graphite and ink on paper, 24 × 19 in. (61 × 48.3 cm)
Don Bachardy Papers

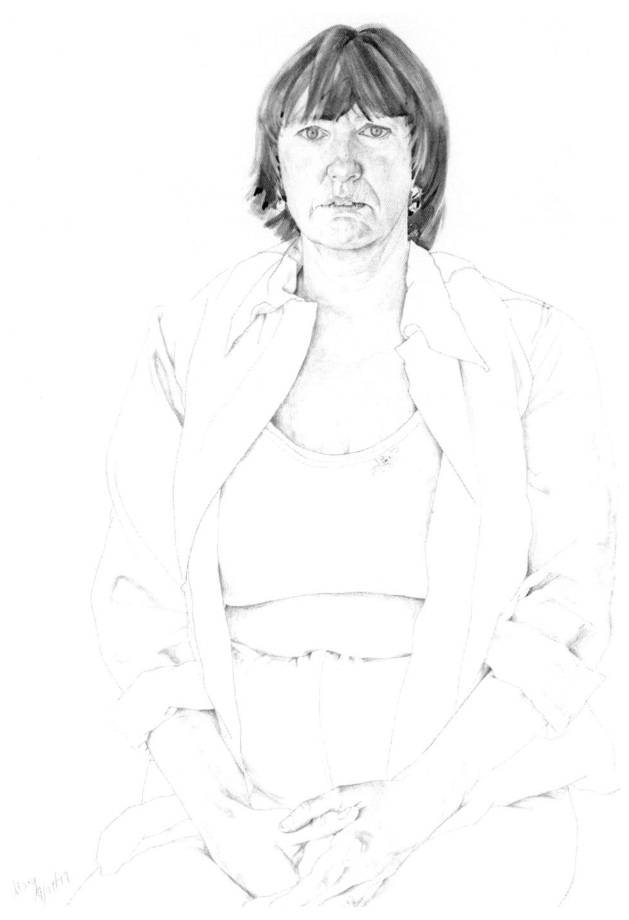

Mary Kienholz, September 29, 1977
Graphite and ink on paper, 24 × 19 in.
(61 × 48.3 cm)
Don Bachardy Papers

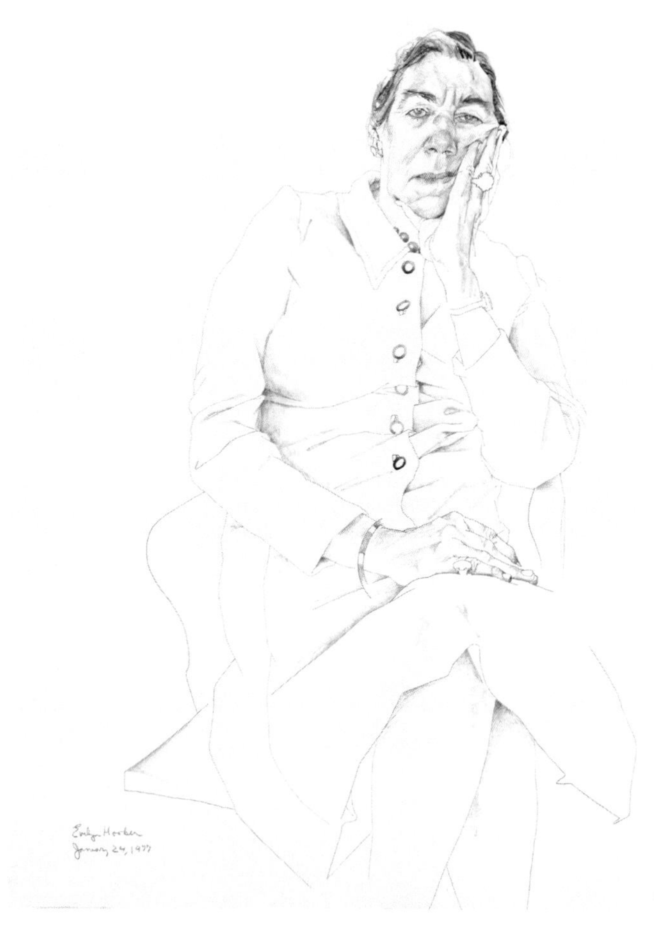

Evelyn Hooker, January 24, 1977 (no. 1)
Graphite and ink on paper, 24 × 19 in. (61 × 48.3 cm)
Don Bachardy Papers

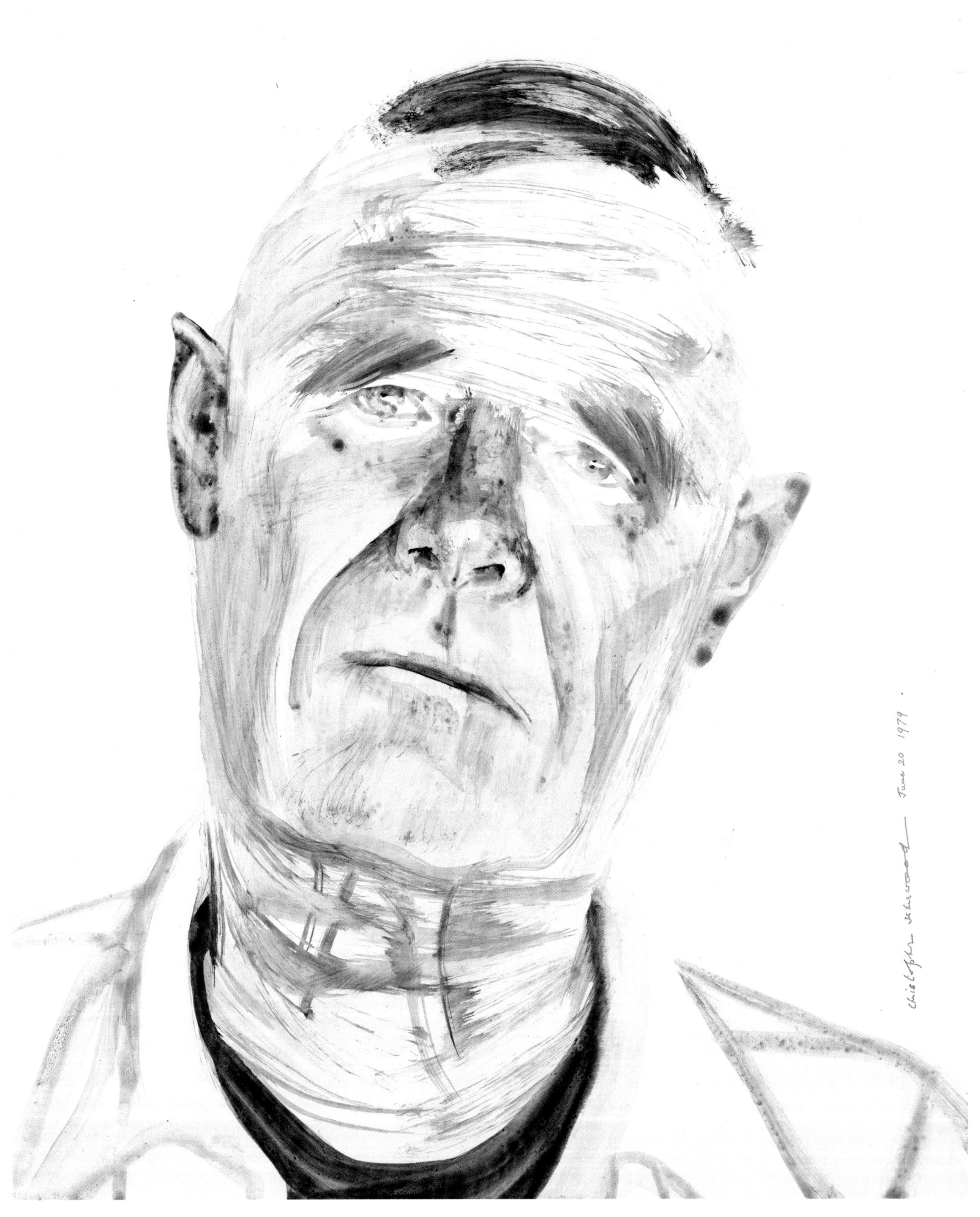

Christopher Isherwood, June 20, 1979
Acrylic on paper, 26 × 20 in. (66 × 50.8 cm)
Don Bachardy Papers

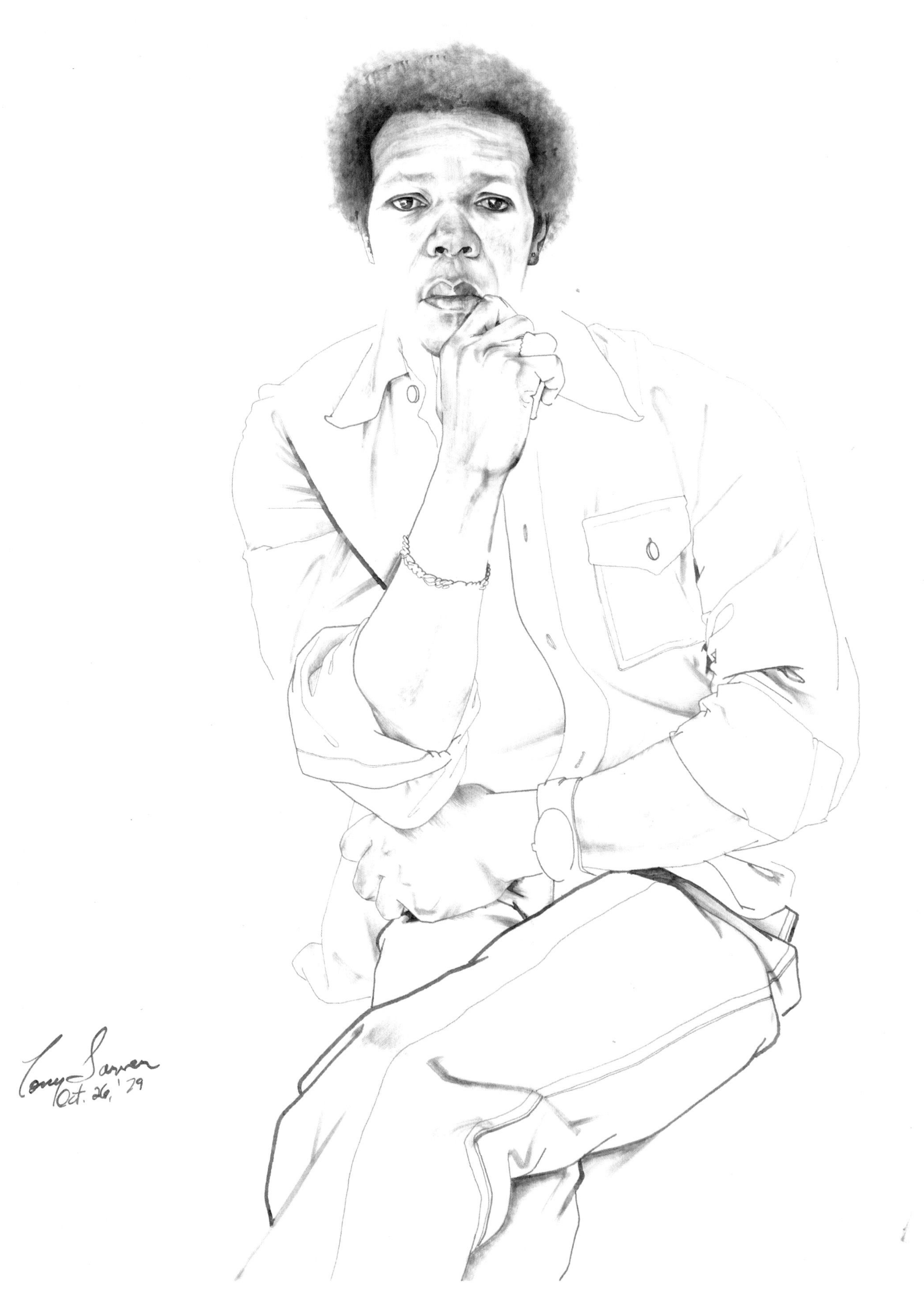

Tony Sarver, October 26, 1979
Pen and ink on paper, 29 × 23 in. (73.7 × 58.4 cm)
Don Bachardy Papers

Eleanor Phillips, January 5, 1980
Pen and ink on paper, 29 × 23 in.
(73.7 × 58.4 cm)
Don Bachardy Papers

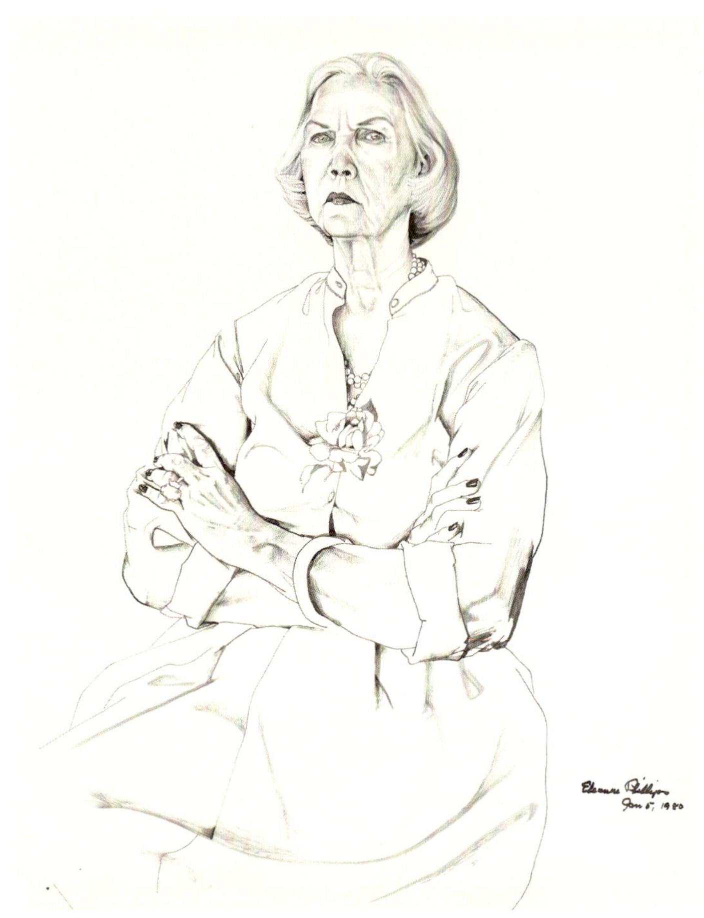

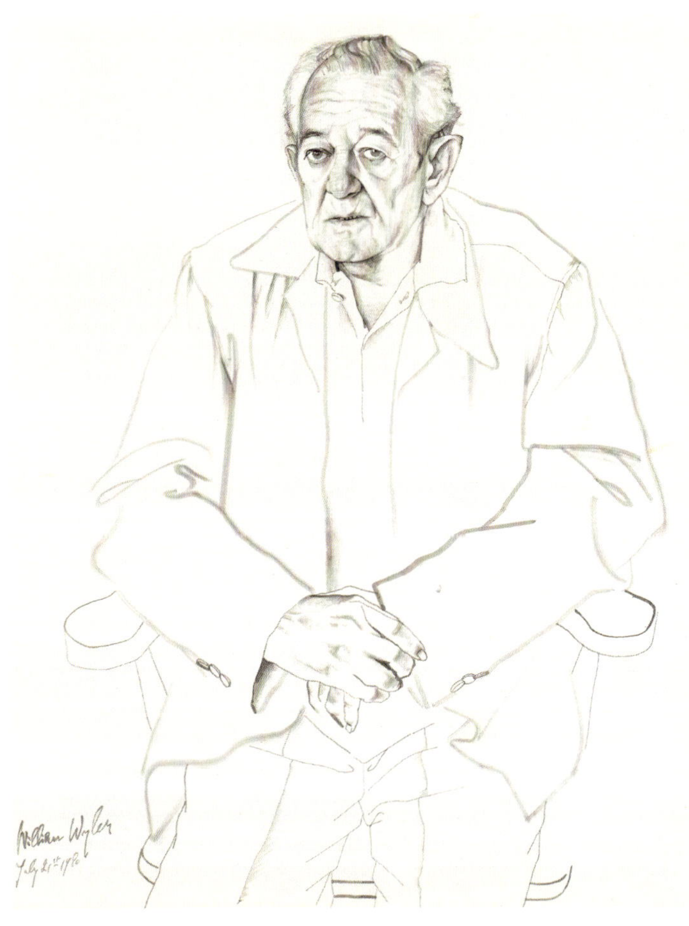

William Wyler, July 21, 1980
Pen and ink on paper, 29 × 23 in. (73.7 × 58.4 cm)
Don Bachardy Papers

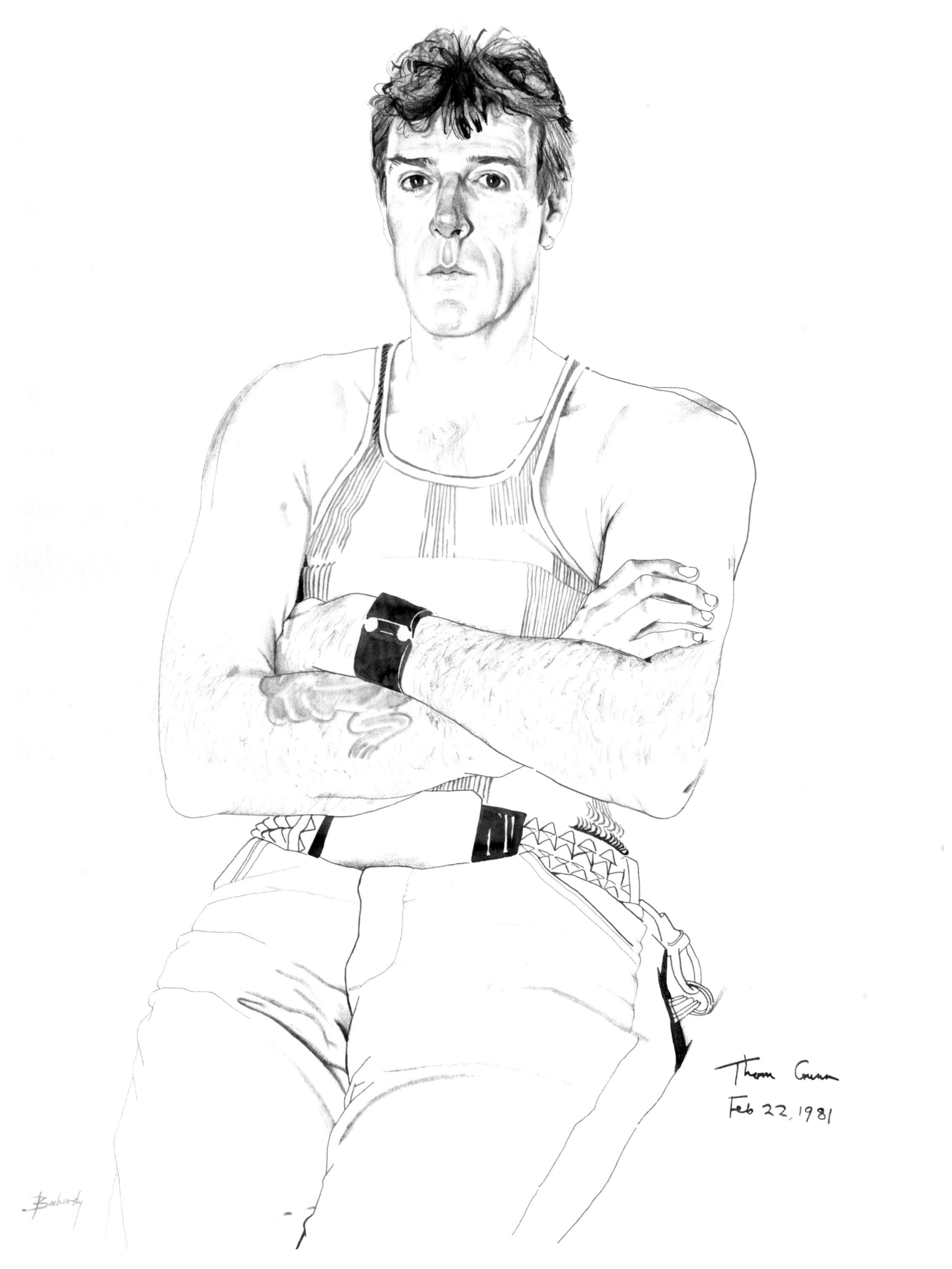

Thom Gunn, February 22, 1981
Ink on paper, 29 × 23⅛ in. (73.7 × 58.7 cm)

Don Bachardy Papers

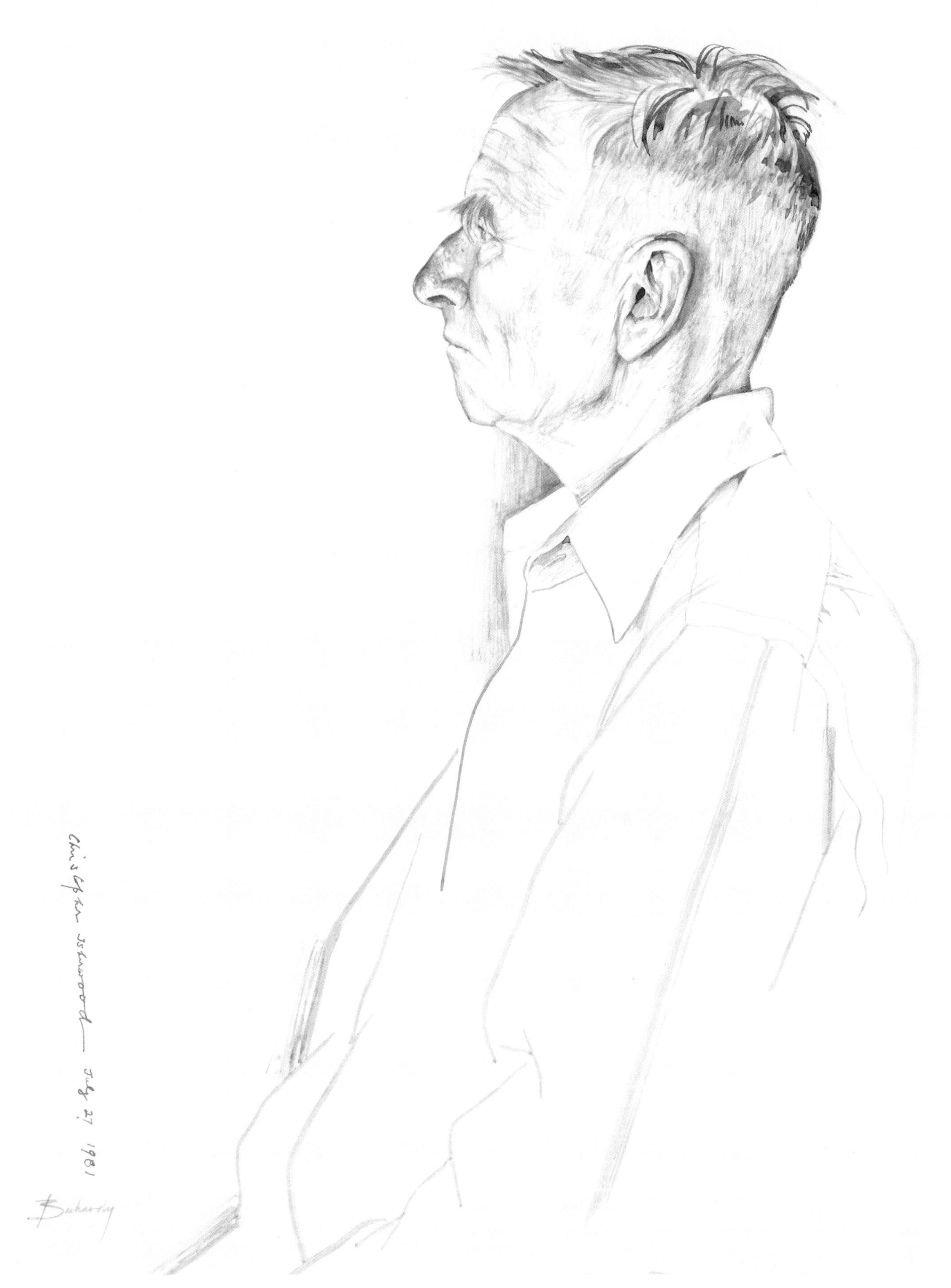

Christopher Isherwood, July 27, 1981
Ink on paper, 24 × 19 in. (61 × 48.3 cm)
Don Bachardy Papers

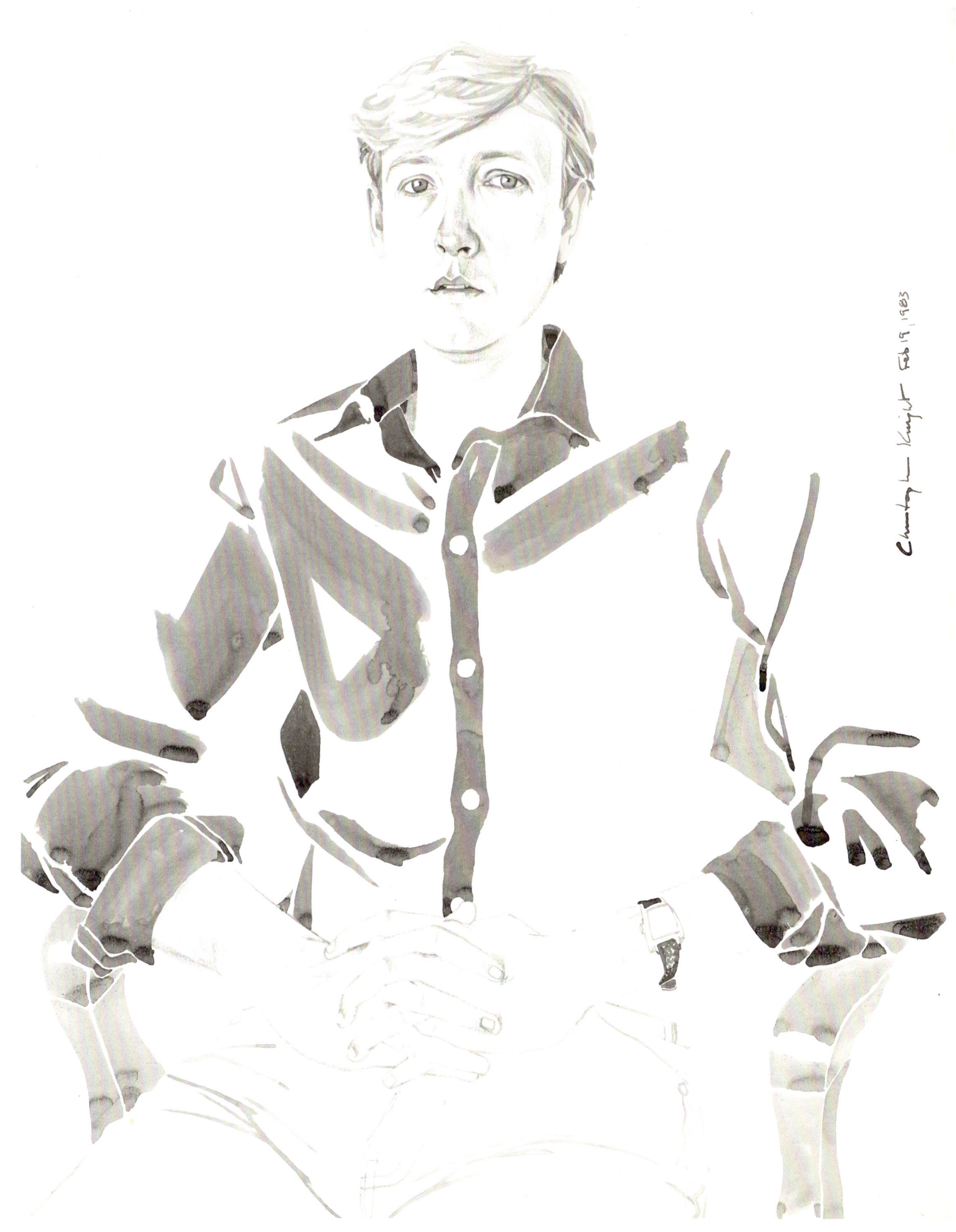

Christopher Knight, February 19, 1983
Ink on paper, 29 × 23 in. (73.7 × 58.4 cm)
Don Bachardy Papers

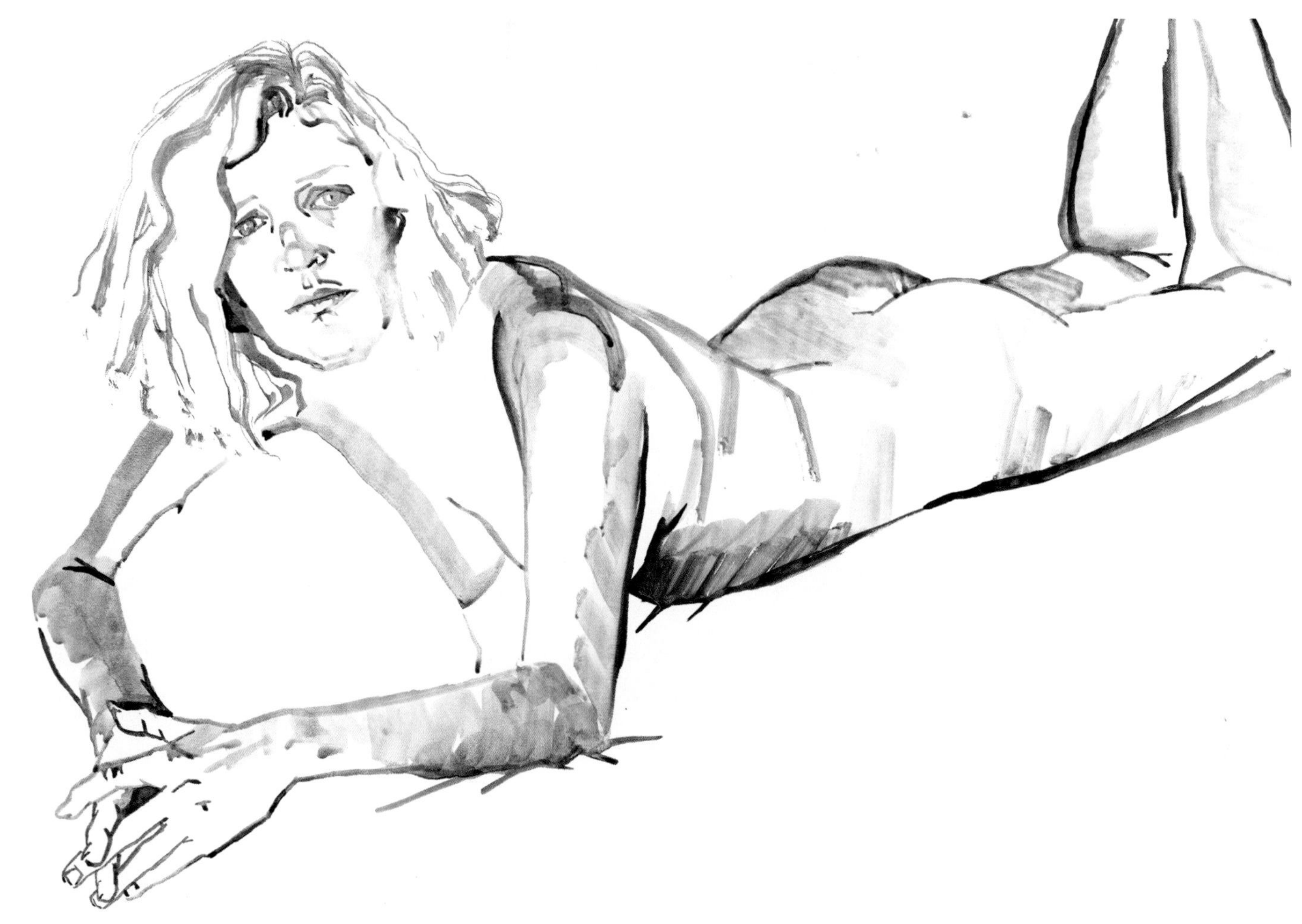

Dagny Corcoran, June 24, 1985 (no. 2)
Acrylic on paper, 22 × 30 in. (55.9 × 76.2 cm)
Don Bachardy Papers

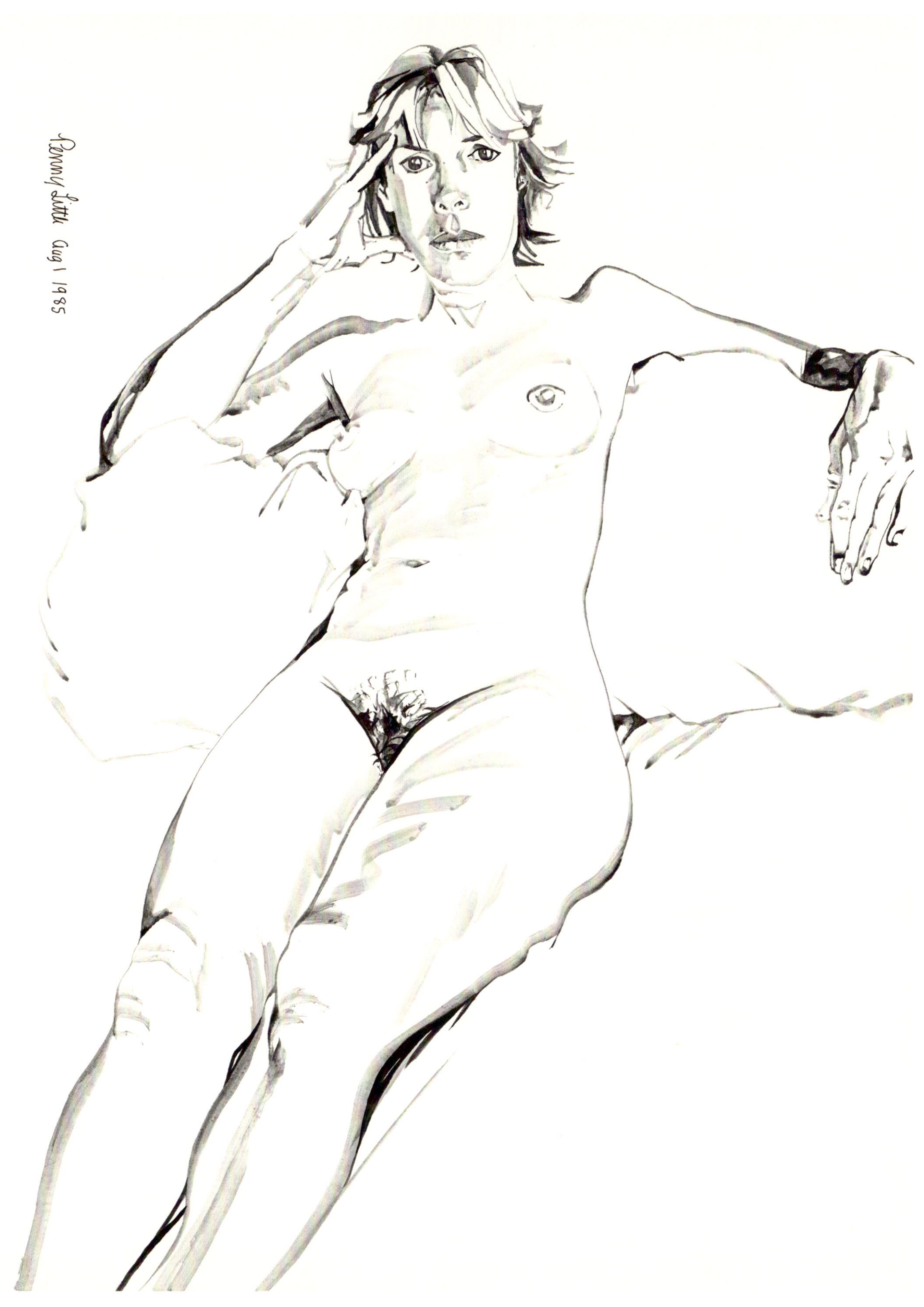

Penny Little, August 1, 1985 (no. 1)
Acrylic on paper, 30 × 22 in. (76.2 × 55.9 cm)
Don Bachardy Papers

Christopher Isherwood, July 9, 1983
Acrylic on board, 48 × 31½ in. (121.9 × 80 cm)
Courtesy of the Christopher Isherwood Foundation

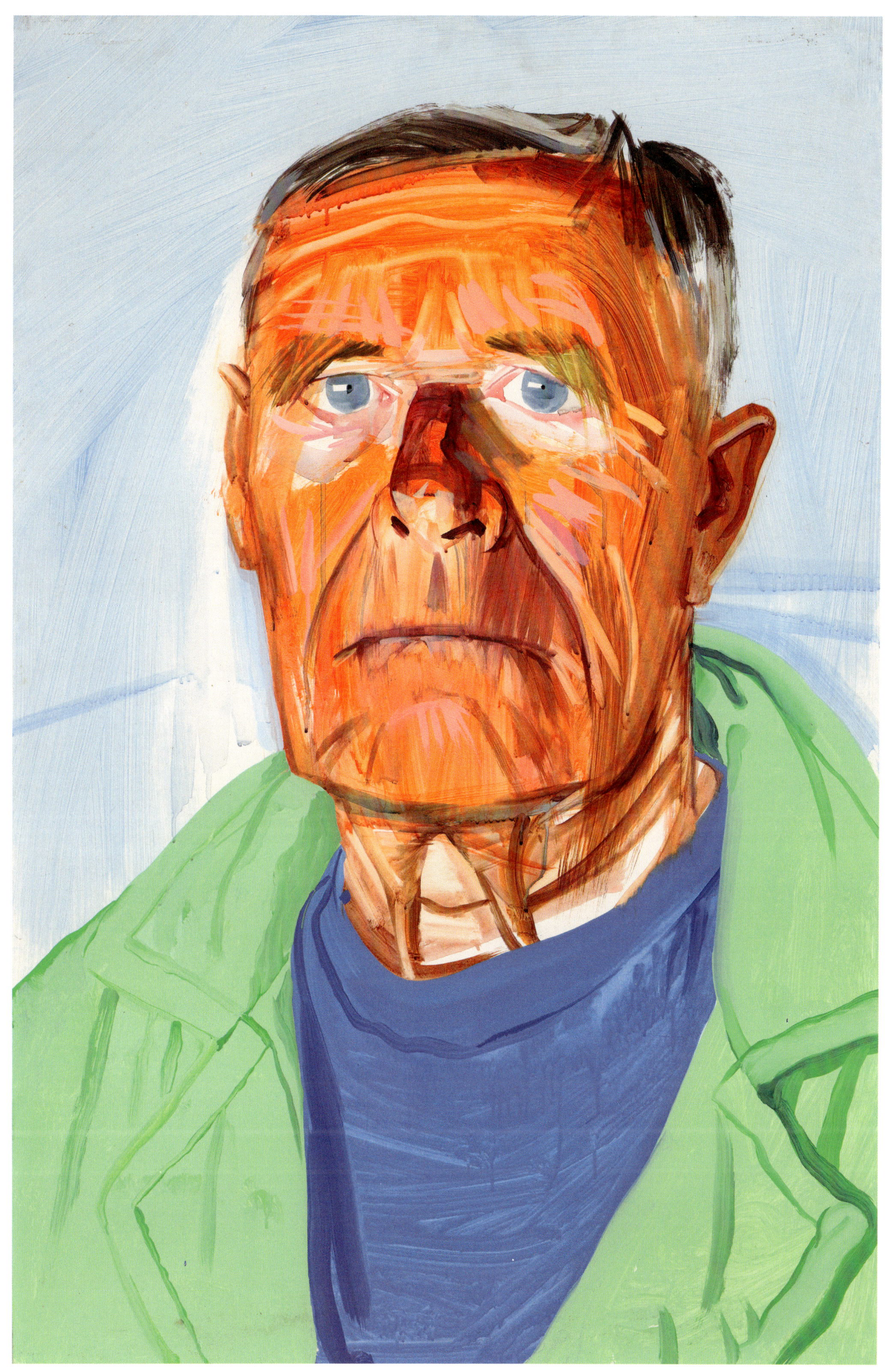

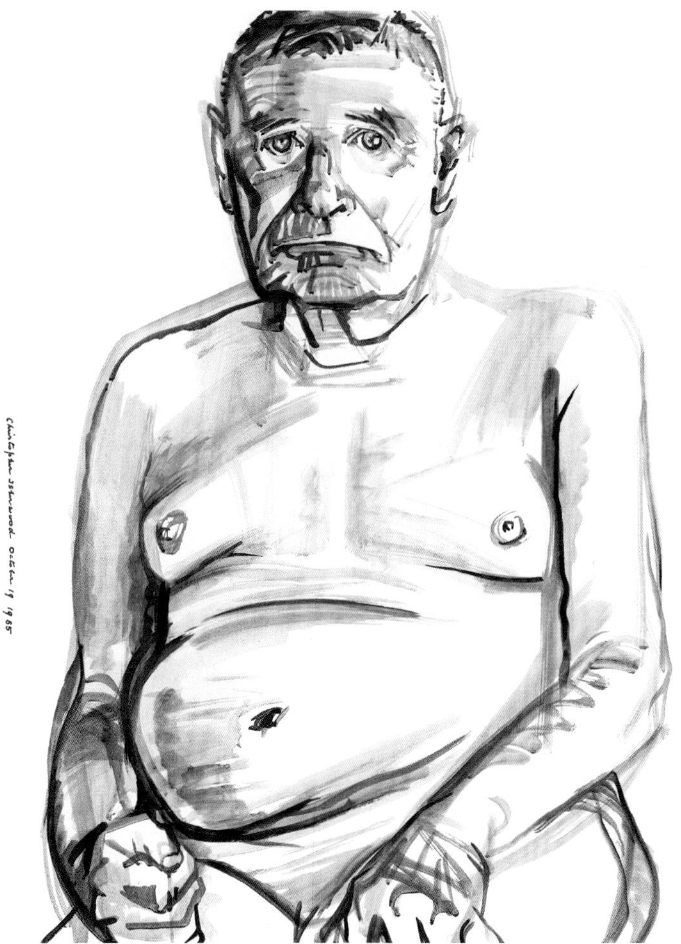

Christopher Isherwood,
October 19, 1985 (no. 3)
Acrylic on paper, 40¼ × 32⅛ in.
(102.2 × 81.6 cm)
Don Bachardy Papers

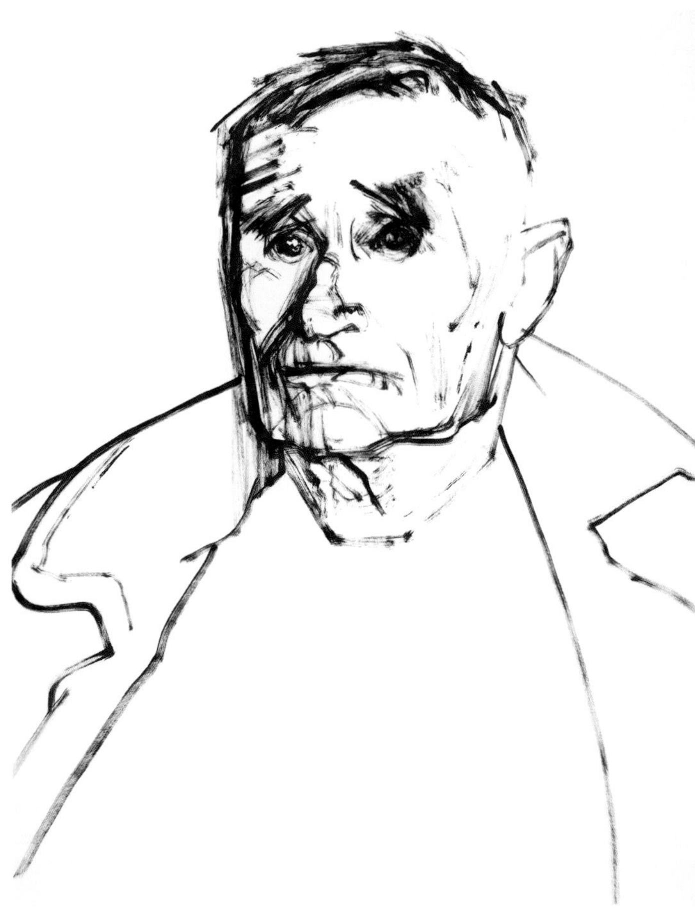

Christopher Isherwood, November 26, 1985 (no. 8)
Acrylic on paper, 39½ × 31¾ in. (100.3 × 80.6 cm)
Courtesy of the Christopher Isherwood Foundation

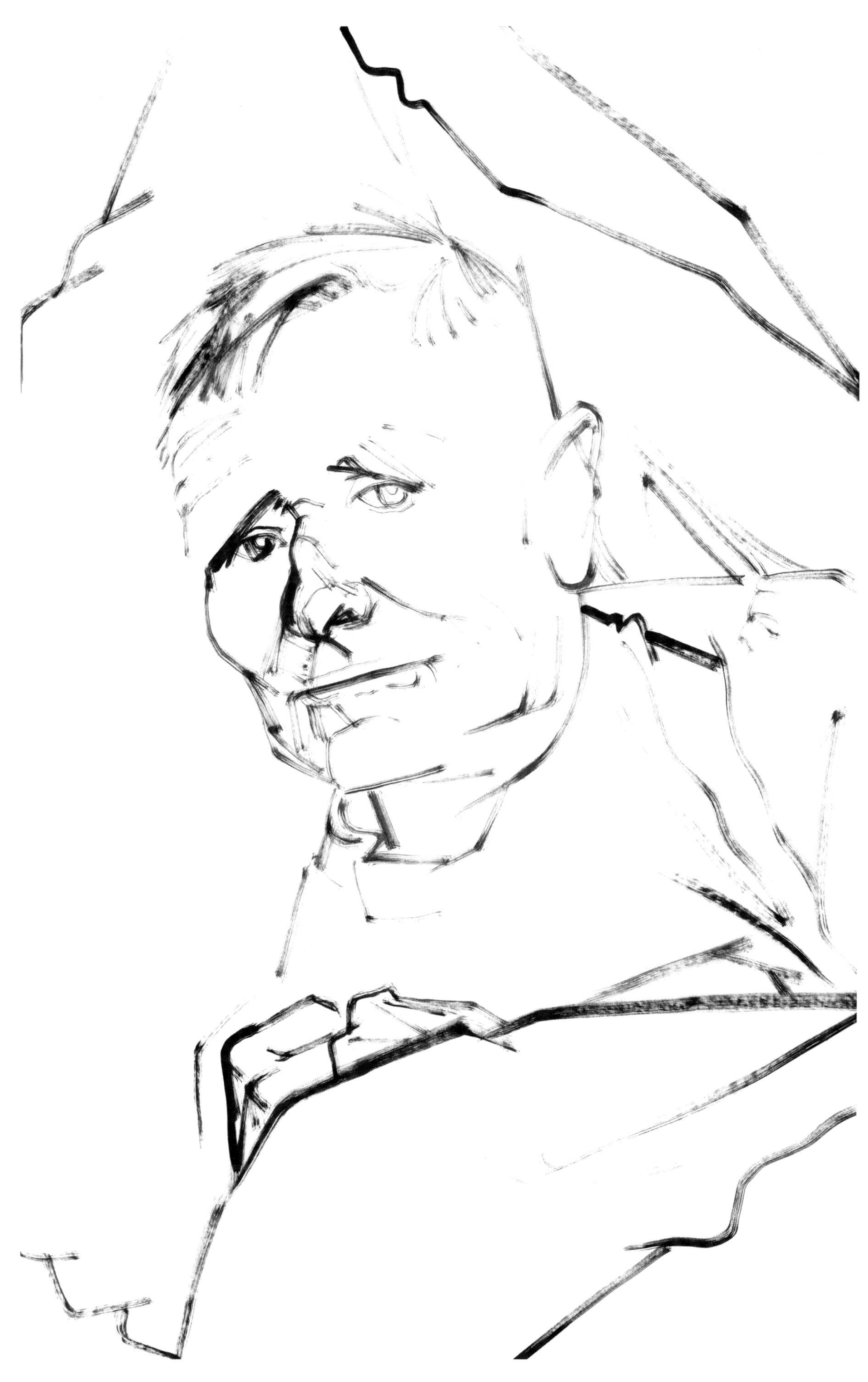

Christopher Isherwood, November 26, 1985 (no. 9)
Acrylic on paper, 39 × 25 in. (99.1 × 63.5 cm)
Courtesy of the Christopher Isherwood Foundation

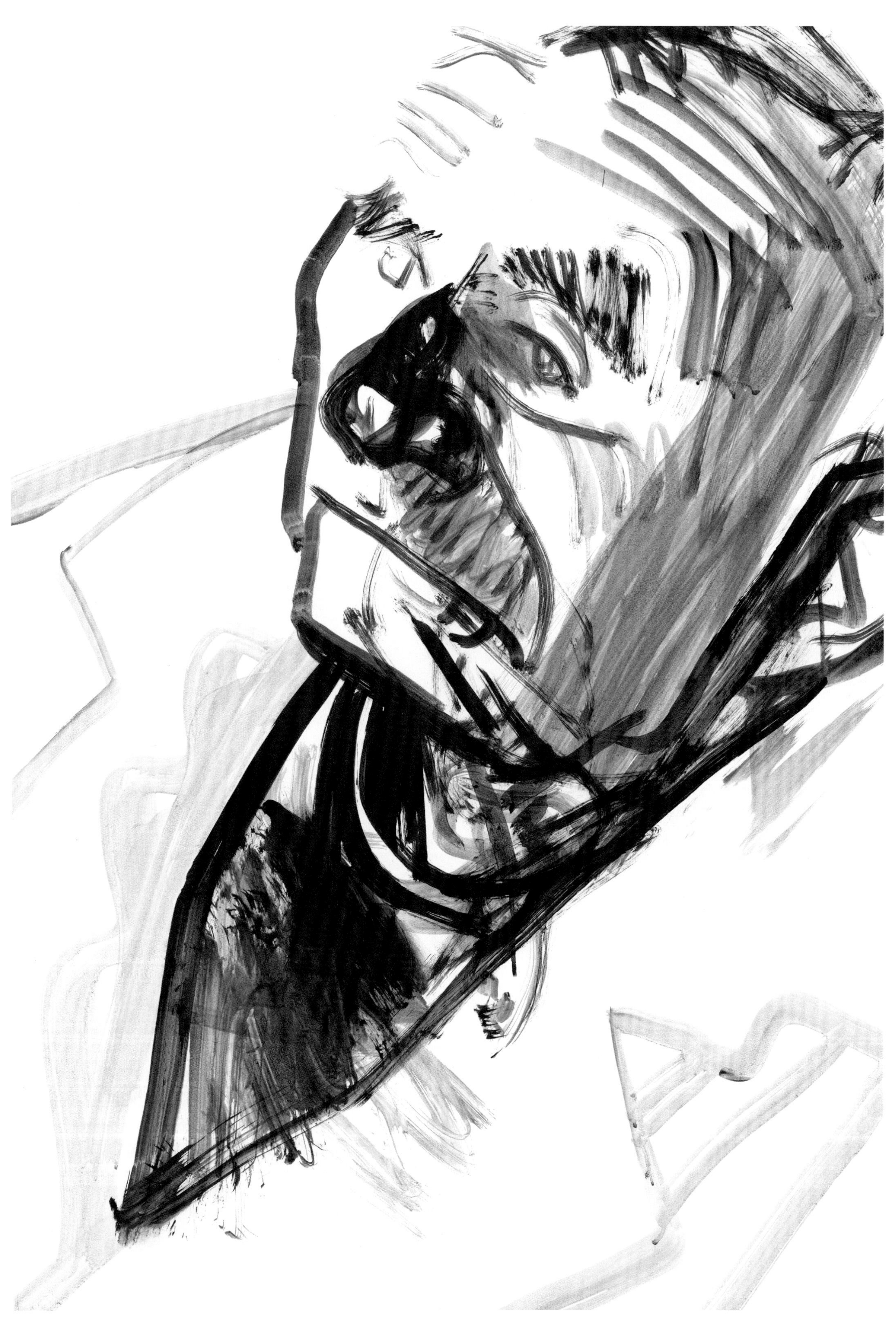

Christopher Isherwood, December 13, 1985
Acrylic on paper, 39 × 27½ in. (99.1 × 69.9 cm)
Courtesy of the Christopher Isherwood Foundation

Self-Portrait, April 16, 1986 (no. 2)
Acrylic on paper, 30 × 22 in. (76.2 × 55.9 cm)
Don Bachardy Papers

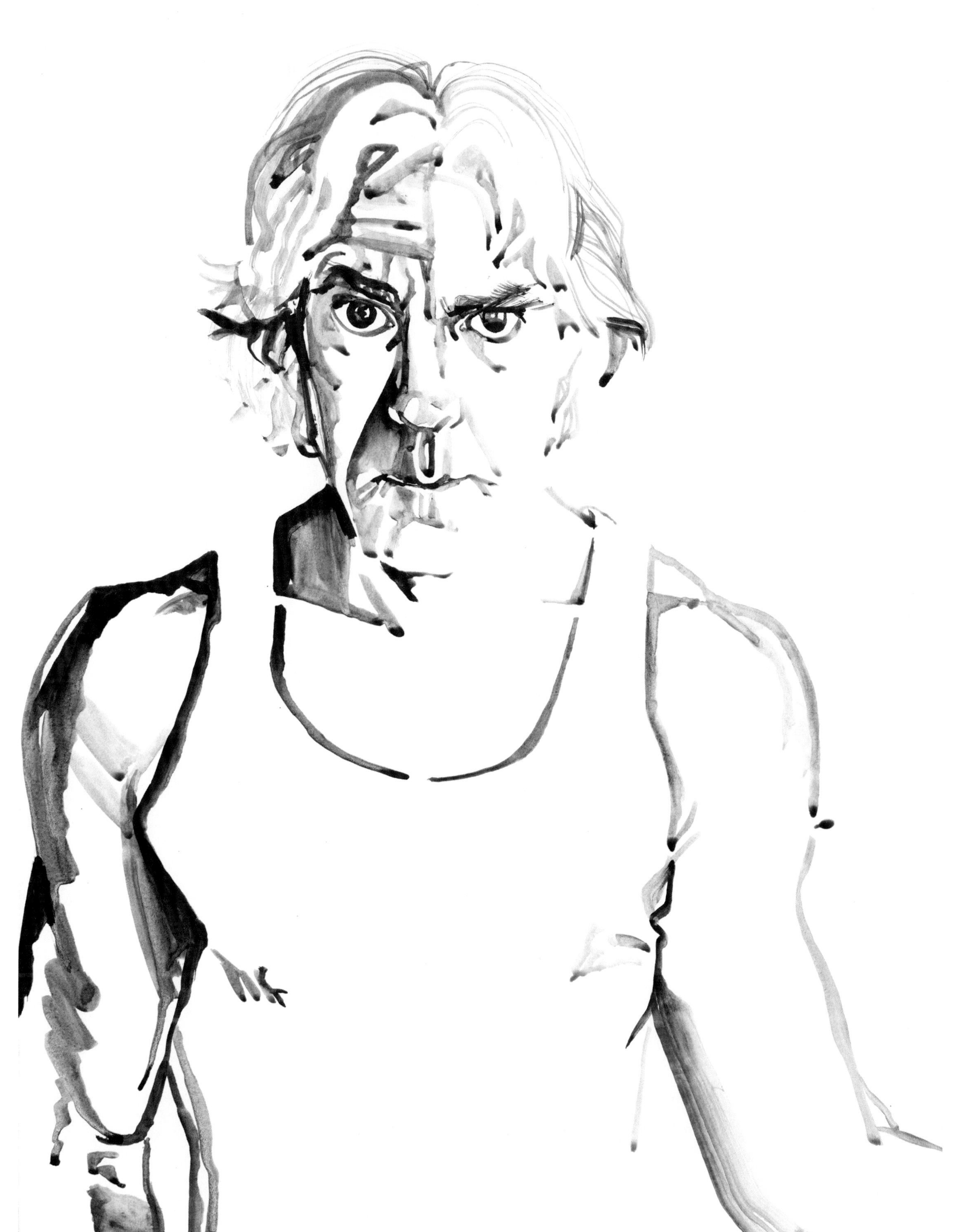

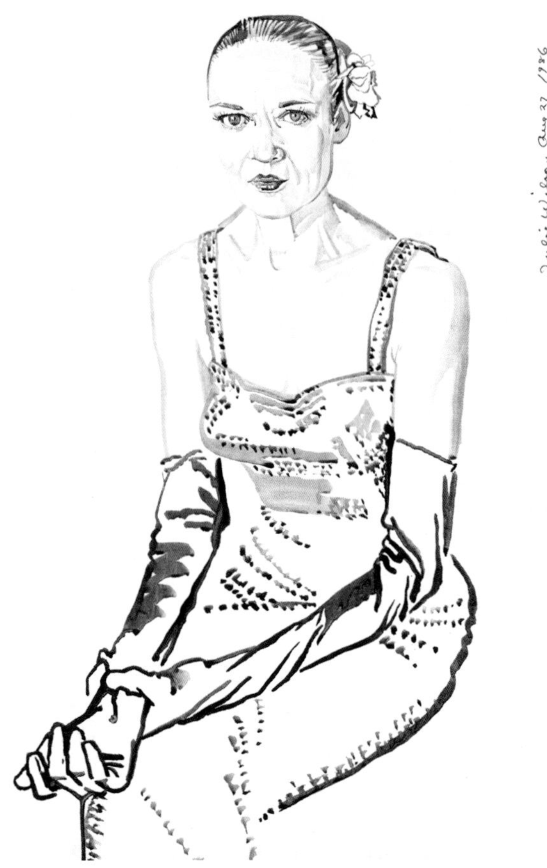

Julie Wilson, August 27, 1986 (no. 1)
Acrylic on paper, 30 × 22 in.
(76.2 × 55.9 cm)
Don Bachardy Papers

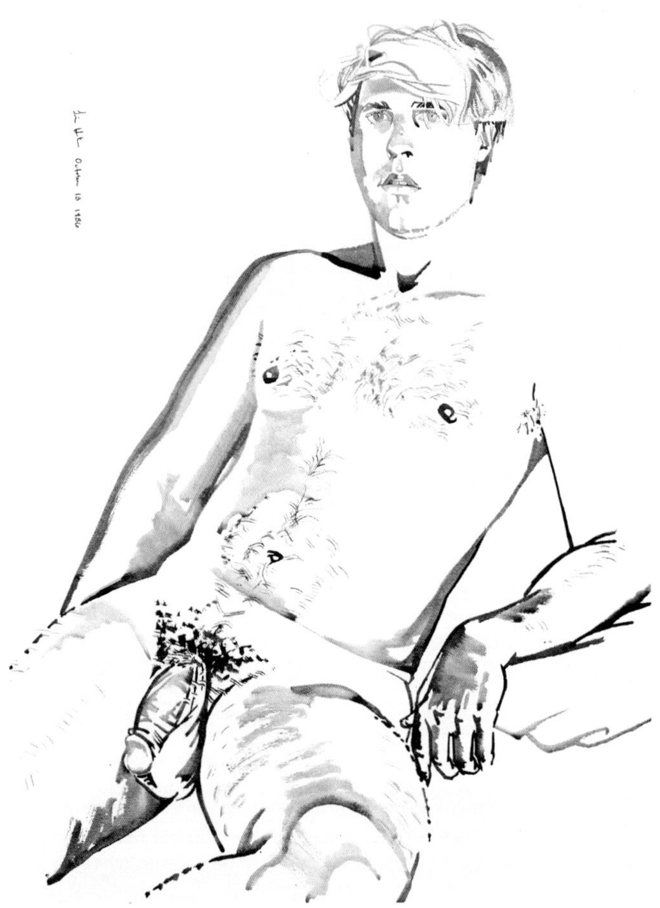

Tim Hilton, October 18, 1986 (no. 3)
Acrylic on paper, 30 × 22 in. (76.2 × 55.9 cm)
Don Bachardy Papers

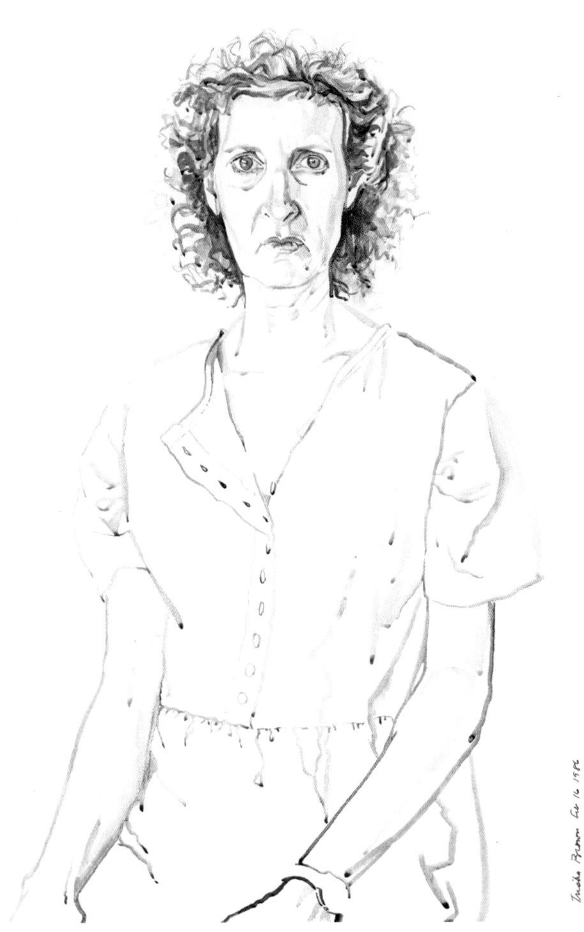

Trisha Brown, February 16, 1986 (no. 1)
Acrylic on paper, 30 × 22 in.
(76.2 × 55.9 cm)
Don Bachardy Papers

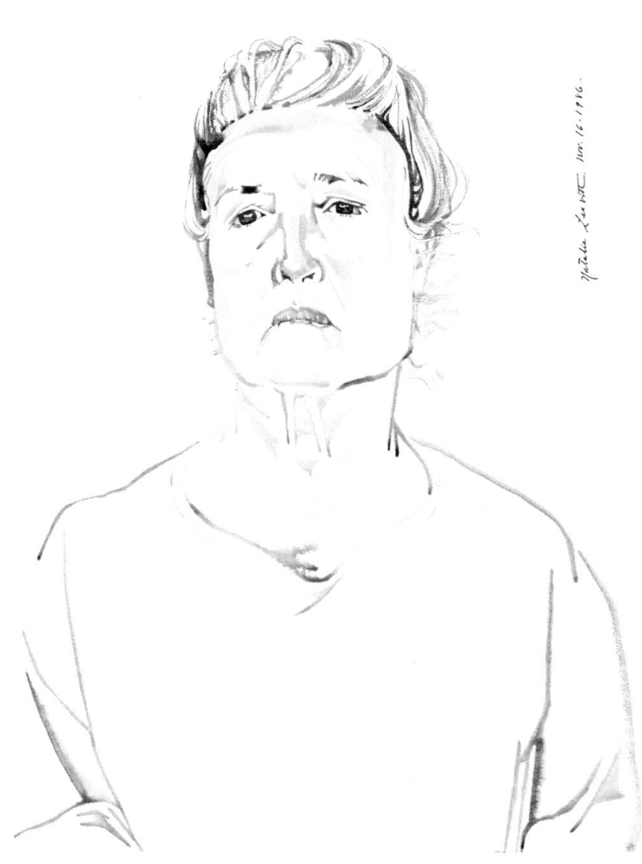

Natalie Leavitt, November 16, 1986 (no. 5)
Acrylic on paper, 30 × 22 in. (76.2 × 55.9 cm)
Don Bachardy Papers

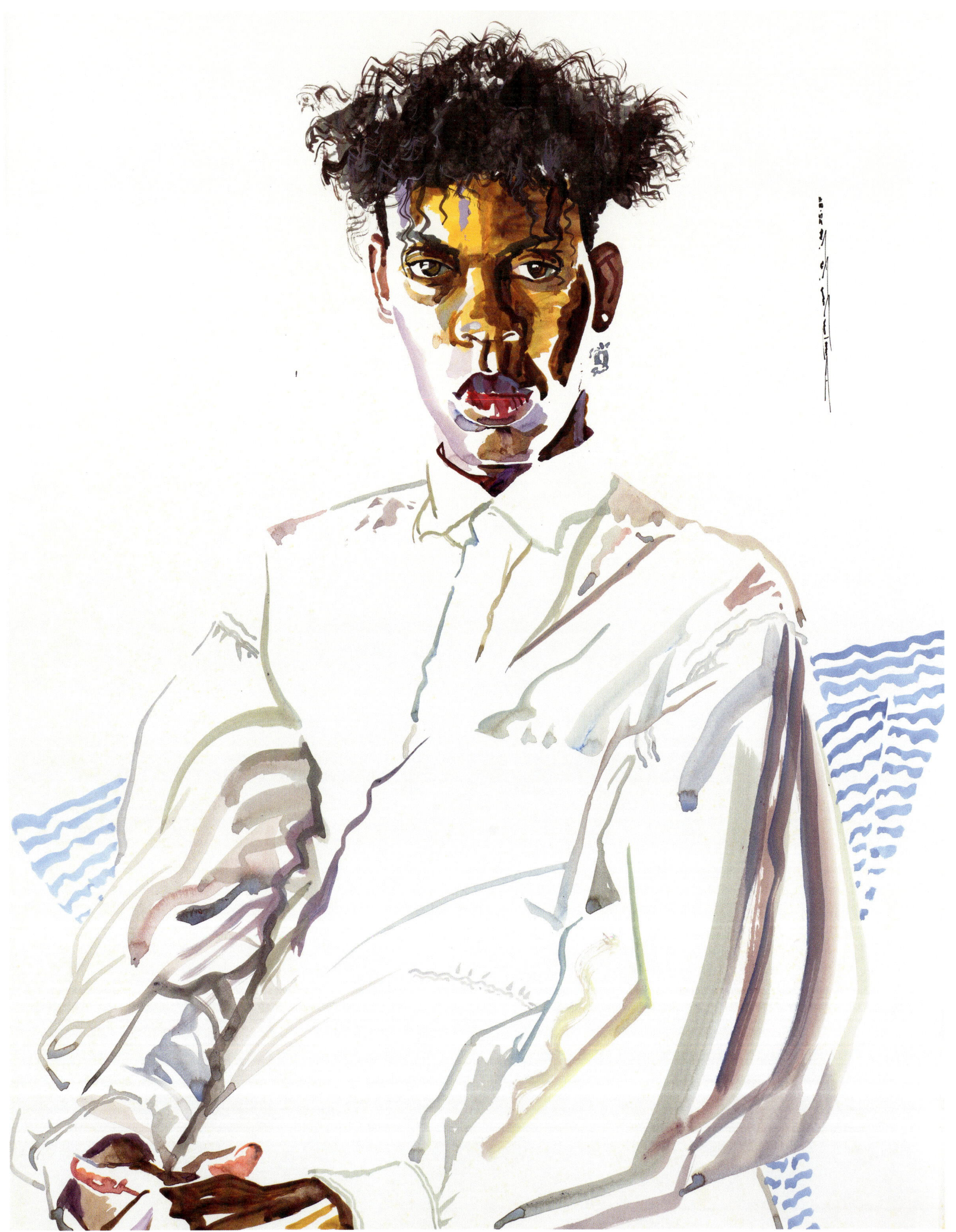

Burton Jones, January 25, 1987 (no. 3)
Acrylic on paper, 29 × 23 in. (73.7 × 58.4 cm)
Don Bachardy Papers

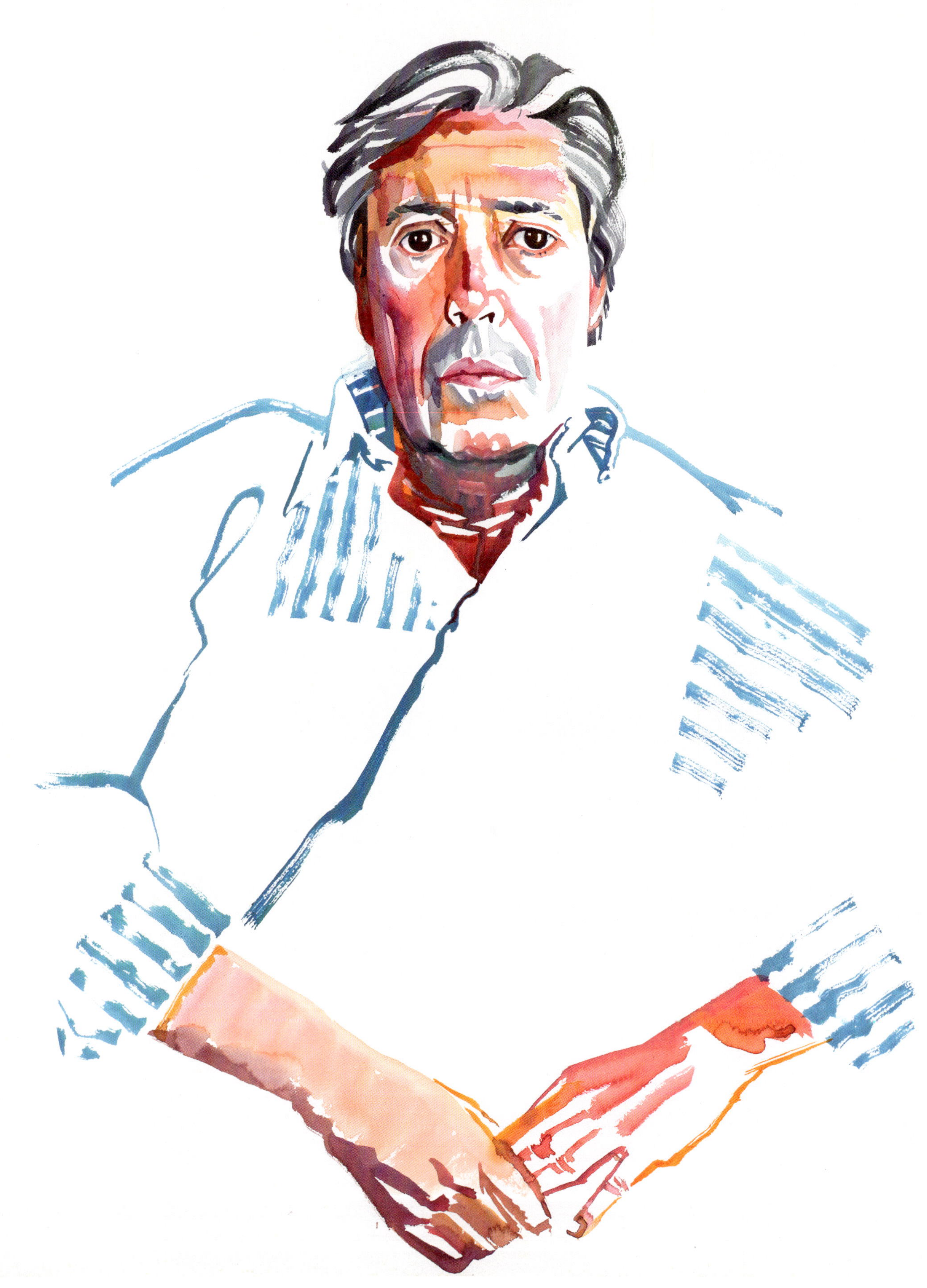

Brian Bedford, May 1992 (no. 2)
Acrylic on paper, 30 × 22 in. (76.2 × 55.9 cm)
Don Bachardy Papers

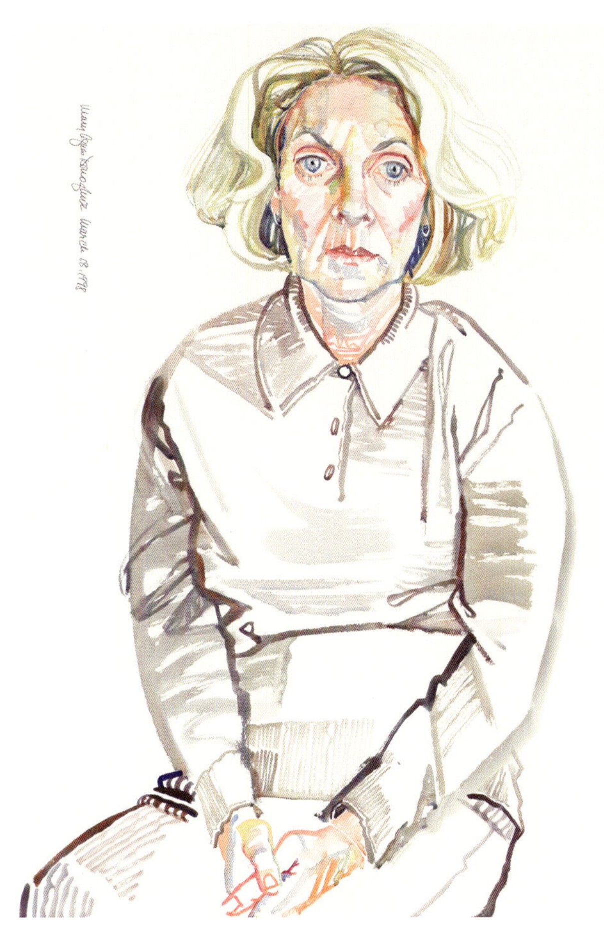

Mary Agnes Donoghue, March 18, 1993
Acrylic on paper, 29 × 23 in.
(73.7 × 58.4 cm)
Don Bachardy Papers

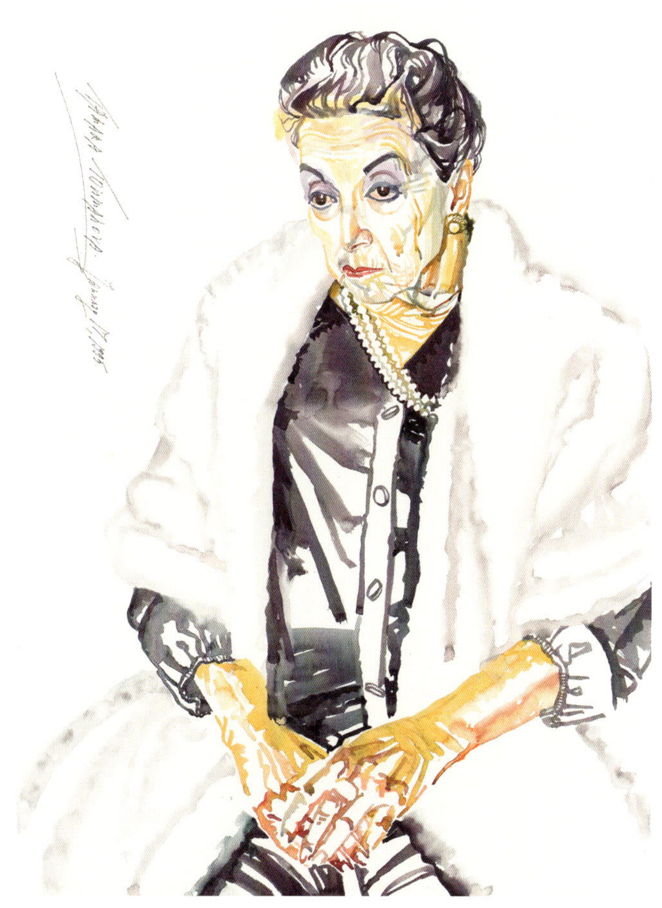

Tamara Toumanova, January 17, 1995 (no. 1)
Acrylic on paper, 30 × 22 in. (76.2 × 55.9 cm)
Don Bachardy Papers

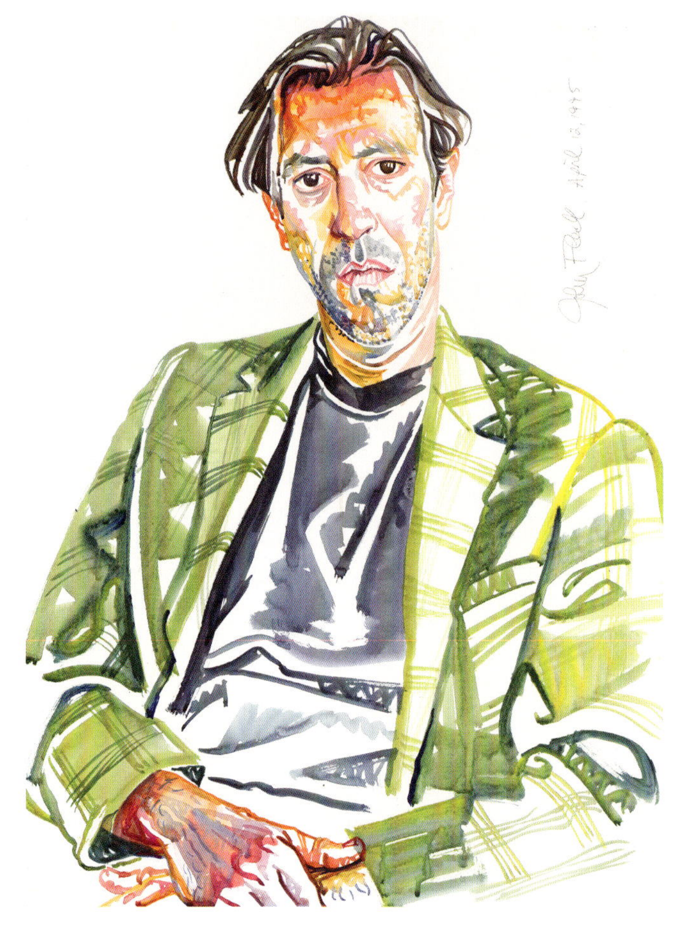

John Fleck, April 12, 1995 (no. 2)
Acrylic on paper, 30 × 22 in.
(76.2 × 55.9 cm)
Don Bachardy Papers

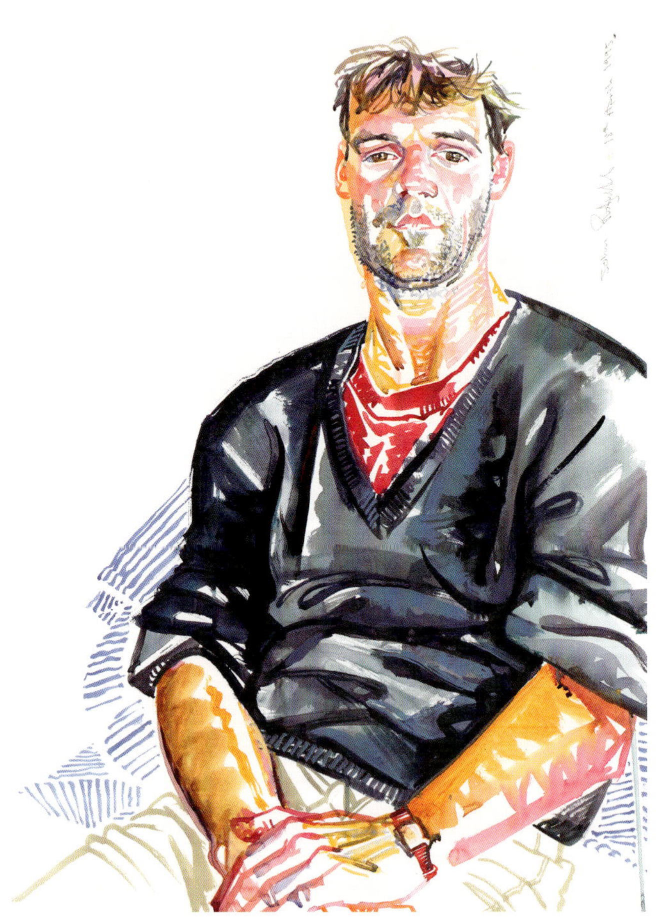

John Fitzherbert, April 18, 1995 (no. 2)
Acrylic on paper, 30 × 22 in. (76.2 × 55.9 cm)
Don Bachardy Papers

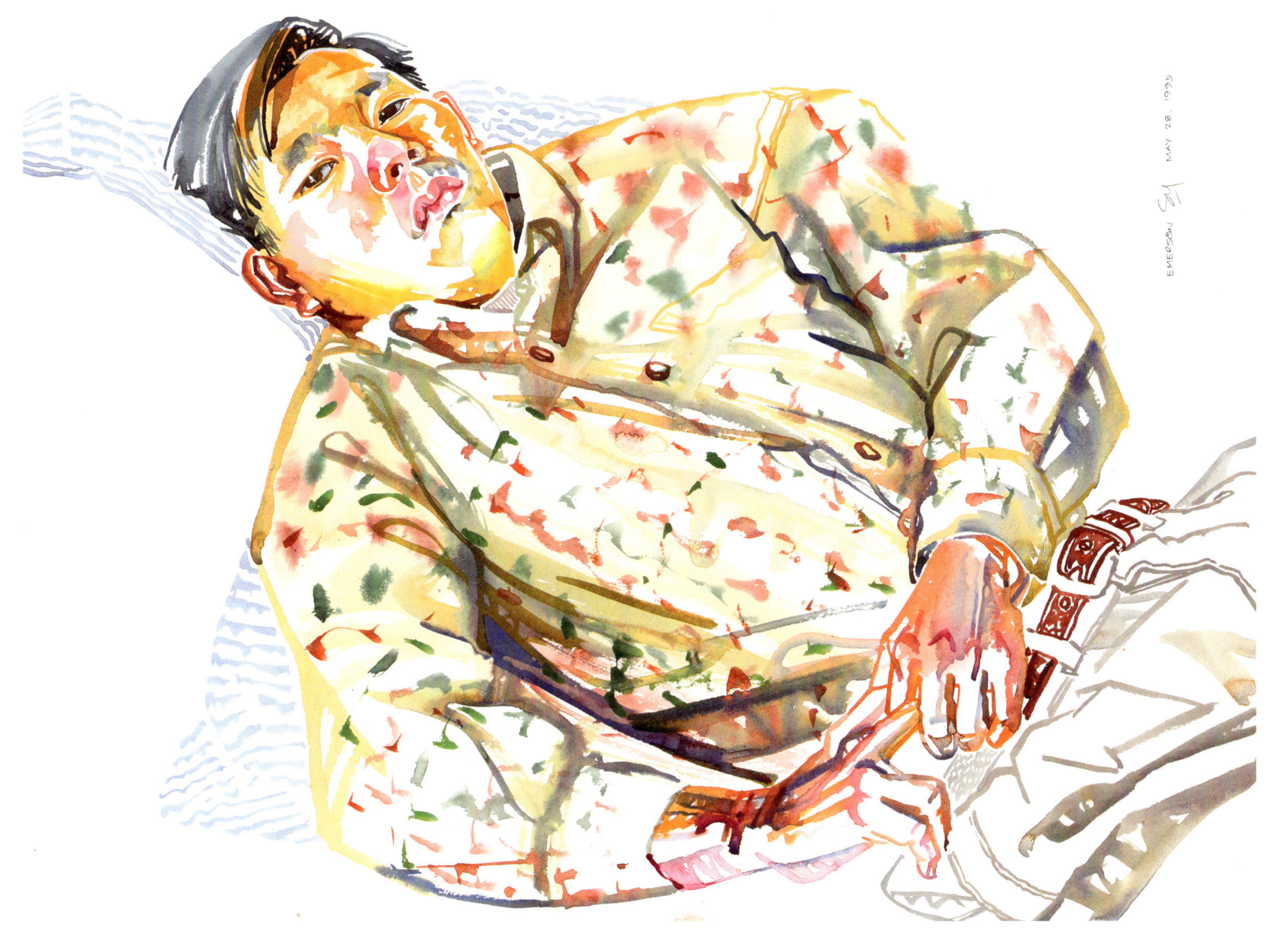

Emerson Sy, May 28, 1995 (no. 2)
Acrylic on paper, 22¼ × 29⅞ in. (56.5 × 75.9 cm)
Don Bachardy Papers

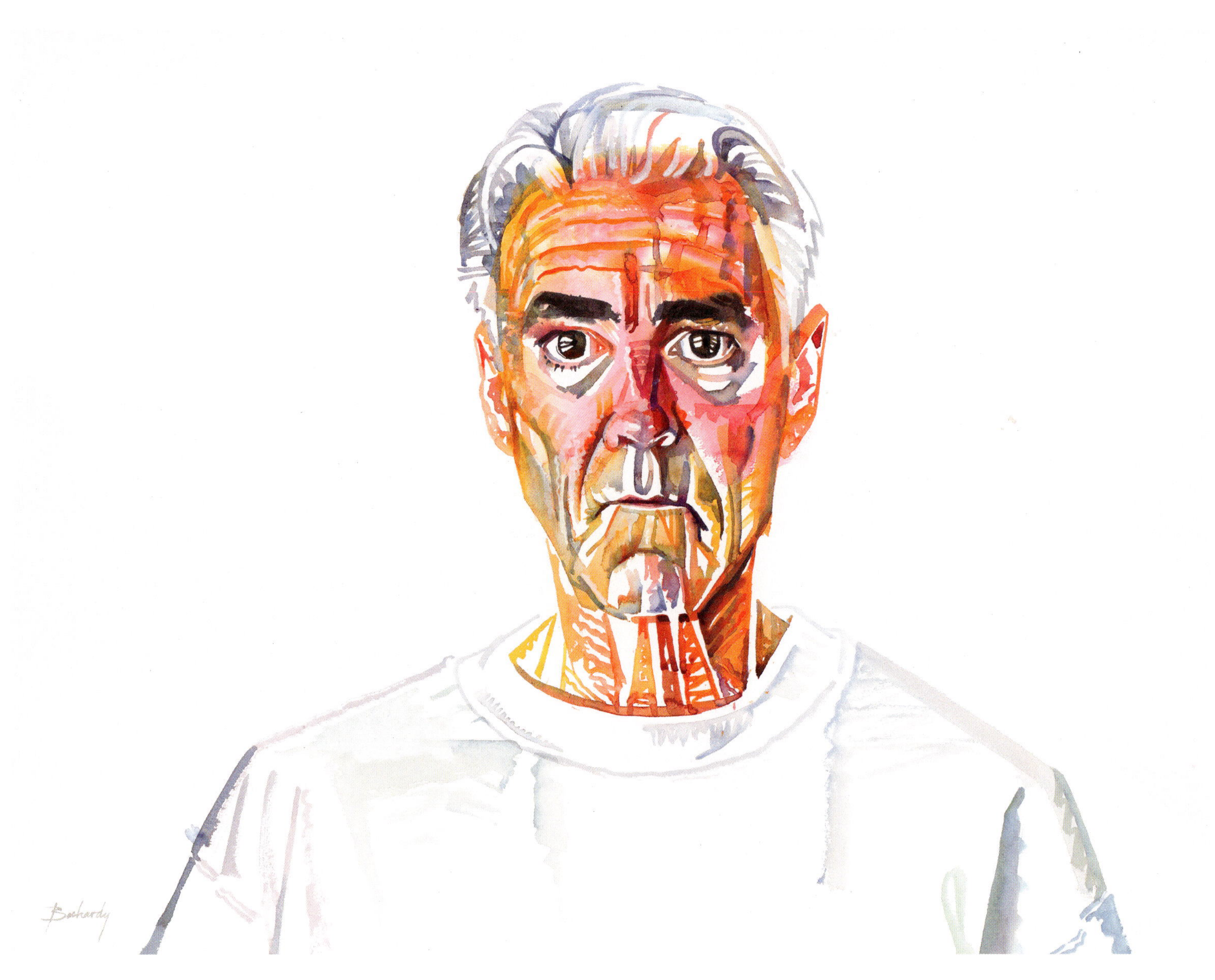

Self-Portrait, early August 1995
Acrylic on paper, 22⅛ × 29⅞ in. (56.2 × 75.9 cm)
Don Bachardy Papers

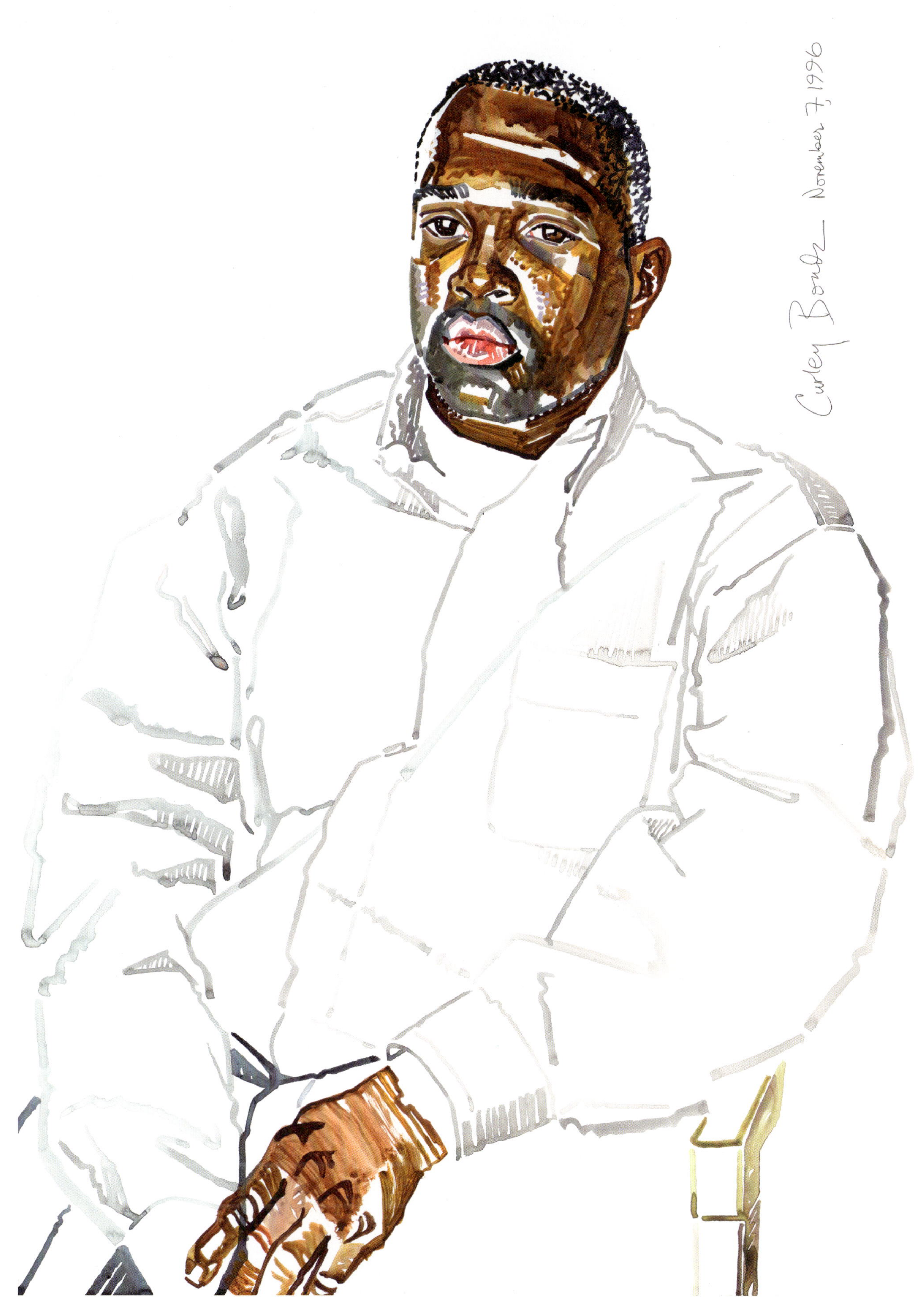

Curley Bonds, November 7, 1996 (no. 1)
Acrylic on paper, 30 × 22 in. (76.2 × 55.9 cm)
Don Bachardy Papers

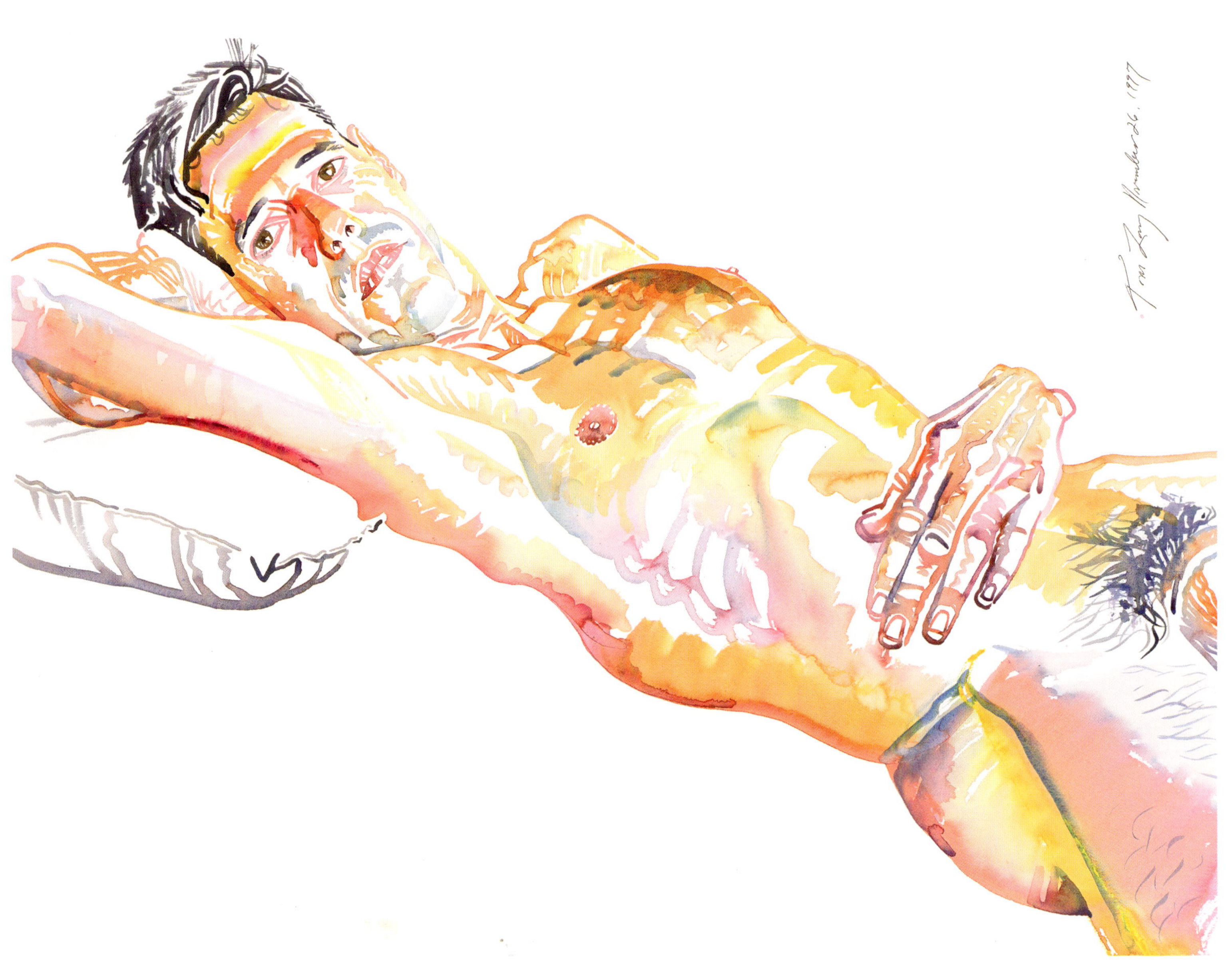

Tom Long, November 26, 1997
Acrylic on paper, 22 × 30 in. (55.9 × 76.2 cm)
Don Bachardy Papers

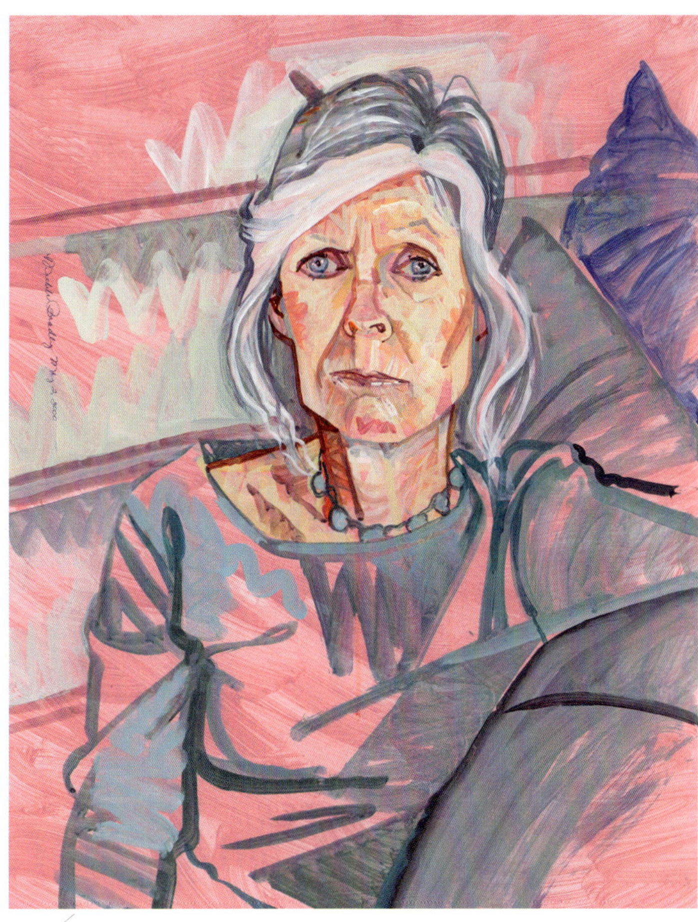

Michele Bradley, May 2, 2000 (no. 3)
Acrylic on paper, 29 × 23 in.
(73.7 × 58.4 cm)
Don Bachardy Papers

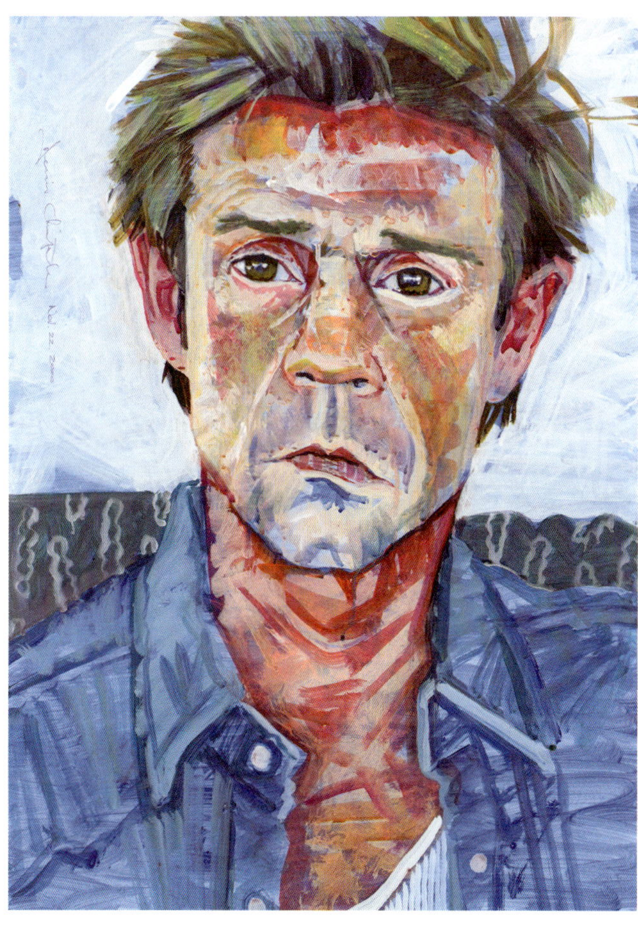

Dennis Christopher, November 22, 2000 (no. 2)
Acrylic on paper, 29⅞ × 21⅞ in. (75.9 × 55.6 cm)
Don Bachardy Papers

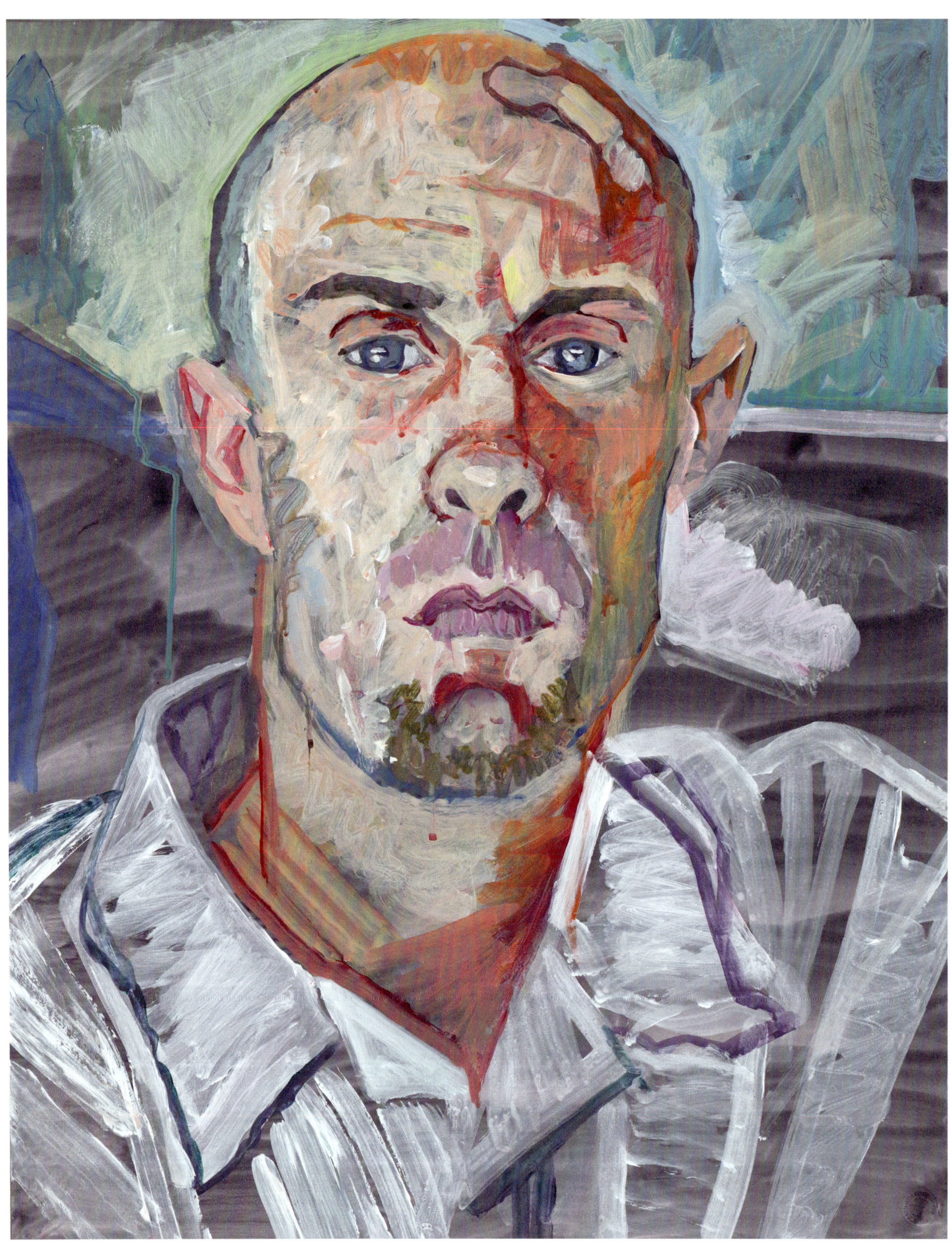

Gus Harper, August 14, 2001 (no. 3)
Acrylic on paper, 28⅞ × 23 in. (73.3 × 58.4 cm)
Don Bachardy Papers

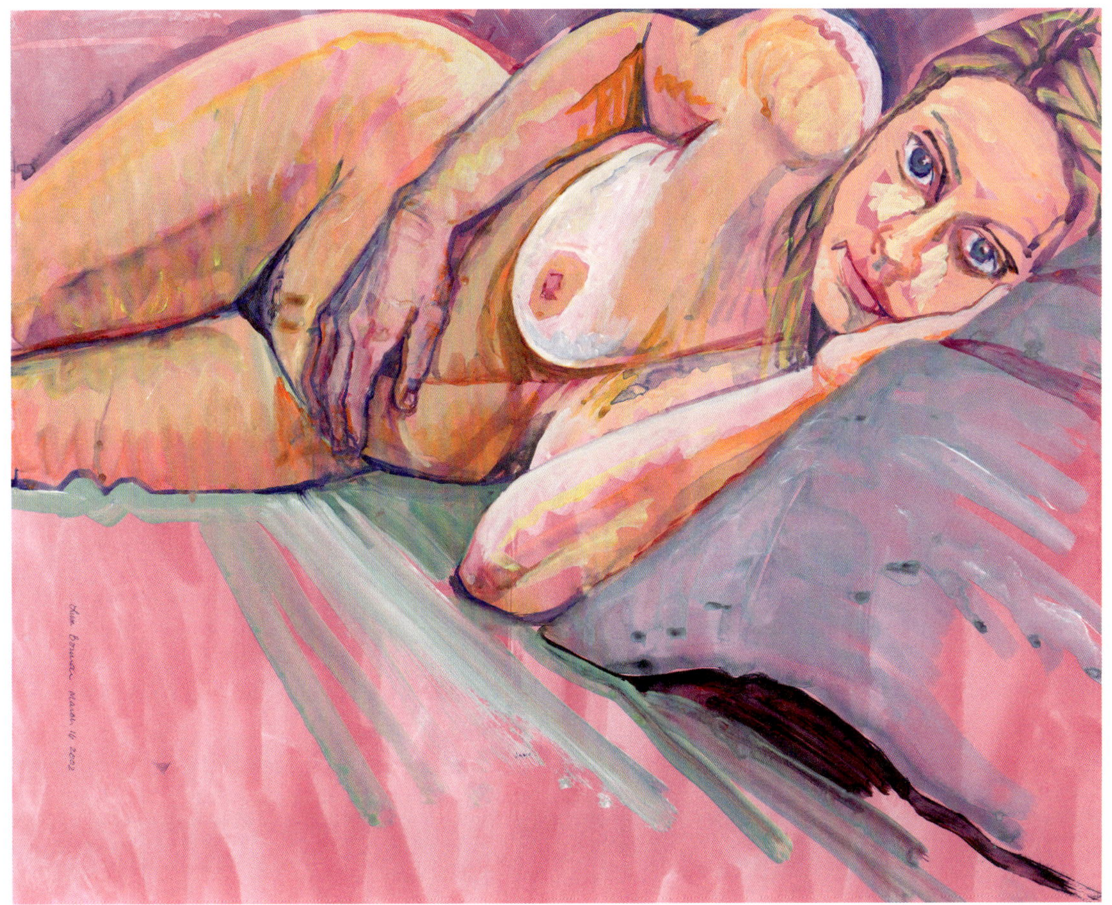

Lisa Bounau, March 16, 2002 (no. 3)
Acrylic on paper, 23 × 28¾ in. (58.4 × 73 cm)
Don Bachardy Papers

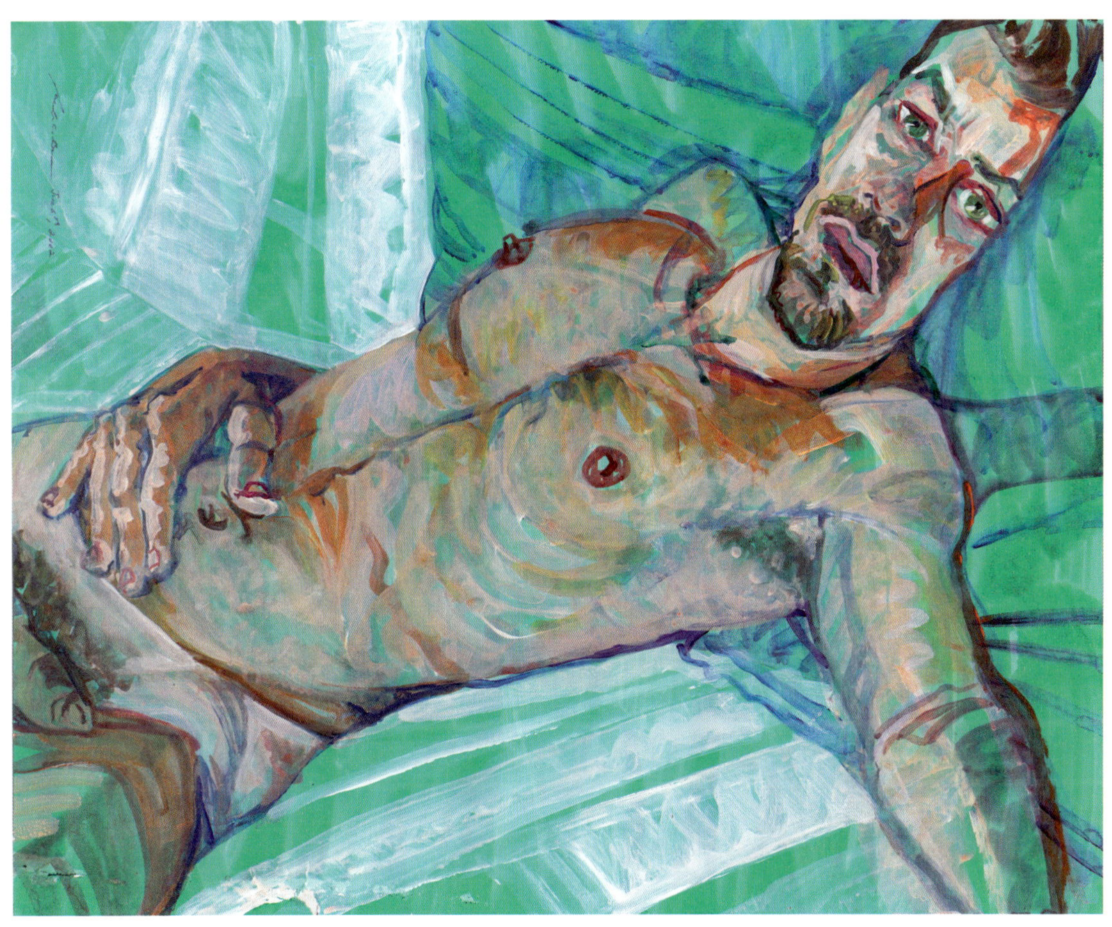

Jake Burgess, June 6, 2002 (no. 3)
Acrylic on paper, 23 × 29 in. (58.4 × 73.7 cm)
The Howarth & Smith Collection of Don Bachardy

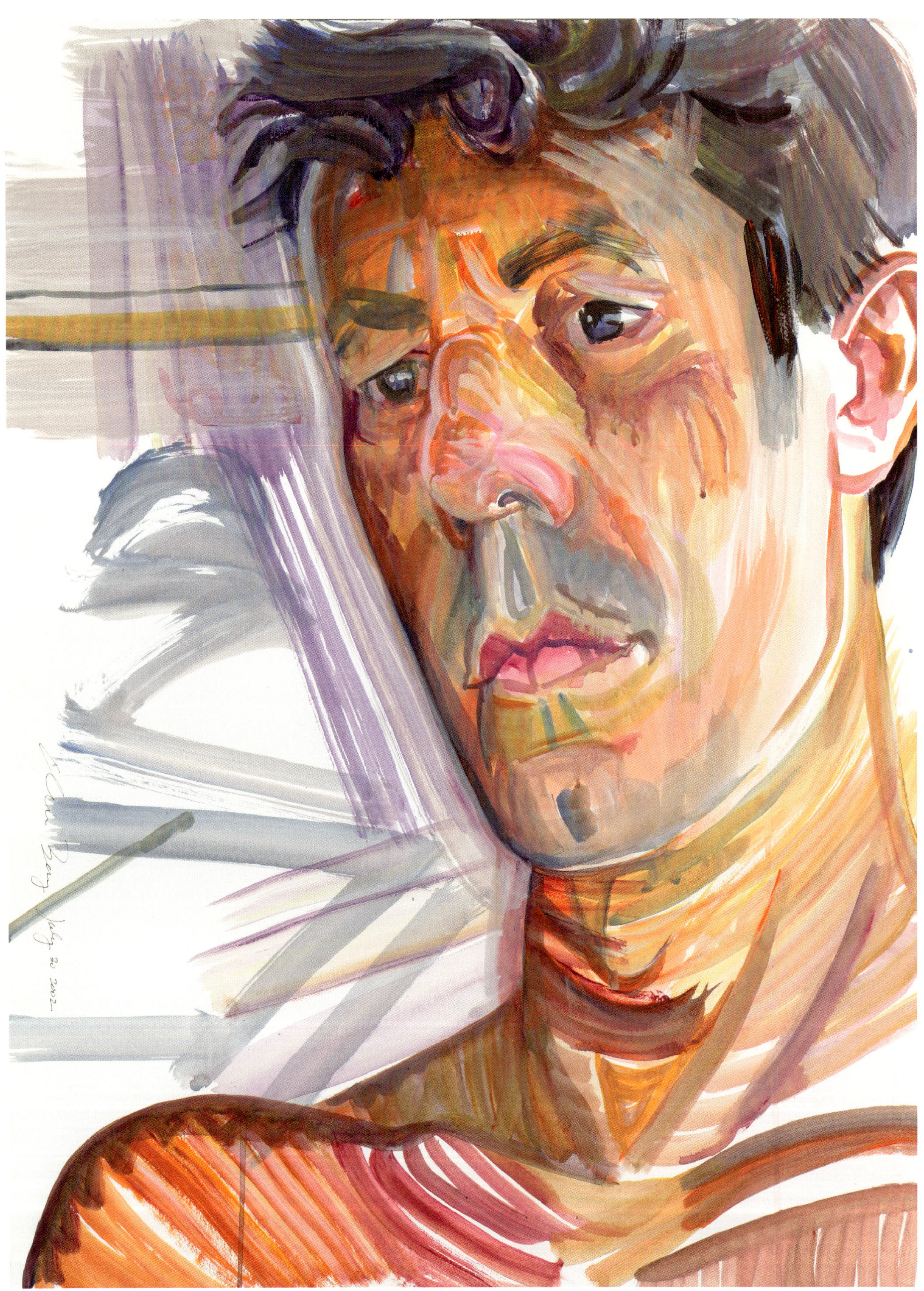

Alan Berry, July 30, 2002 (no. 1)
Acrylic on paper, 30 × 22 in. (76.2 × 55.9 cm)
The Howarth & Smith Collection of Don Bachardy

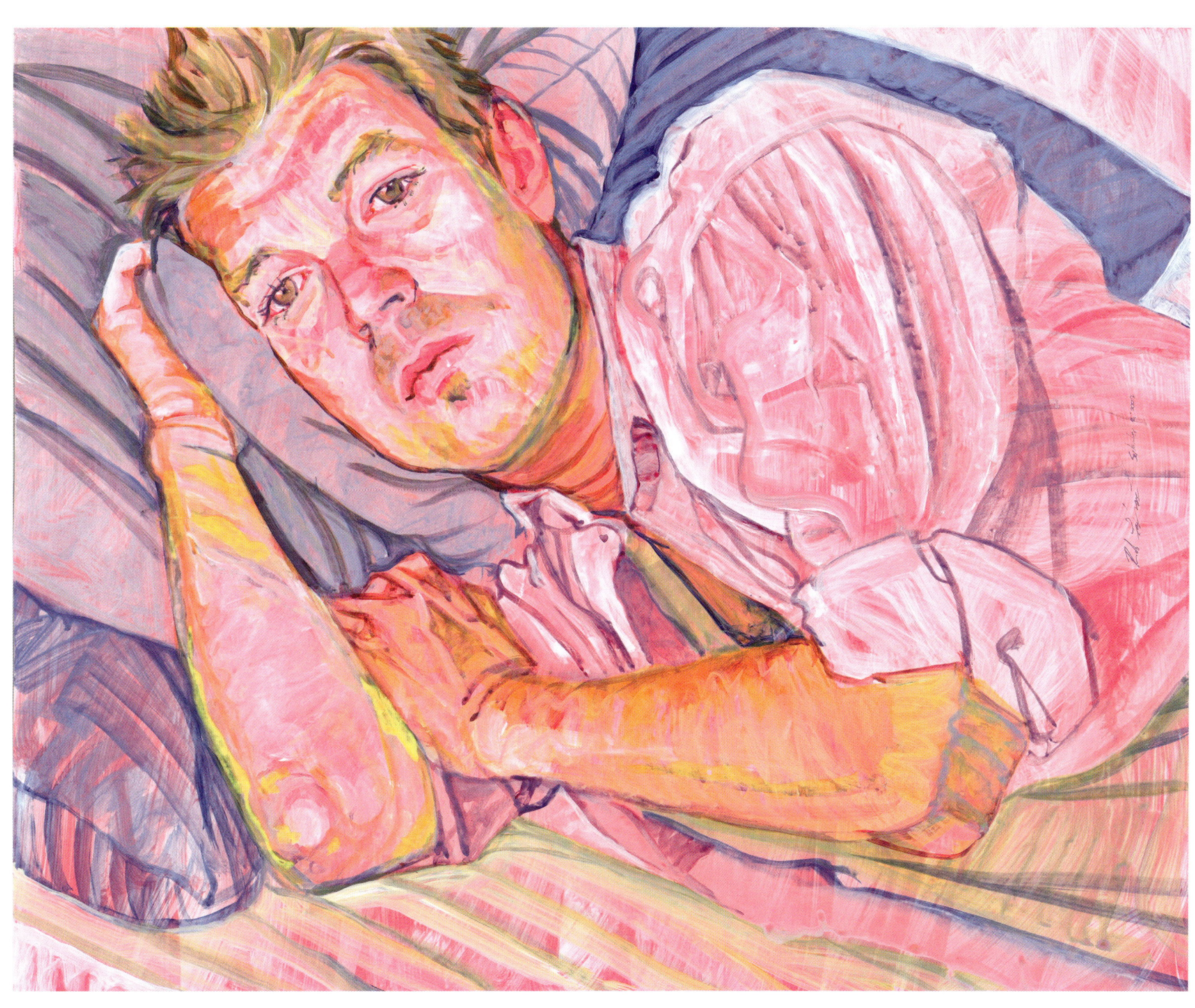

Rob III, September 2, 2002 (no. 2)
Acrylic on paper, 23 × 29 in. (58.4 × 73.7 cm)

143

The Howarth & Smith Collection of Don Bachardy

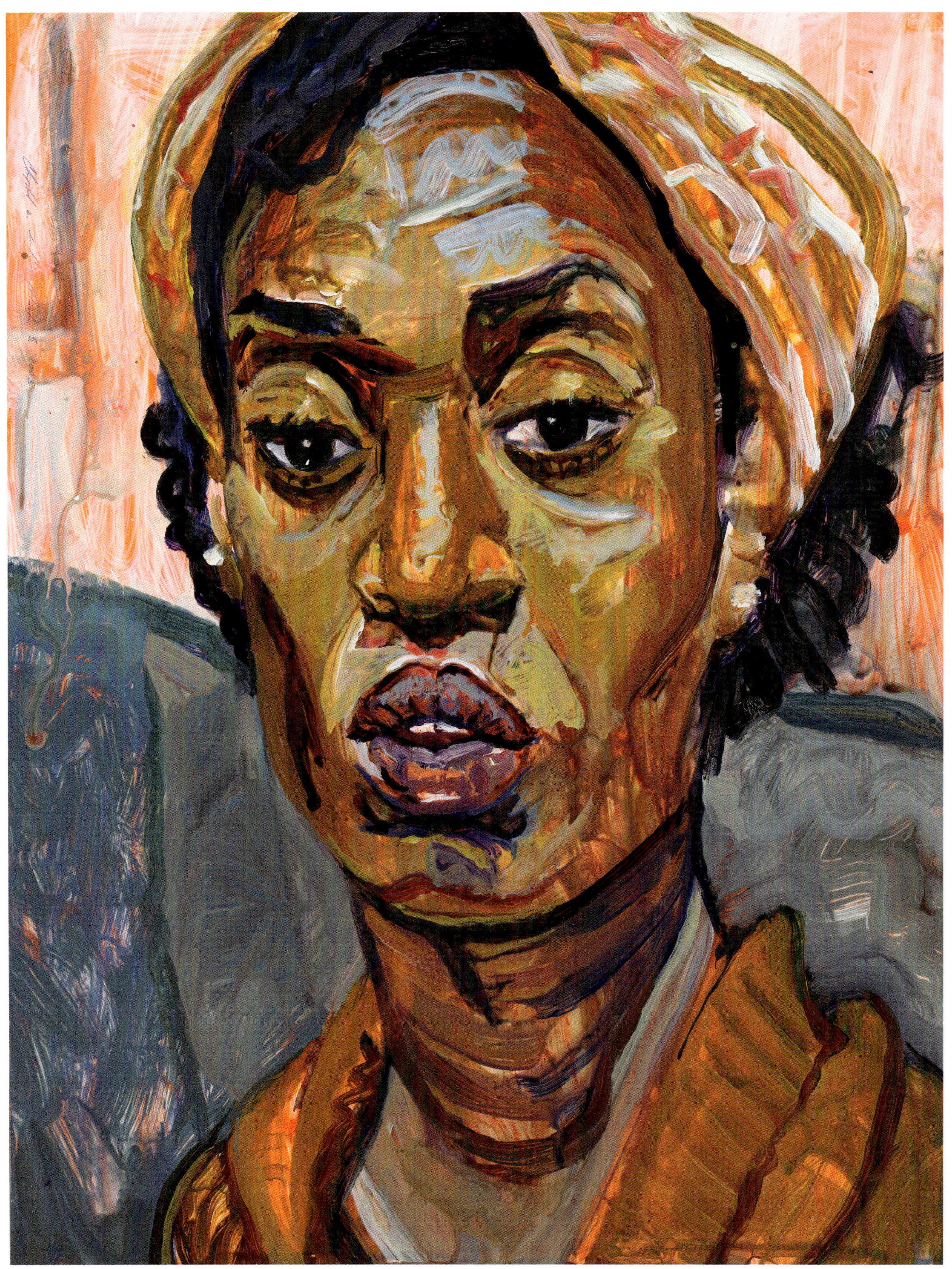

Crystal Martin, March 5, 2003 (no. 4)
Acrylic on paper, 26 × 20 in. (66 × 50.8 cm)
The Howarth & Smith Collection of Don Bachardy

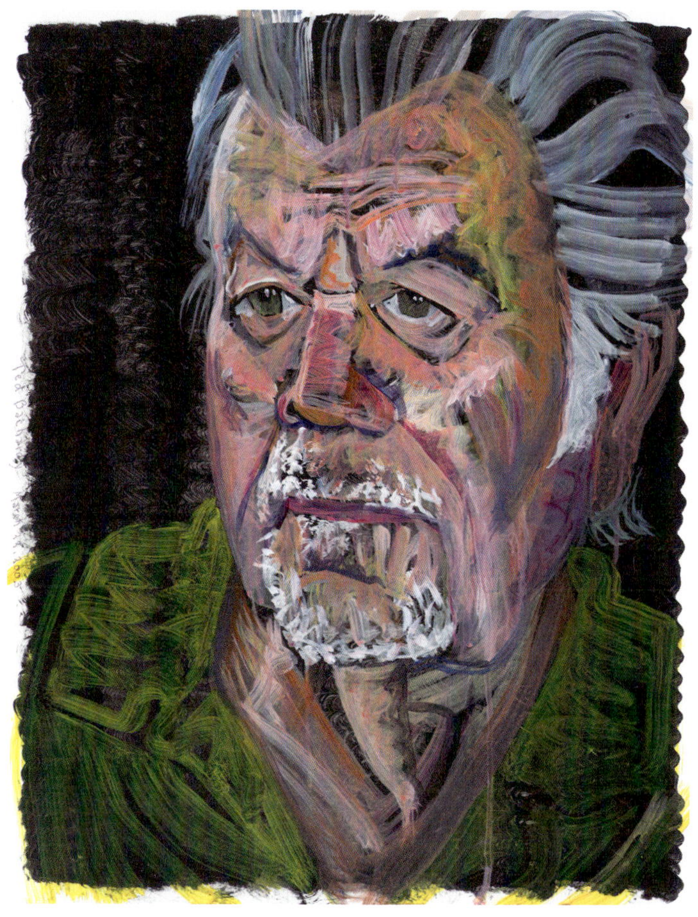

Ted Bachardy, March 23, 2003 (no. 3)
Acrylic on paper, 29 × 23 in.
(73.7 × 58.4 cm)
Don Bachardy Papers

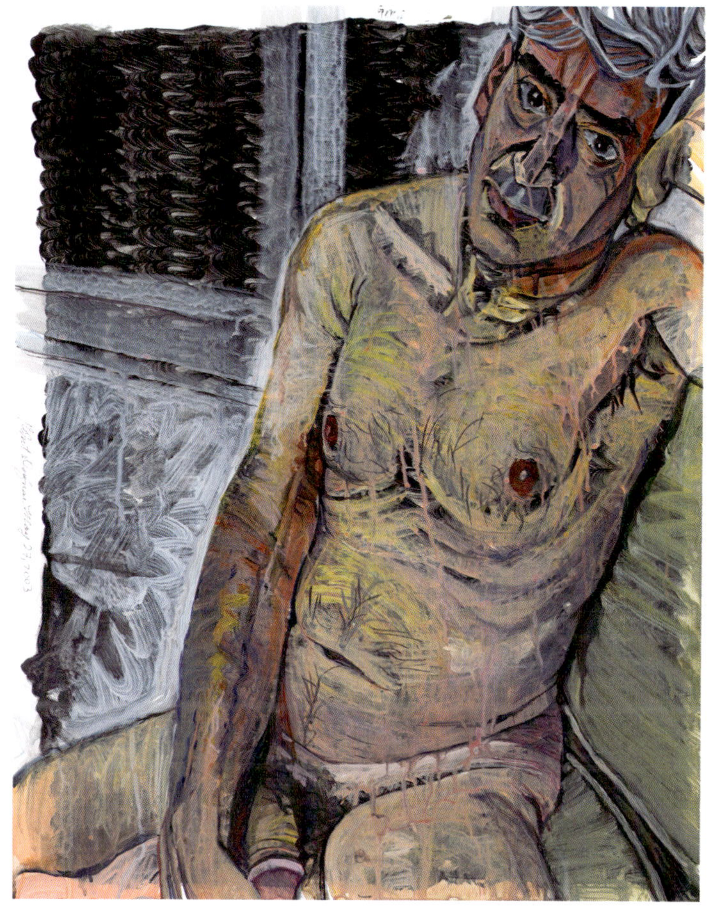

Robert Dorfman, May 27, 2003 (no. 3)
Acrylic on paper, 29 × 23 in. (73.7 × 58.4 cm)
Don Bachardy Papers

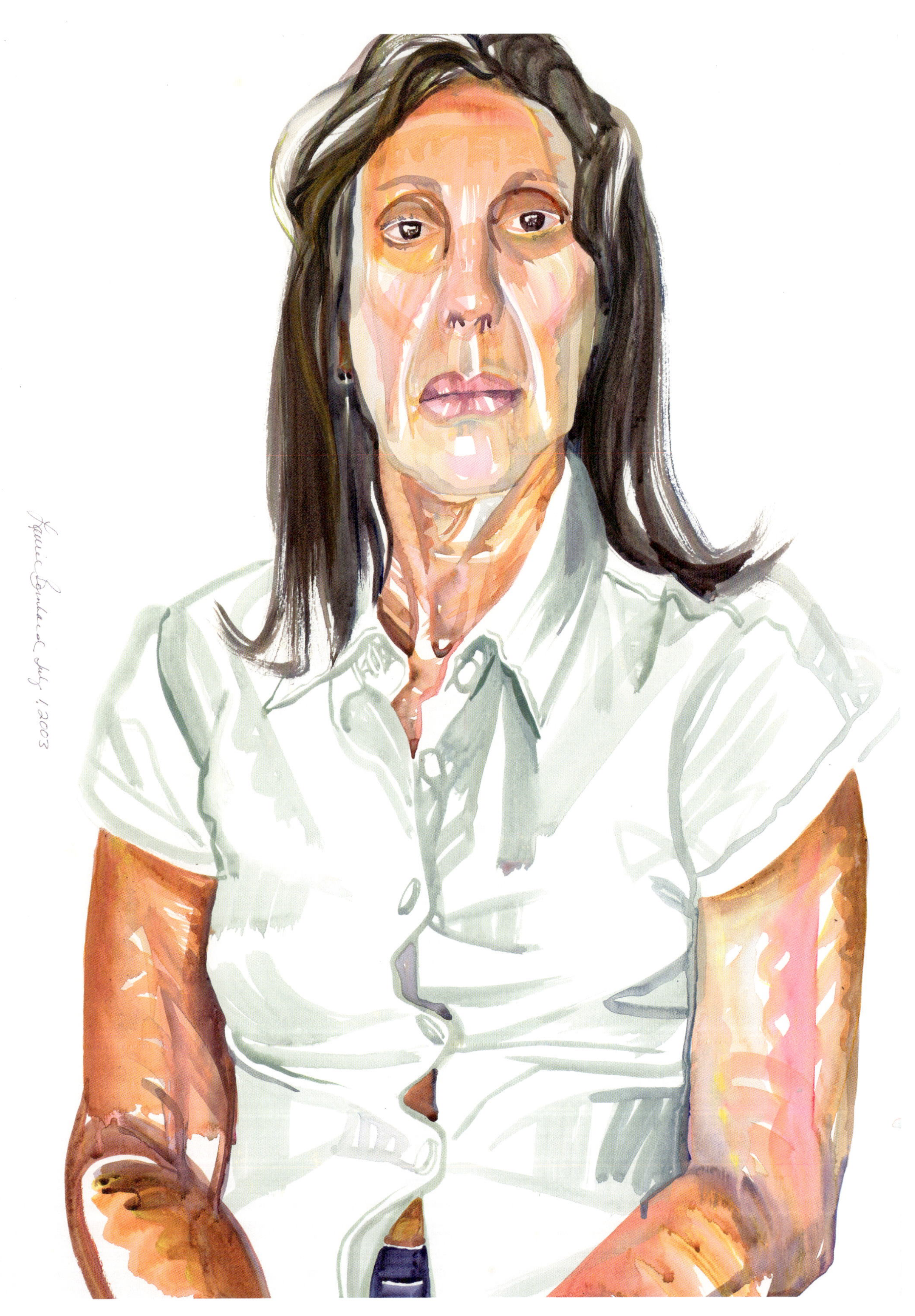

Laurie Bernhard, July 1, 2003 (no. 2)
Acrylic on paper, 29¾ × 22⅛ in. (75.6 × 56.2 cm)
Don Bachardy Papers

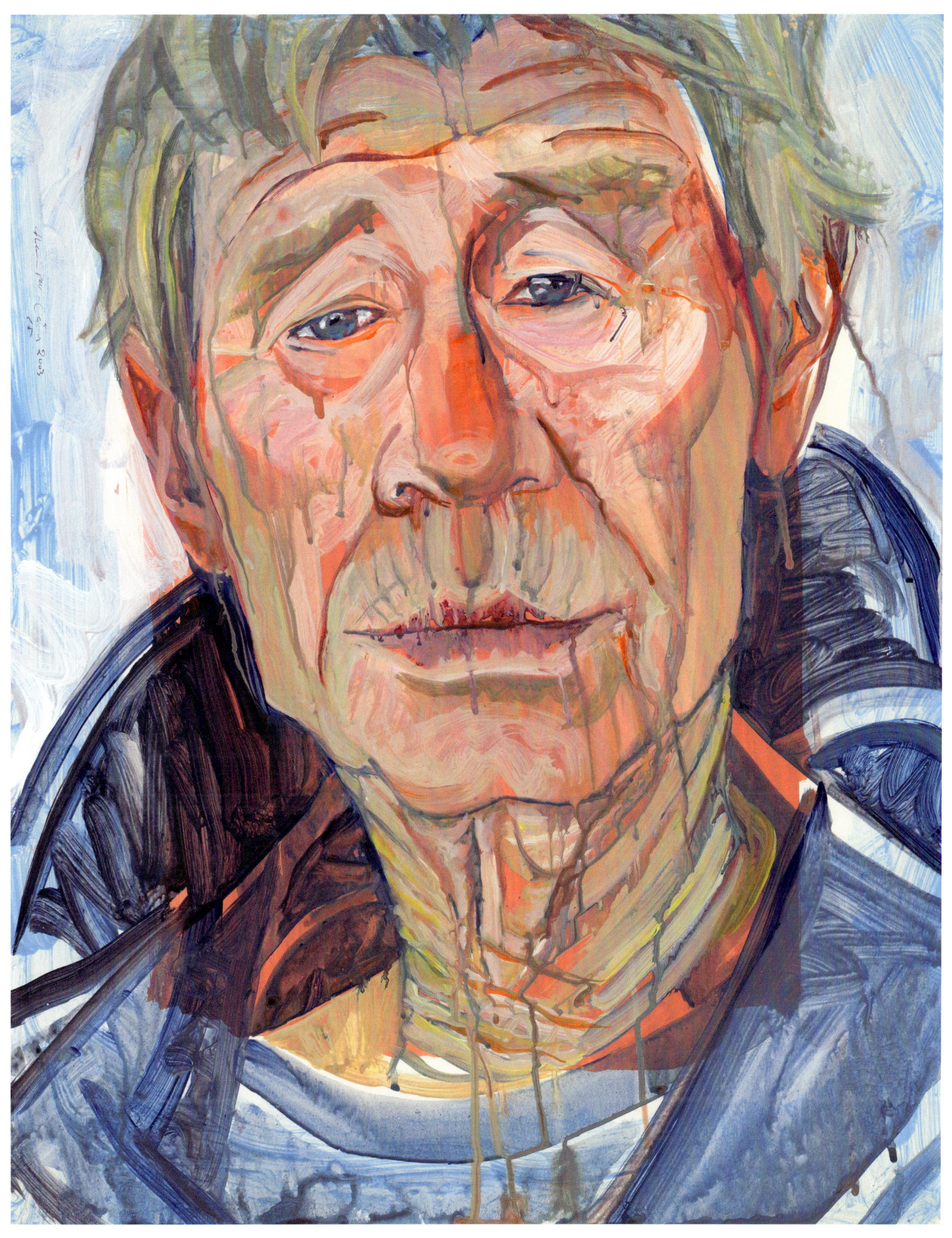

Michael Parks, October 15, 2003 (no. 3)
Acrylic on paper, 29 × 23 in. (73.7 × 58.4 cm)
Don Bachardy Papers

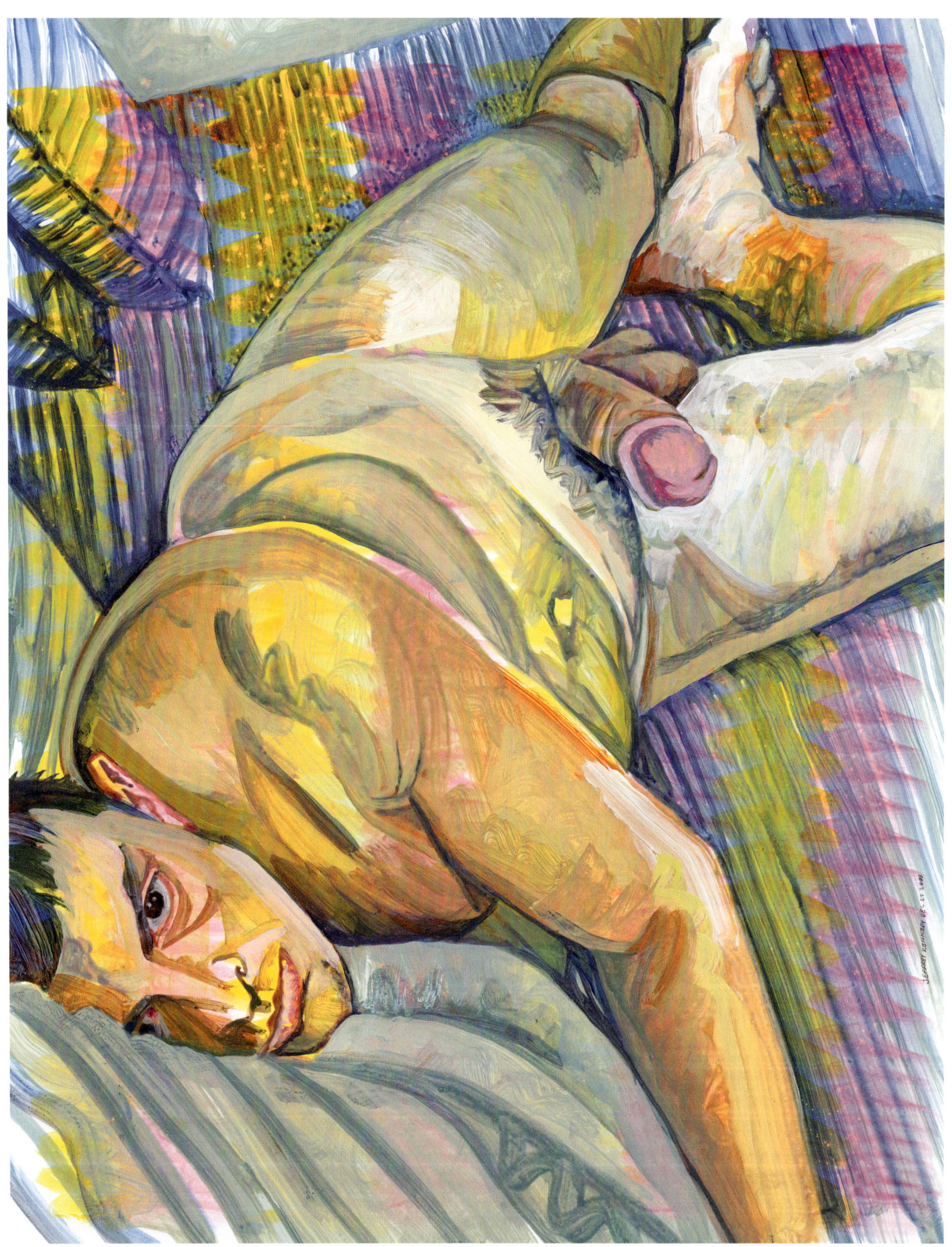

Jeffrey Kennedy, December 27, 2003 (no. 3)
Acrylic on paper, 28⅞ × 23 in. (73.3 × 58.4 cm)
Don Bachardy Papers

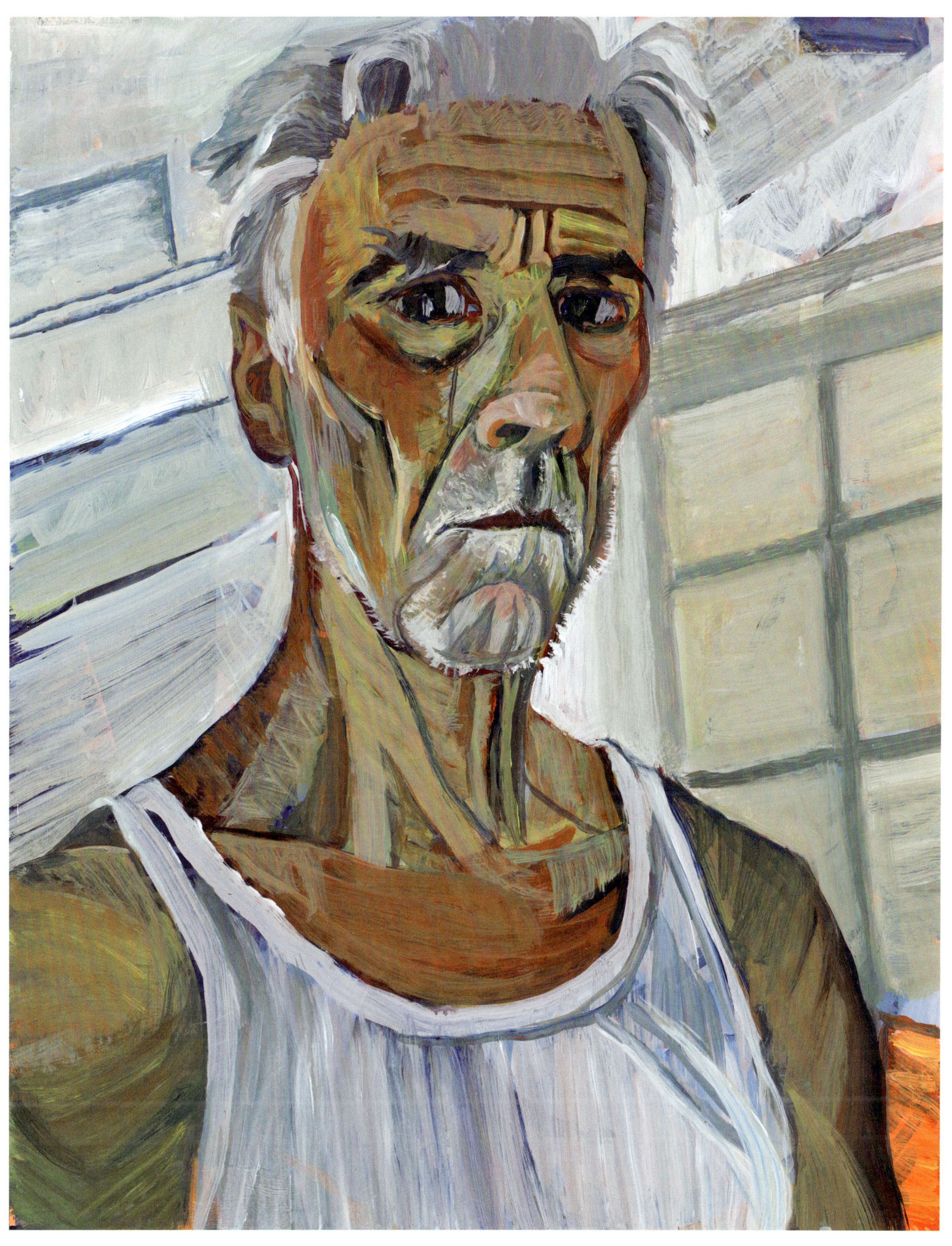

Self-Portrait, July 4, 2004
Acrylic on paper, 28⅞ × 23 in. (73.3 × 58.4 cm)
Don Bachardy Papers

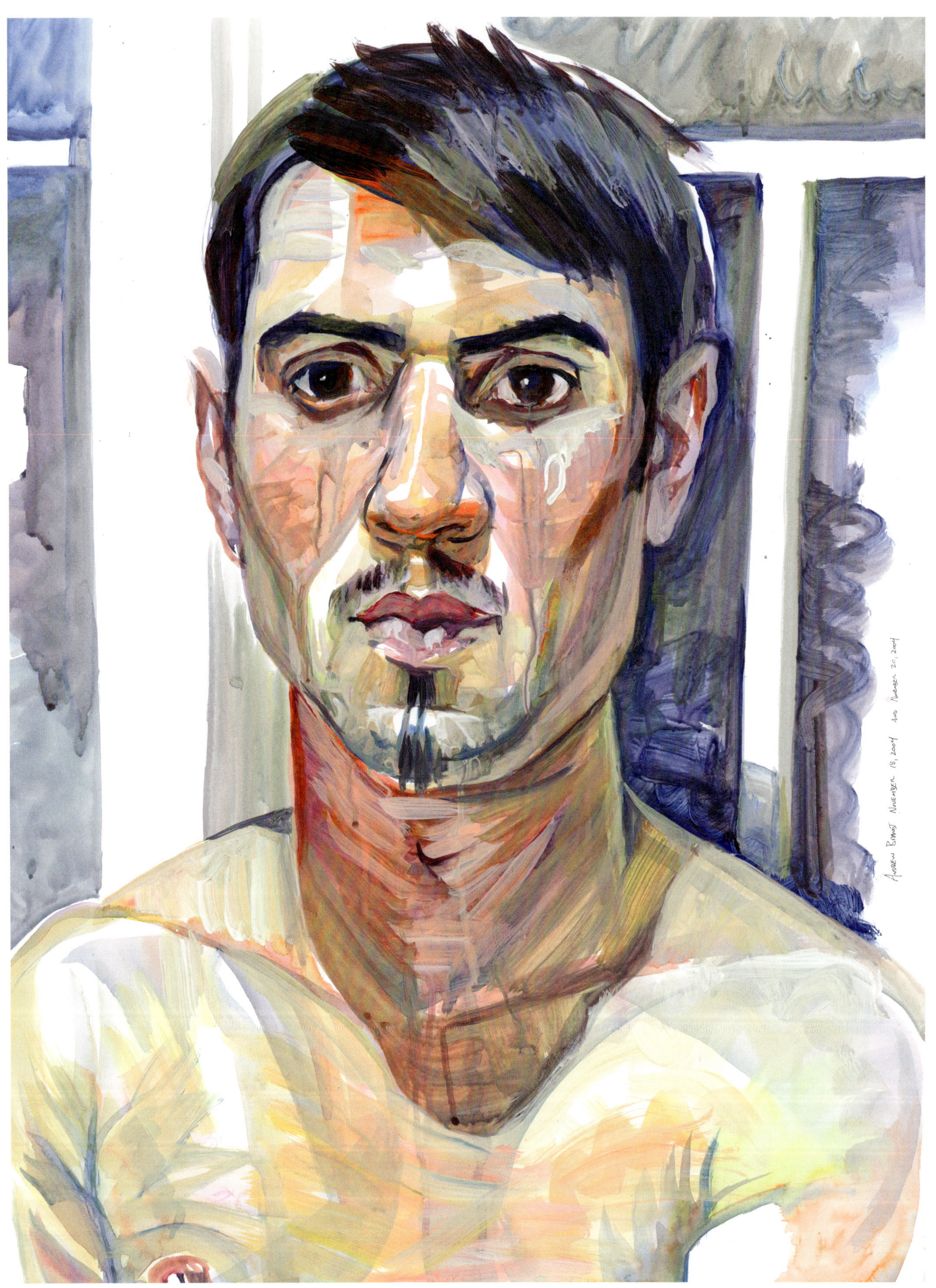

Andrew Brandt, November 18 and 20, 2004 (no. 4)
Acrylic on paper, 29⅞ × 22¼ in. (75.9 × 56.5 cm)
Don Bachardy Papers

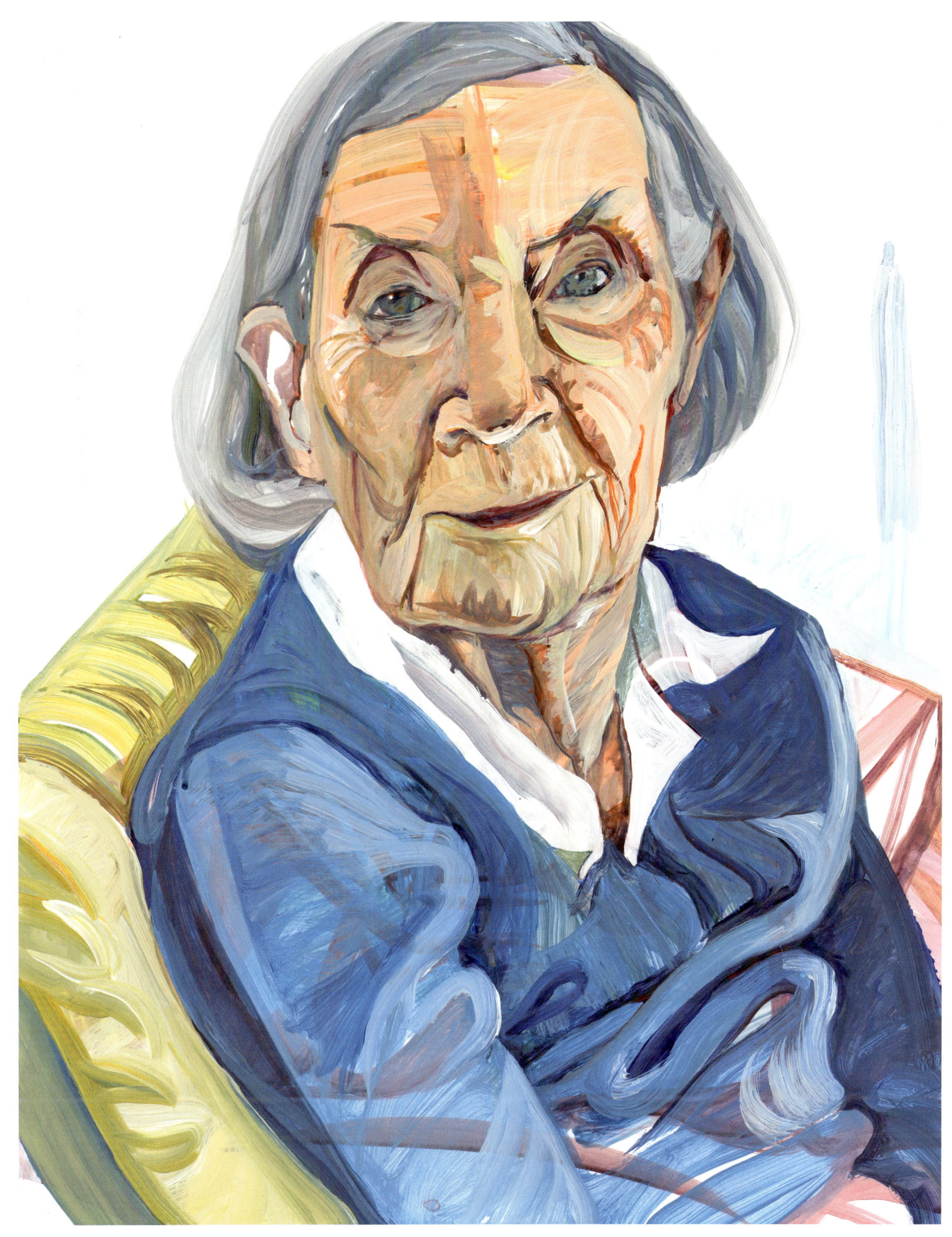

Barbara Diamond, September 12, 2005 (no. 3)
Acrylic on paper, 29 × 23 in. (73.7 × 58.4 cm)
Don Bachardy Papers

Sandro Kopp, November 10, 2011 (no. 1)
Acrylic on paper, 29 × 23 in.
(73.7 × 58.4 cm)
Don Bachardy Papers

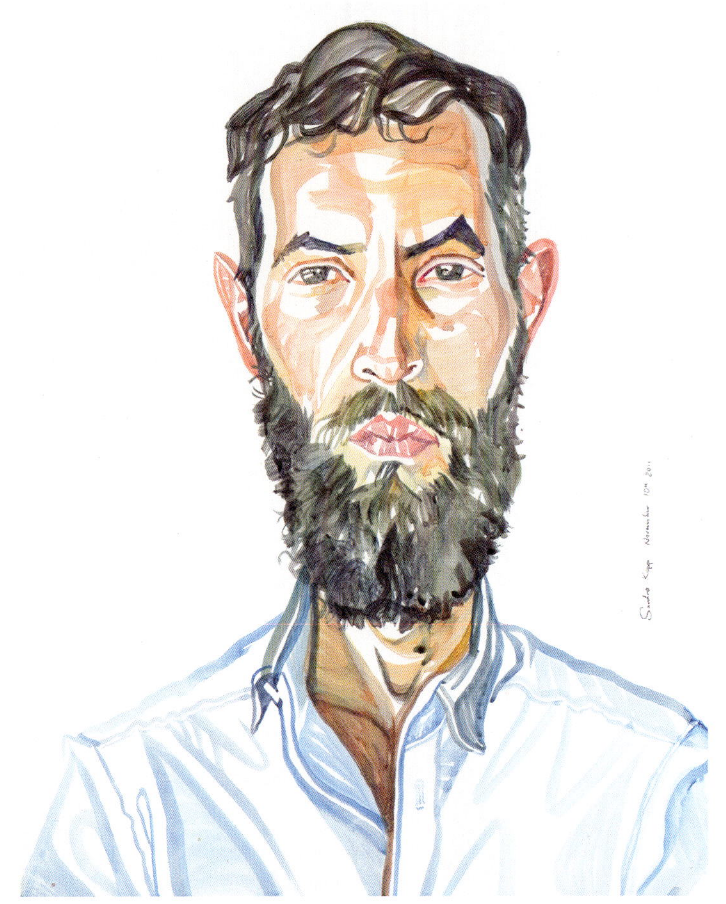

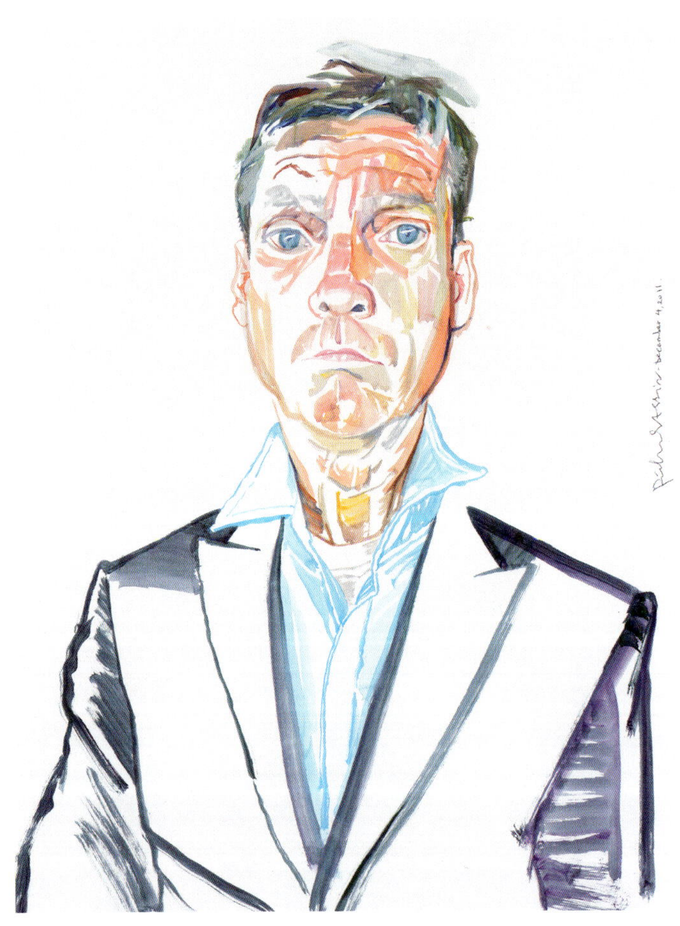

Richard Sassin, December 4, 2011 (no. 2)
Acrylic on paper, 29 × 23 in. (73.7 × 58.4 cm)
Don Bachardy Papers

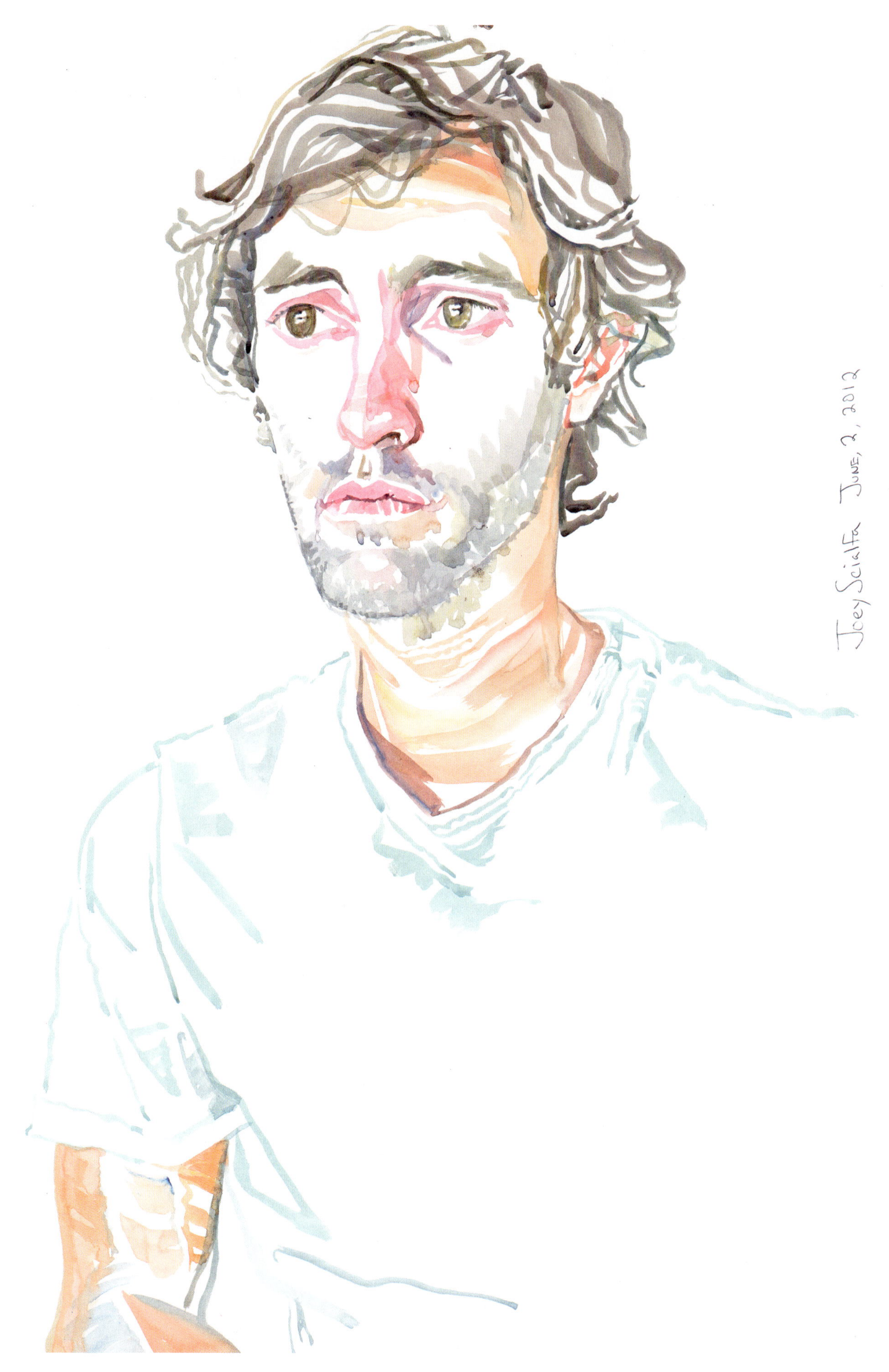

Joey Scialfa, June 2, 2012 (no. 1)
Acrylic on paper, 28⅞ × 22⅞ in. (73.3 × 58.1 cm)
Don Bachardy Papers

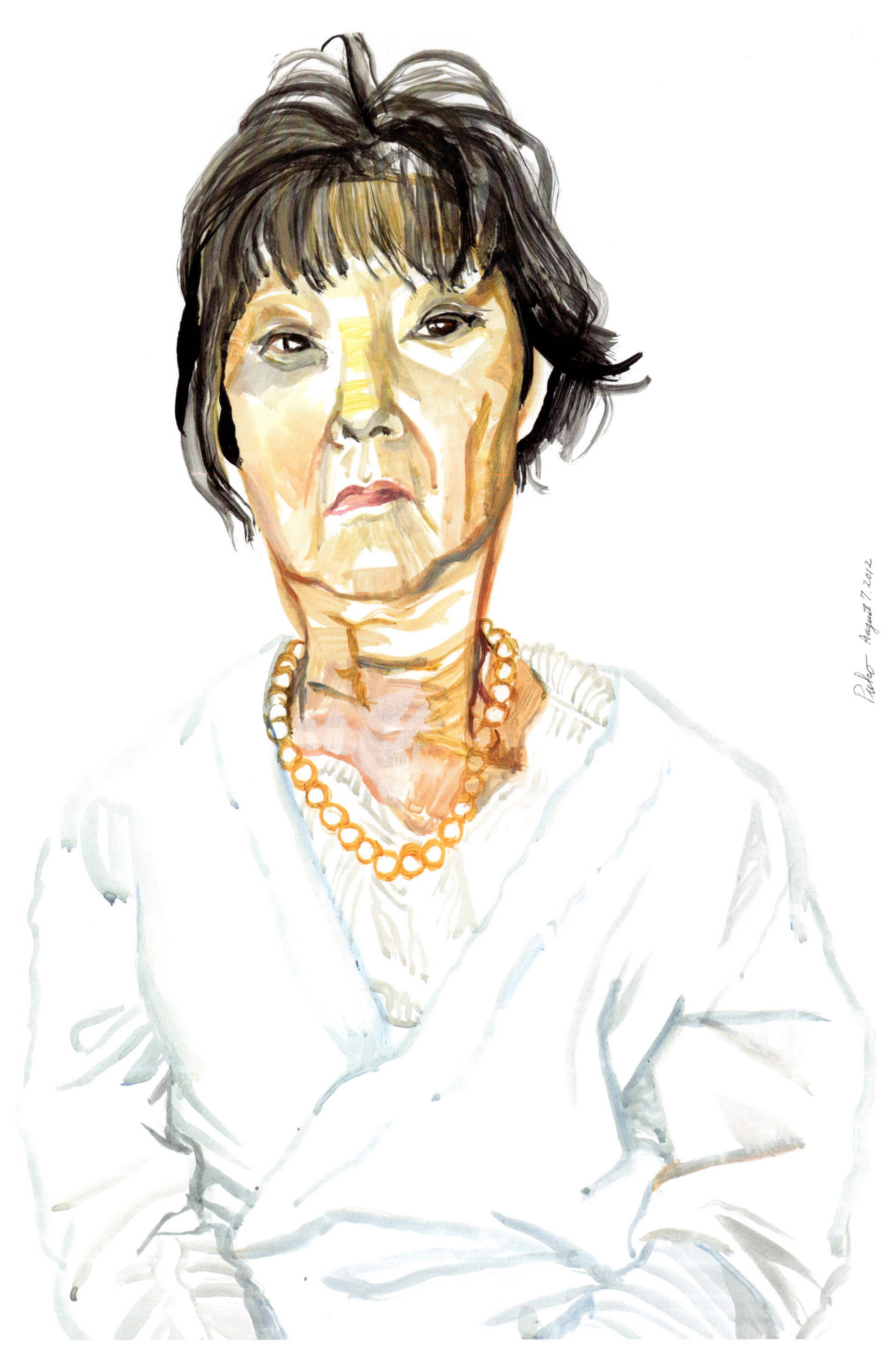

Puko, August 7, 2012 (no. 2)
Acrylic on paper, 29 × 23 in. (73.7 × 58.4 cm)
Don Bachardy Papers

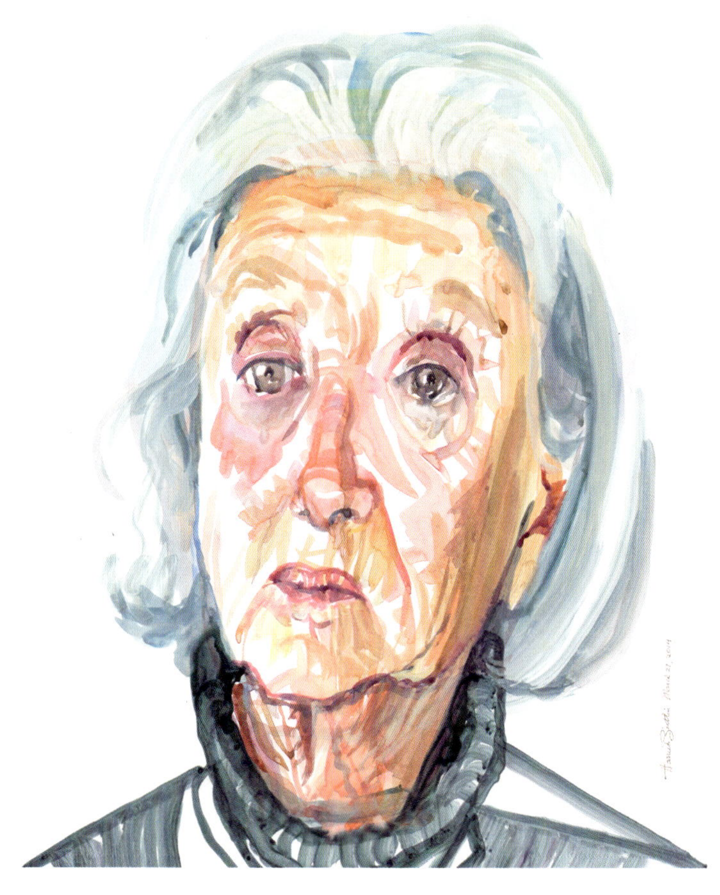

Harriet Zeitlin, March 27, 2014
Acrylic on paper, 33½ × 25⅛ in.
(85.1 × 63.8 cm)
Don Bachardy Papers

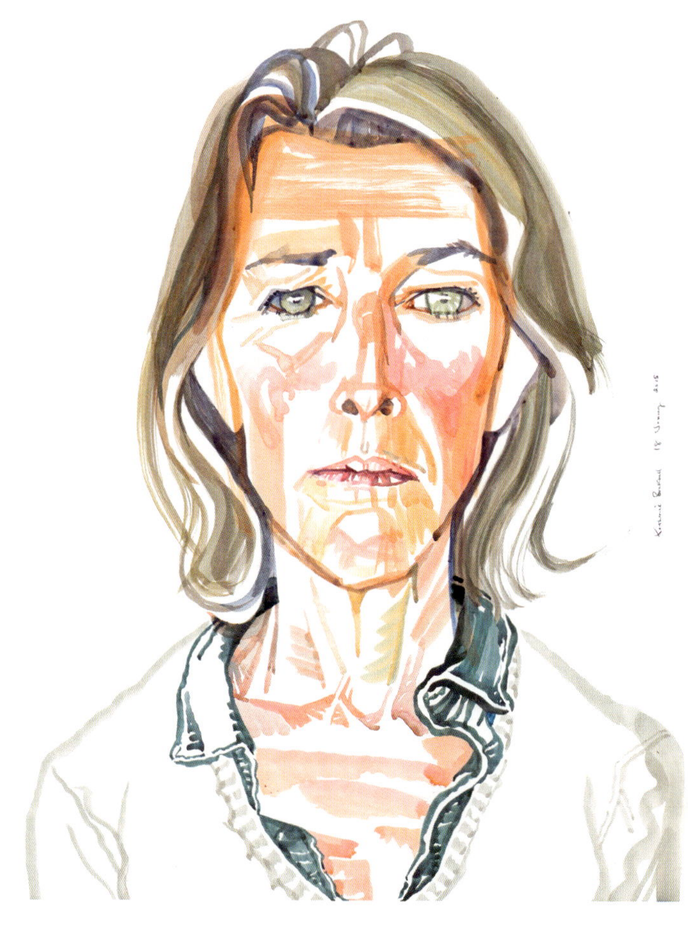

Katherine Bucknell, January 18, 2015
Acrylic on paper, 28⅞ × 23 in. (73.3 × 58.4 cm)

Don Bachardy Papers

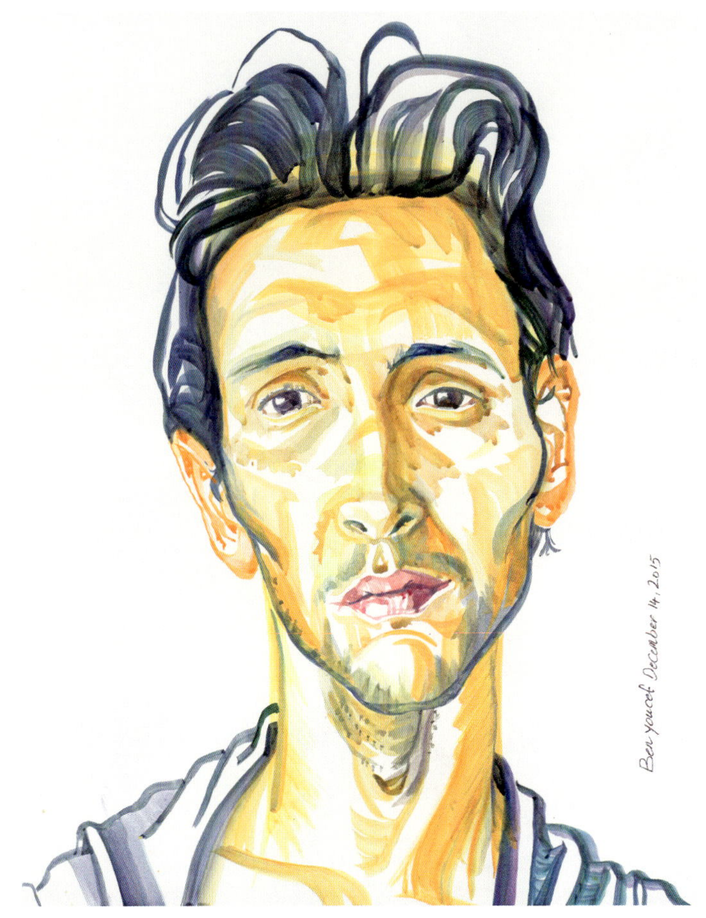

Ben Youcef, December 14, 2015
Acrylic on paper, 29 × 23 in.
(73.7 × 58.4 cm)
Don Bachardy Papers

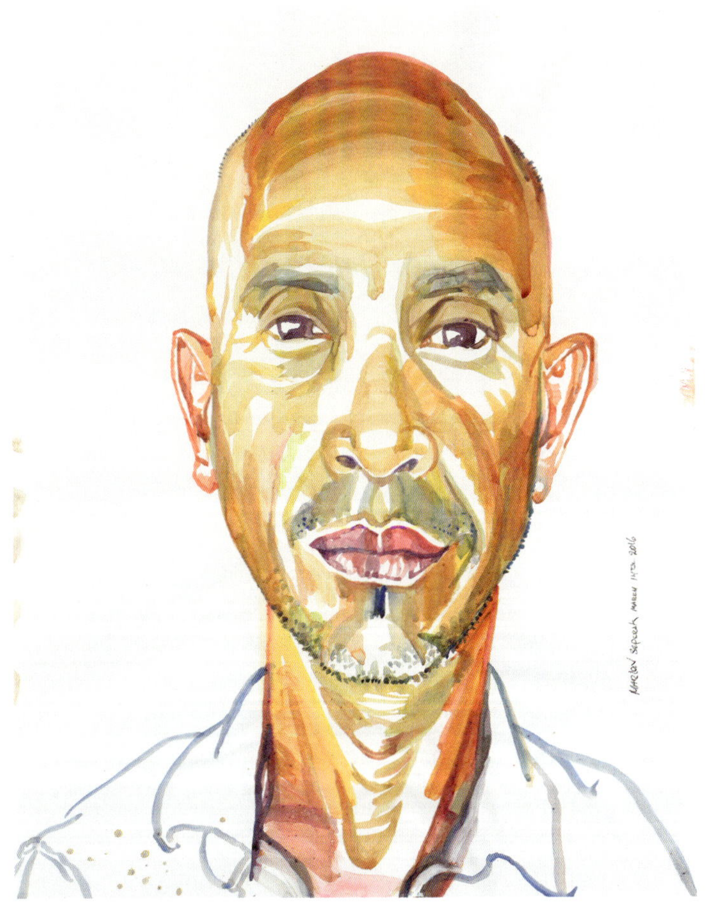

Marlon Seperak, March 14, 2016 (no. 1)
Acrylic on paper, 29 × 23 in. (73.7 × 58.4 cm)
Don Bachardy Papers

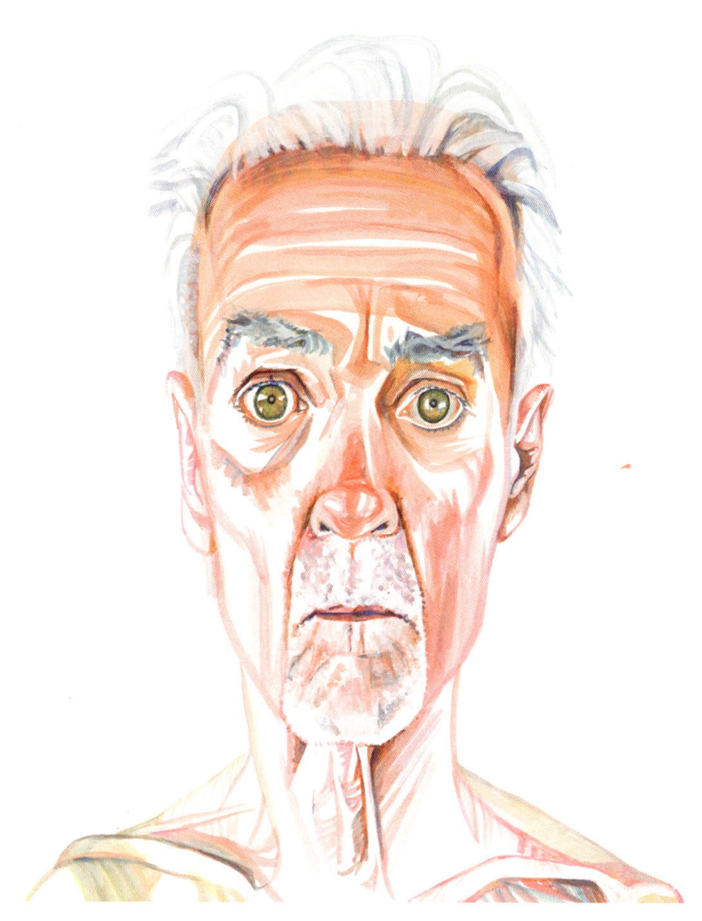

Self-Portrait, March 19, 2016 (no. 1)
Acrylic on paper, 29 × 23 in.
(73.7 × 58.4 cm)
Don Bachardy Papers

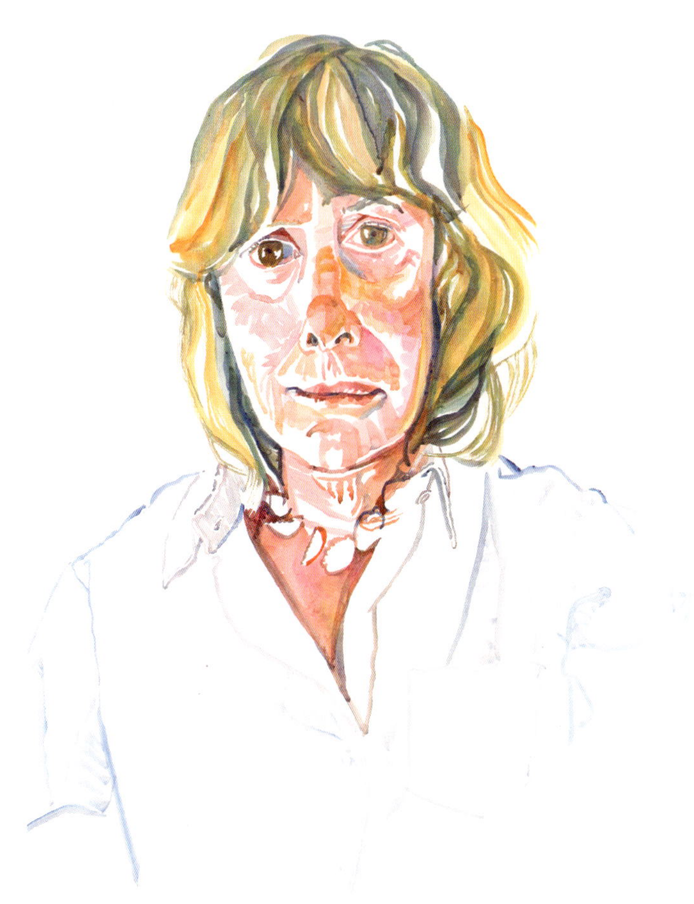

Penny Little Hawks, May 30, 2016
Acrylic on paper, $28\frac{7}{8}$ × 23 in. (73.3 × 58.4 cm)
Don Bachardy Papers

Peter Macaulay, February 20, 2017
Acrylic on paper, 29 × 23 in.
(73.7 × 58.4 cm)
Don Bachardy Papers

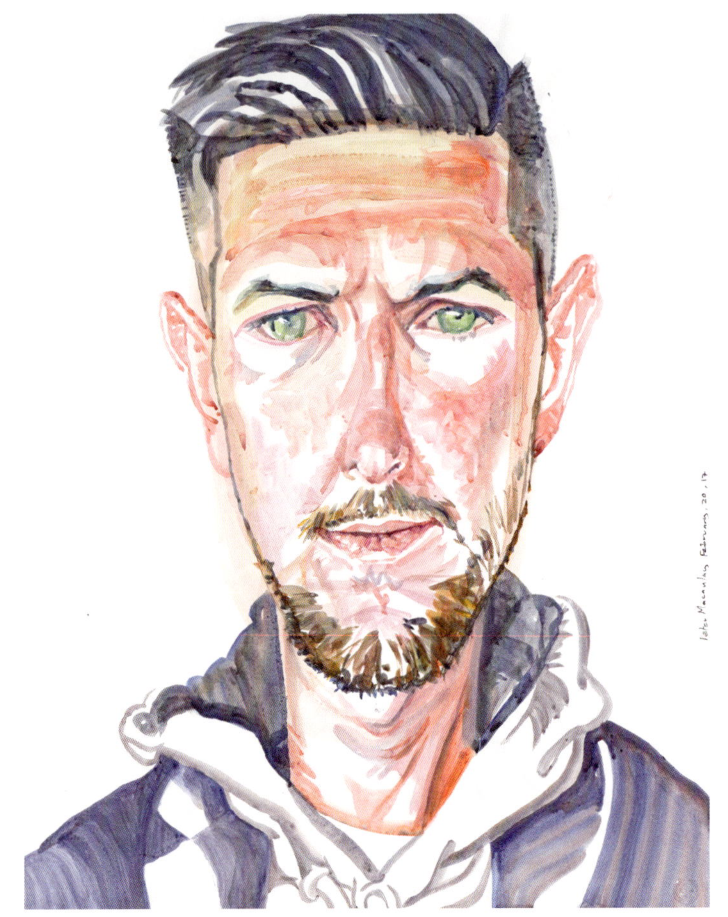

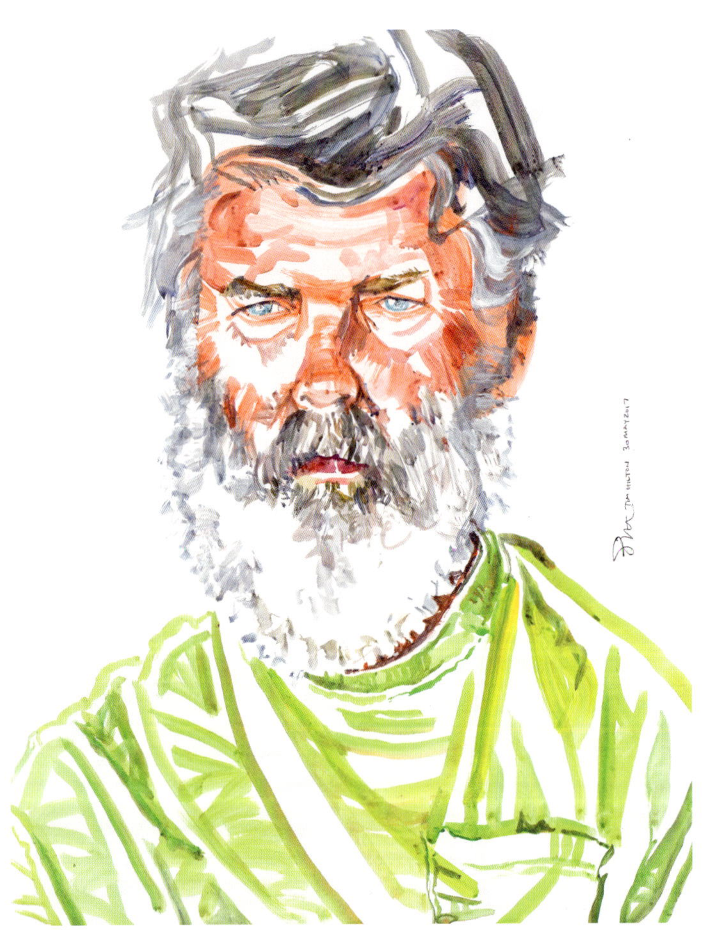

Tim Hilton, May 30, 2017
Acrylic on paper, 29 × 23 in. (73.7 × 58.4 cm)
Don Bachardy Papers

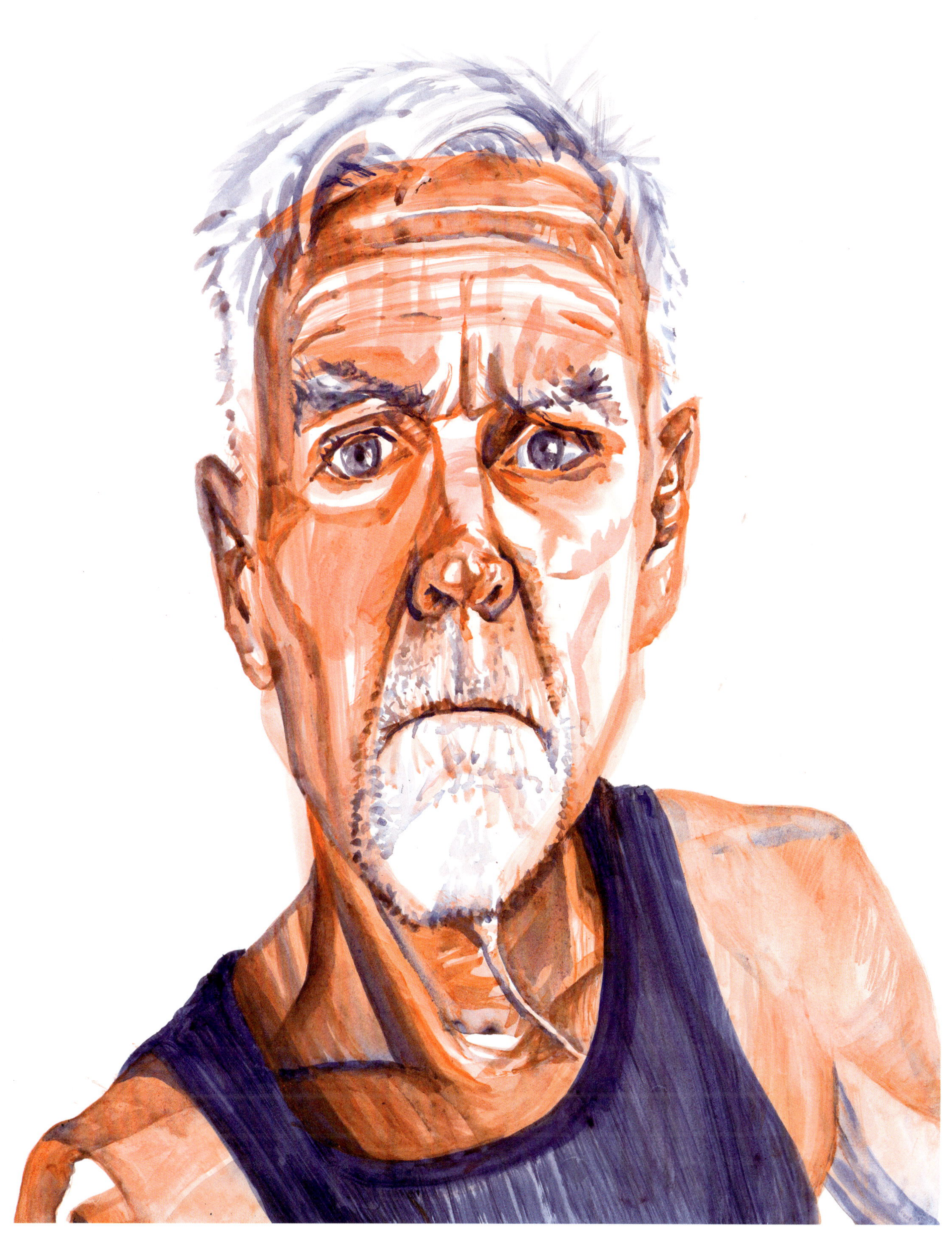

Self-Portrait, August 8, 2018
Acrylic on paper, 29 × 23 in. (73.7 × 58.4 cm)
Don Bachardy Papers

Self-Portrait, November 19, 2018
Acrylic on paper, 23 × 29 in.
(58.4 × 73.7 cm)
Don Bachardy Papers

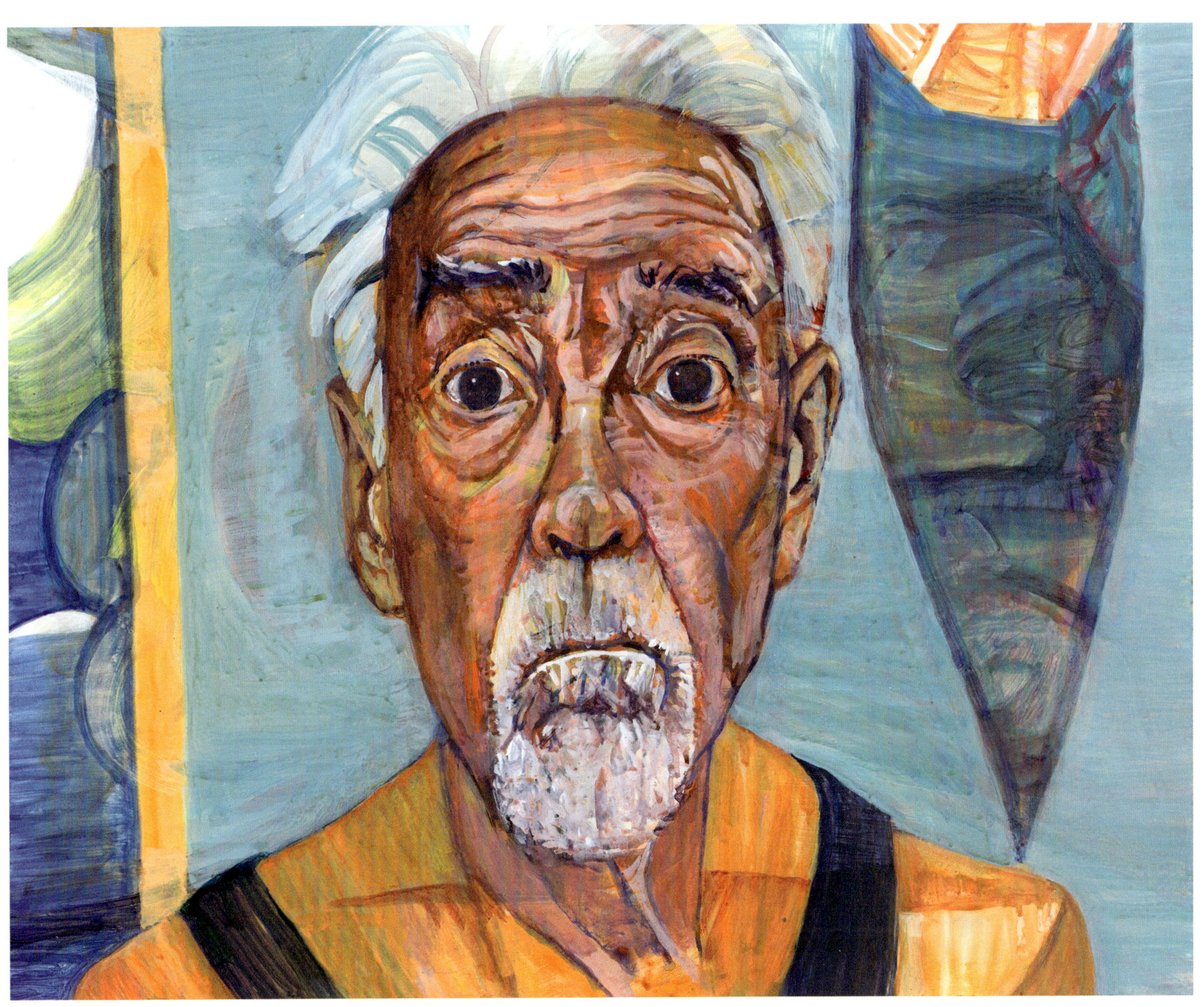

Guido Santi, January 1, 2019 (no. 2)
Acrylic on paper, 28⅞ × 23 in.
(73.3 × 58.4 cm)
Don Bachardy Papers

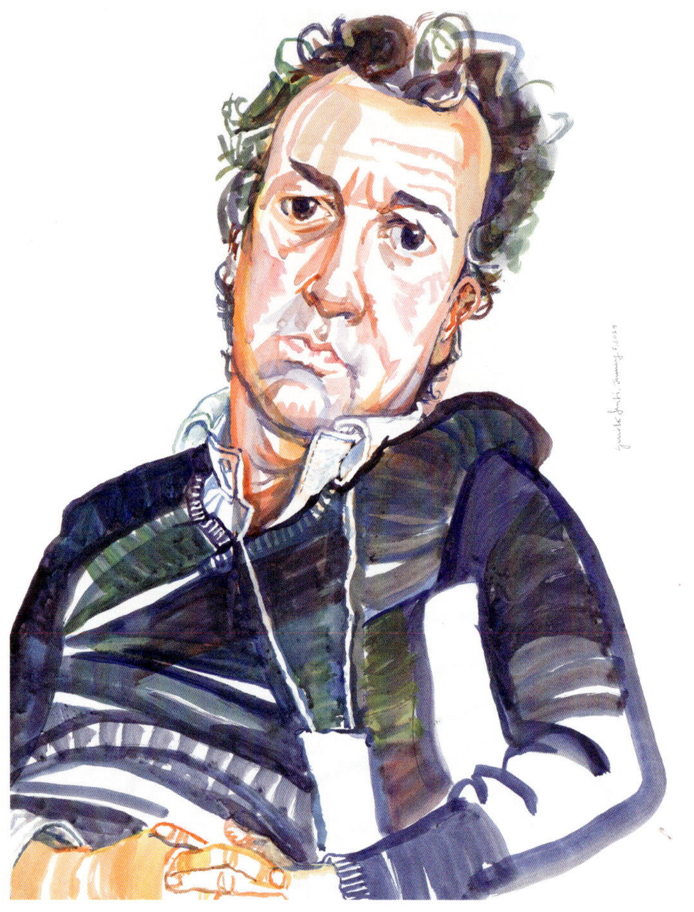

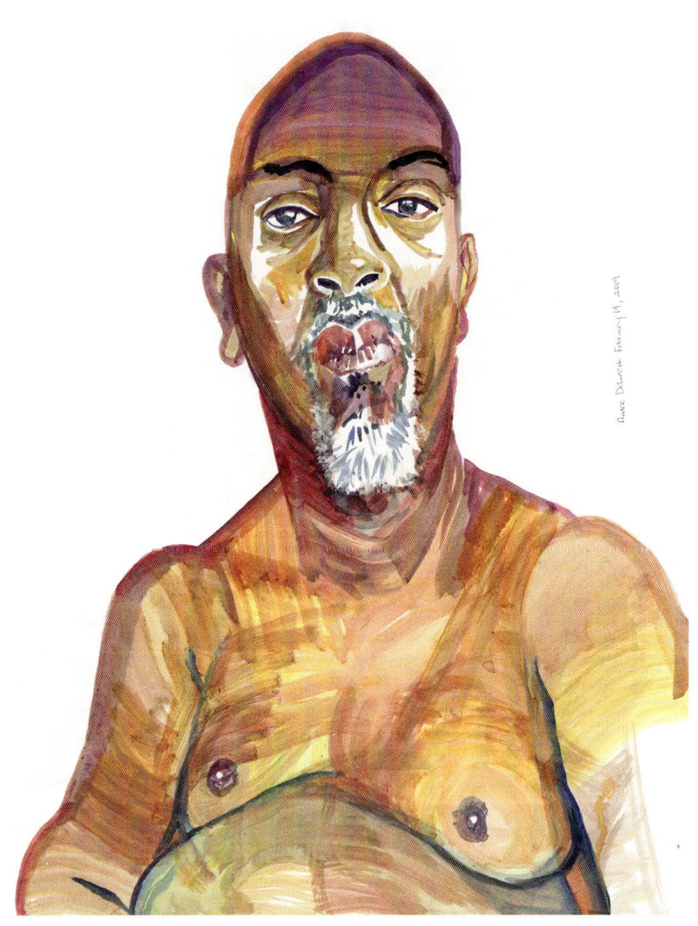

Andre DeLoach, February 19, 2019
Acrylic on paper, 28⅞ × 23 in. (73.3 × 58.4 cm)
Don Bachardy Papers

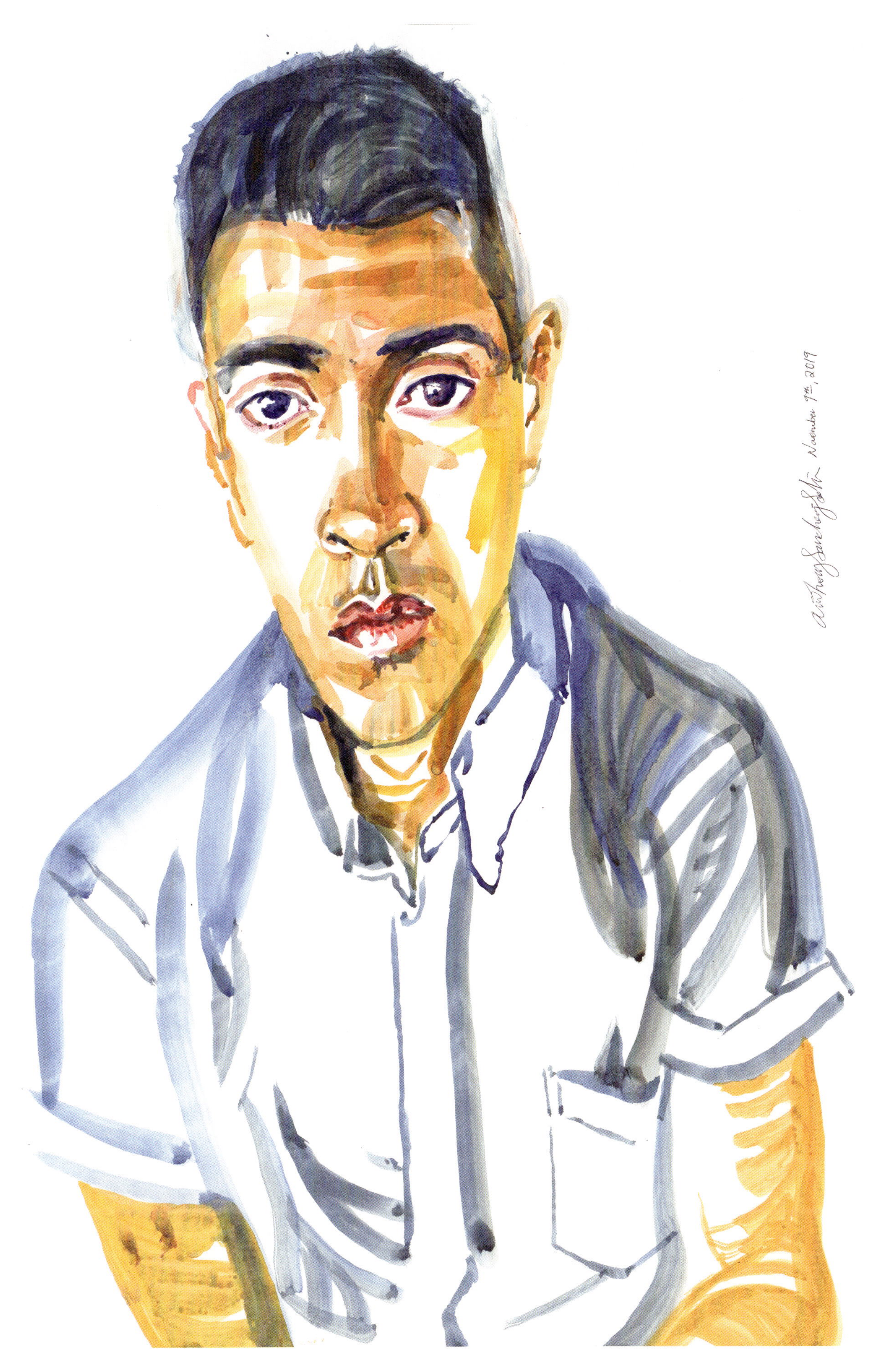

Anthony Sanchez-Solis, November 9, 2019 (no. 1)
Acrylic on paper, 29 × 23 in. (73.7 × 58.4 cm)
Don Bachardy Papers

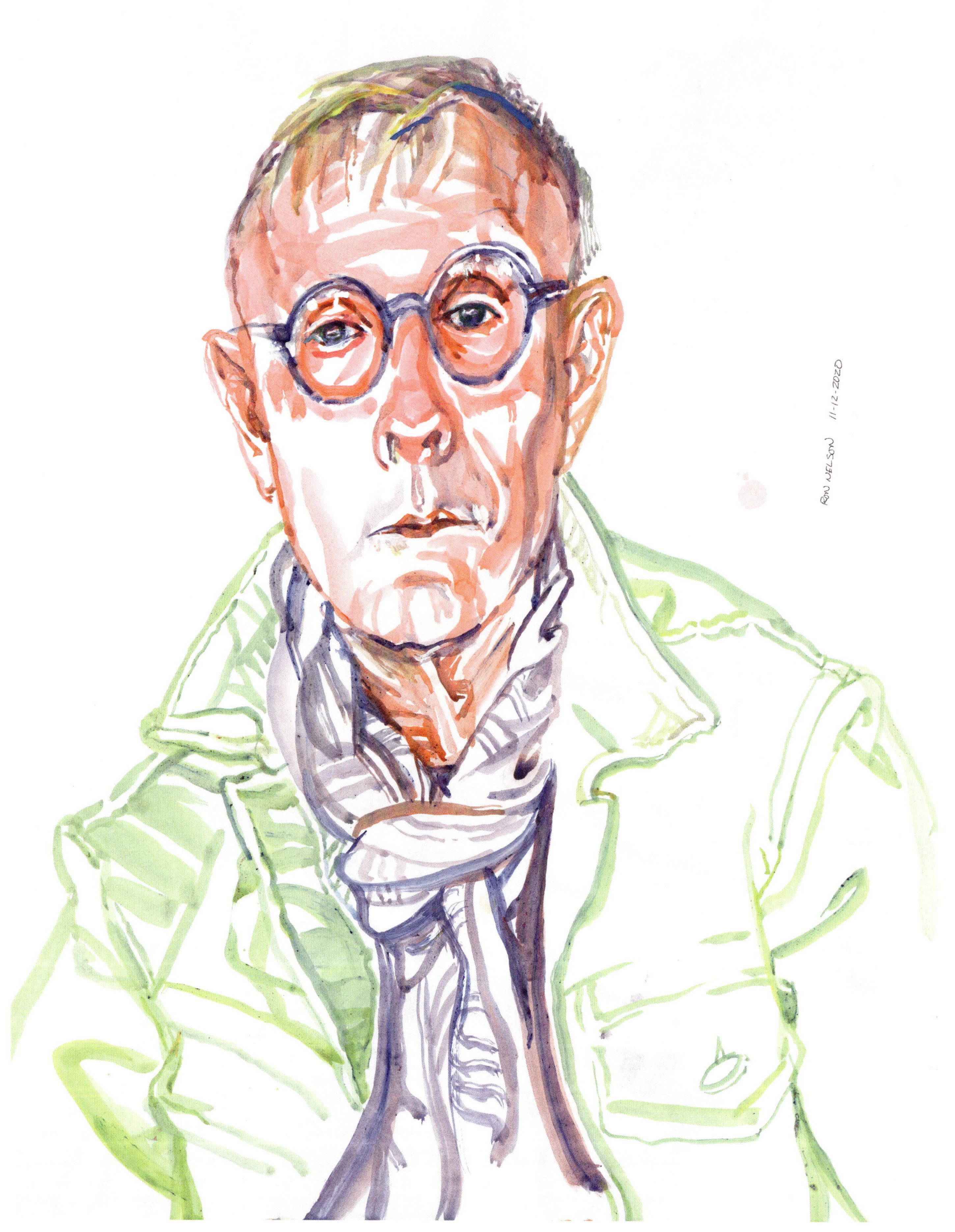

Ron Nelson, November 12, 2020
Acrylic on paper, 28⅞ × 23 in. (73.3 × 58.4 cm)
Don Bachardy Papers

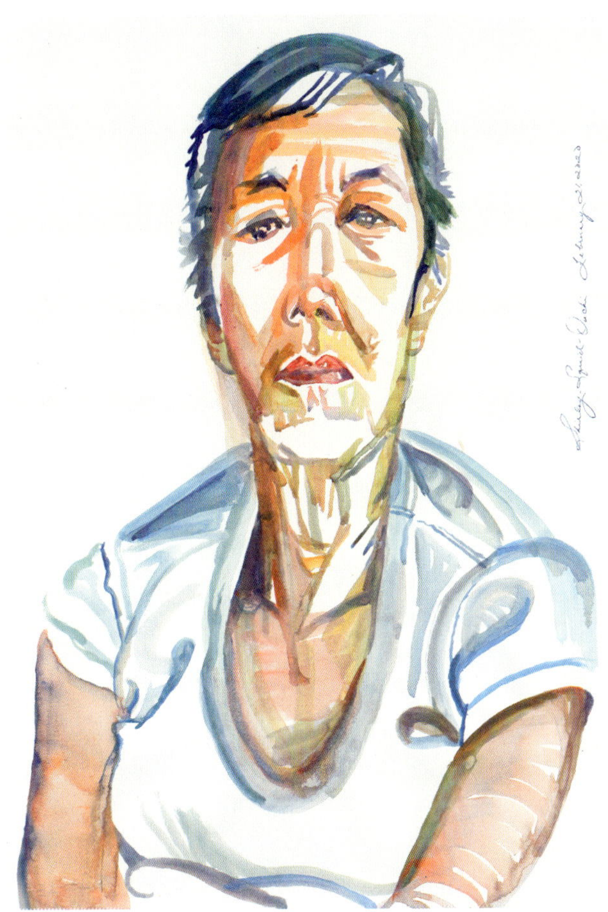

Shirley Squid-Ouchi, February 21, 2020
(no. 1)
Acrylic on paper, 30 × 22 in.
(76.2 × 55.9 cm)
Don Bachardy Papers

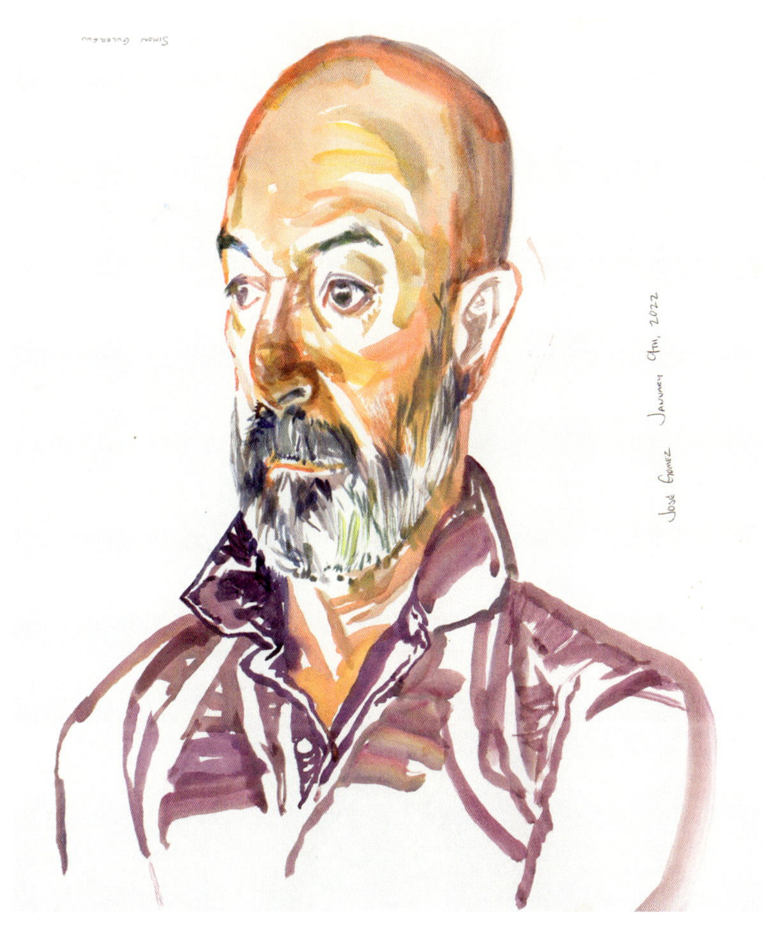

Jose Gomez, January 9, 2022 (no. 1)
Acrylic on paper, 26⅛ × 23 in. (66.4 × 58.4 cm)
Don Bachardy Papers

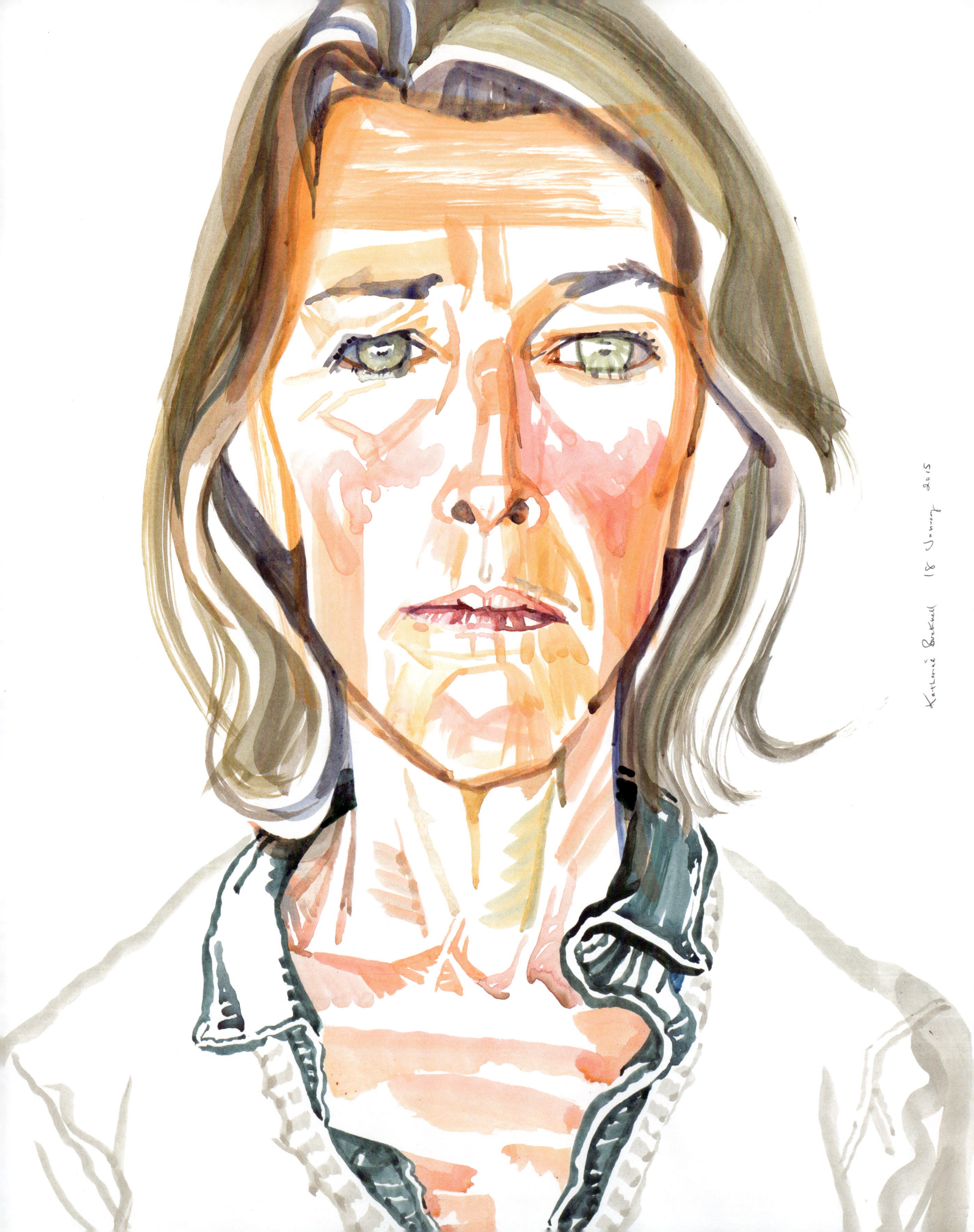

Katherine Bracknell   18 January   2015

CONTRIBUTORS

Katherine Bucknell is the author of the major biography *Christopher Isherwood Inside Out* (2024). She edited three volumes of Isherwood's diaries; his posthumous memoir, *Lost Years* (2000); and *The Animals* (2013), a volume of letters between Isherwood and Bachardy. She also edited W. H. Auden's *Juvenilia: Poems 1922–1928* (1996) and co-edited the series *Auden Studies*. She has published four novels— *Canarino* (2004), *Leninsky Prospekt* (2005), *What You Will* (2011), and *+1* (2013)—and she has created an audiobook, *The Flynn Guarneri* (2013).

James Cahill is an author, critic, and art historian. His debut novel, *Tiepolo Blue* (2022), was shortlisted for the Author's Club Best First Novel Award. His second novel, *The Violet Hour*, is forthcoming in 2025. His writing has appeared in *Artforum*, the *Daily Telegraph*, the *London Review of Books*, and the *Times Literary Supplement*, among others.

Simon Callow is an English actor, director, and writer.

Dennis Carr is the Virginia Steele Scott Chief Curator of American Art at The Huntington.

Mary Agnes Donoghue is an American filmmaker and playwright.

Gregory Evans served as a projects assistant (1978–85) and curator and business manager (1993–2020) for David Hockney and has worked as a textile designer (1987–2007). From 2022 to 2024 he worked as an independent archivist and curator of the Don Bachardy personal archive.

Sandra Brooke Gordon is the Avery Director of the Huntington Library.

Tina Mascara is a filmmaker who lives in Los Angeles and is on the board of the Christopher Isherwood Foundation. Her works include the critically acclaimed films *Chris & Don: A Love Story* (2007) and *Monk with a Camera* (2014).

Christina Nielsen is the Hannah and Russel Kully Director of the Huntington Art Museum.

Karla Nielsen is the Senior Curator of Literary Collections at The Huntington.

First published in 2025 by The Huntington
Published in conjunction with the exhibition
Don Bachardy: A Life in Portraits, organized by
The Huntington, on view April 12–August 4, 2025

Generous support for the exhibition and its catalogue were provided by the Douglas and Eunice Erb
Goodan Endowment and the Robert F. Erburu Exhibition Endowment. Additional funding was provided
by The Ahmanson Foundation Exhibition and Education Endowment, The Melvin R. Seiden-Janine Luke
Exhibition Fund in memory of Robert F. Erburu, and
the Boone Foundation.

ISBN: 978-1-64657-044-7
Library of Congress Control Number: 2024950735
A Cataloguing-in-Publication record for this book is
available from the British Library.

Available through:
ARTBOOK | D.A.P.
75 Broad Street, Suite 630
New York, NY 10004
artbook.com

For The Huntington:
1151 Oxford Road
San Marino, CA 91108
huntington.org
Project management by Jean Patterson
Publication coordination by Shirin Sadjadpour
    and Mindy Chen
Principal photography by Dana Barsuhn and
    Manuel Flores
Photographs on pp. 46, 47, 101 (top), and 103
(top and bottom) © Alan Shaffer 2024

Produced by Marquand Books, Seattle
marquandbooks.com

Copyedited by Jane Friedman
Proofread by Jennifer Snodgrass
Designed by Ryan Polich
Typeset in Messina Sans by Maggie Lee
Image management by I/O Color
Printed and bound in Canada by Friesens

Front cover: detail of p. 159
Back cover: detail of p. 106
Page ii: detail of p. 136
Page iv: detail of p. 134 top
Page 82: detail of p. 156 top
Page 166: detail of p. 155 bottom